GEORGES CLEMENCEAU

CLEMENCEAU
THE MAN AND HIS TIME

WORKS BY GEORGES CLEMENCEAU.

De la Génération des Eléments Anatomiques. 8vo. Paris: Baillière et fils. 1865.
Notions d' Anatomie et de Physiologie Générale. De la Génération des Eléments Anatomiques. Précédée d'une introduction par M. Charles Robin. 8vo. Paris: Germer Baillière. 1867.
J. Stuart Mill: *Auguste Comte et le Positivisme.* Traduction. 18mo. Paris: Germer Baillière. 1868. Alcau. 1893.
L'Amnistie devant le Parlement. Discours Chambre des Députés, 16 Mai, 1876. 18mo. Paris. Imp.: Wittersheim. 1876.
Affaires Egyptiennes. Discours Chambre des Députés, 19 and 20, Juillet, 1882. 18mo. Paris: Imp. Wittersheim. 1882.
Discours prononcé au Cirque Fernando le 25 Mai, 1884. (Account of Clemenceau's stewardship.) 18mo. Paris: Imp. Schiller. 1884.
Affaire du Tonkin. Discours Chambre des Députés, 27 Nov., 1884. 18mo. Paris: Imp. Schiller. 1884.
Politique Coloniale. Discours Chambre des Députés, 30 Juillet, 1884. 18mo. Paris: Imp. Schiller. 1885.
Discours prononcé à Draguignan, 13 Septembre, 1885. 18mo. Paris: Imp. Schiller. 1885.
La Mêlée Sociale. 18mo. Paris: Charpentier et Fasquelle. 1895.
Le Grand Pan. 18mo. Paris: Charpentier et Fasquelle. 1896.
Les Plus Forts. Roman contemporain. 18mo. Paris: Fasquelle. 1898.
Au Pied du Mont Sinai. 4to. Paris. Floury. 1898.
L'Iniquité. Notes sur l'affaire Dreyfus. 18mo. Paris: Stock. 1899.
Au Fil des Jours. 18mo. Paris: Stock. 1899.
Le Voile du Bonheur. Pièce en un acte. 18mo. Paris: Fasquelle. 1901.
La Honte. 18mo. Paris: Stock. 1903.
Aux Embuscades de la Vie. Dans la foi, dans l'ordre établi, dans l'amour. 18mo. Paris: Fasquelle. 1903.
L'Enseignement dans le Droit Républicain. Discours au Sénat. 18mo. Paris: Fasquelle. 1904.
Figures de la Vendée. 4to. Paris: Hessèle. 1904.
La France devant l'Allemagne. Imp. 8vo. Payot. 1918.

The above is a list of Clemenceau's most important works. His speeches in the Chamber of Deputies from 1876 up to 1893, and in the Senate, since 1902, will be found in the *Journal Officiel* and the *Annales du Sénat.* There are several studies of Clemenceau and his career: the most recent is *Clemenceau* (8vo, Paris—Charpentier, 1918), of which M. Georges Lecomte is the author. But he has been disinclined to have any detailed personal biography published. Though he must be well aware of the eminent part he has played in the history of his own country and of Europe, he has always preferred to speak of himself, and to be spoken of, as only one of the people of the France whom he has so well served.

CLEMENCEAU

THE MAN AND HIS TIME

BY

H. M. HYNDMAN

29438

NEW YORK
FREDERICK A. STOKES COMPANY
PUBLISHERS

Copyright, 1919, by
FREDERICK A. STOKES COMPANY

All Rights Reserved

CONTENTS

CHAPTER		PAGE
	INTRODUCTION	vii
I.	EARLY LIFE	1
II.	PARIS UNDER THE EMPIRE	12
III.	DOWNFALL AND RECONSTRUCTION	20
IV.	THE COMMUNE	34
V.	CLEMENCEAU THE RADICAL	49
VI.	FROM GAMBETTA TO CLEMENCEAU	62
VII.	THE TIGER	80
VIII.	THE RISE AND FALL OF BOULANGER	98
IX.	PANAMA AND DRAGUIGNAN	111
X.	PHILOSOPHER AND JOURNALIST	136
XI.	CLEMENCEAU AS A WRITER	152
XII.	CLEMENCEAU AND THE DREYFUS AFFAIR	164
XIII.	THE DREYFUS AFFAIR (II)	177
XIV.	AS ADMINISTRATOR	187
XV.	STRENGTH AND WEAKNESS OF CLEMENCEAU	224
XVI.	END OF CLEMENCEAU'S MINISTRY	246
XVII.	CLEMENCEAU AND GERMANY	261
XVIII.	THE GREAT WAR	278
XIX.	THE ENEMY WITHIN	289
XX.	"LA VICTOIRE INTEGRALE"	317
XXI.	CONCLUSION	333
	INDEX	339

President of the Council
  Minister of War
                                        Paris, July 1st, 1918
Dear Mr. Hyndman,
  I really must thank you for the more than flattering letter, prompted by your old friendship. I have nothing to say concerning myself, except that I am doing the best I can, and always with the feeling that it can never be enough. France is making day by day incredible sacrifices. No effort can be thought too great a price for assuring the triumph of saving humanity. Success is certain, when all free peoples have arisen to oppose the final convulsions of barbarism.
  In so great a drama, my dear friend, my own personality does not count. Whether at certain times I have been in the wrong or in the right, no longer even interests me, since it belongs to the past. I have kept no record of what I may have said or written. It would be impossible for me to give you further information or to refer you to any one else in a position to do so. I must therefore content myself with expressing my appreciation of your kindly purpose. I ask only to see the day of the great victory. After that, I shall feel repaid, quite beyond my deserts, especially when you add the expression of your own fraternal regard.
                       Affectionately yours,
                            G. CLEMENCEAU.

INTRODUCTION

I BEGAN to write this book in June. We were then holding our breath as we looked on, after the disasters of Cambrai and St. Quentin, upon the British troops still fighting desperately against superior numbers and defending the Channel Ports "with their backs to the wall" and barely left with room to maneuver. The enemy was at the same time seriously threatening Amiens and Epernay and the possible withdrawal of the French Government from Paris was being again discussed. It was a trying four months on both sides of the Channel. But England and France never despaired of the future. Both nations were determined to fight on to the last.

In July came the second great victory of the Marne, followed by the wonderful triumphant advance of the Allied Armies all along the line, side by side with our brethren of the United States, who were pouring into France at the rate of 300,000 men a month. And now I finish when the all-important matter of discussion is what shall be the terms of permanent peace imposed upon Germany, what shall be the punishment inflicted upon her and so far as is possible the compensation exacted from her for her unforgivable crimes against our common humanity. The transformation scene of the huge world war within four months has been one of the most astounding episodes in the history of mankind and the tremendous struggle on the West Front has proved, as it was bound to prove from the first, the crisis of the whole conflict.

Throughout the terrible period from November, 1917, when for the second time in his long political career he took office as Premier of the French Republic, Georges Clemenceau has borne the full burden of political responsibility in his war-worn and devastated country. It has been no light task for any man, especially for one within easy hail of eighty years of age. When he became President of Council and Minister of War the prospect of anything approaching to complete success seemed remote indeed. It was a thankless post he assumed and neither friends nor enemies believed at first that physically, mentally or politically could he bear the strain, and overcome the intrigues which were at once set on foot against him. But those who had the advantage of knowing Clemenceau well took a much more hopeful view of his chances of remaining Prime Minister until the close of the war. His mind as well as his body has been in strict training all his life. The one is as alert and as vigorous as the other. In the course of his stirring career his lightness of heart and gayety of spirit, his power of taking the most discouraging events as part of the day's work have carried him triumphantly through many a difficulty. Personally, I felt confident that nothing short of unforeseen disease, or a bomb from the foreign or domestic enemy, would bring him down before he had done his work. For below his exterior vigor and his brilliancy of conversation he possesses the most relentless determination that ever inspired a human being. Moreover a Frenchman may be witty and light-hearted and very wise at the same time. The world of the Middle Ages found that out.

INTRODUCTION

I read therefore with some amusement in Mrs. Humphry Ward's recent book of Victorian Recollections that, having met Clemenceau at dinner, in the eighties, she came to the conclusion that he was "too light a weight to ride such a horse as the French democracy." A very natural mistake, no doubt, for one of us staid and solemn Victorians to make, according to the young cynics and jesters of to-day who gird at us! It is precisely this inexhaustible fund of animal spirits and his never-failing cheerfulness and brilliancy which have given Clemenceau the power over France which he possesses to-day. Frenchmen have felt the more assured confidence in themselves and their future when they saw, day after day, their own representative and ruler full of go and of belief in himself at the time when the issue for them all was hanging in the balance. No real leader of men can ever afford to be a pessimist. He must assume a certitude if he have it not. There was no need for Clemenceau to assume anything. It was all there.

I have known this great Frenchman at many critical stages in his exciting life. What I most admire about him is that he is always the same man, no matter what his personal position at the moment may be. Never excessively elated: never by any chance cast down. Good or bad fortune, success or failure make no difference to him. The motto of the Tenth Legion might well be taken as his own. *"Utrinque paratus"* has been the watchword of this indefatigable and undaunted political warrior throughout. It is well to recall also that he has invariably told his country the full truth about the situation as it appeared to him at the time, alike in opposition and in office, as a deputy, as a Senator and as a journalist at large.

Beginning his political career as the intimate friend and almost pupil of the out-and-out Radical Republican, Etienne Arago, a sympathizer with the nobler men of the Commune, whom he endeavored to save from the ruthless vengeance of the reactionaries headed by Thiers, he had previously voted at Bordeaux in the minority of genuine Republicans who were in favor of continuing the war against Germany when all but enthusiastic patriots held that further resistance was hopeless. Many a time of late those events of *l'Année Terrible* must have come back to his mind during these still more terrible four years. His attitude now is but the continuation and fulfillment of the policy he advocated then. Thereupon, five years devoted to service on the Municipal Council of Paris and to gratuitous ministrations as a doctor to the poor of one of the poorest districts of the French metropolis: a continuous endeavor to realize in some degree, by political action, the practical ends for which the Communards had so unfortunately and injudiciously striven. Then political work again on the floor of the Assembly at one of the most stirring periods of French history: supporting Gambetta vigorously in his fight as the head of the Republican Party against the dangerous reactionism of the Duc de Broglie and Marshal MacMahon, and opposing and denouncing the fiery orator whom he succeeded as the leader of the Left, when that statesman adopted trimming and opportunism as his political creed.

The long fight against Colonization by Conquest, the exposure of shameless traffic in decorations, the support and overthrow of Boulanger, the Panama Scandal, the

INTRODUCTION xiii

denunciation of the Alliance with despotic Russia, the advocacy of a close understanding with England: in each and all of these matters Clemenceau was well to the front. Then came the crash of exclusion from political life, due to the many enemies he had made by his inconvenient honesty and bitter tongue and pen. Once more, after the display of almost unequaled skill and courage as a journalist, exceptionally manifested in the championship of Dreyfus, a return to political life and unexpected acceptance of office.

From first to last Clemenceau has been a stalwart Republican and a thoroughgoing democratic politician of the advanced Left, with strong tendencies to Socialism. These tendencies I begged him more than once to turn into actual realities and to join, or at least to act in complete harmony with, the Socialists. This seemed possible towards the close of the Dreyfus affair. But I must admit here that, much as I regret that Socialism has never enjoyed the full advantage of his services, Clemenceau, as an avowed member of the Socialist Party, could not have played the glorious part for France as a whole which he has played since the beginning of the war. It was far more important, at such a desperate crisis, to carry with him the overwhelming majority of his countrymen, including even the reactionaries, than to act with a minority that has shown itself at variance with the real sentiments of the Republic, when France was fighting for her existence.

That Clemenceau has, at one time or another, made great mistakes is beyond dispute. It could not be otherwise with a man of his character and temperament. But this, as he himself truly writes me, is all of the past. At no moment, in any case, has he ever failed to do his best for the greatness, the glory, the dignity of France as they presented themselves to his mind. This is incontestable. In the following pages I have endeavored not to write a biography of the statesman who has been constantly in public life for more than fifty years, but to give a study of the growth of a commanding personality, who is an honor to his country, and of the surroundings in which his faculties were developed.

CLEMENCEAU

CHAPTER I

EARLY LIFE

WE are all accustomed to think of La Vendée as that Province of France which is most deeply imbued with tradition, legend and religion. Even in this period of almost universal skepticism and free thought, the peasants of La Vendée keep tight hold of their ancient ideas, in which the pagan superstitions of long ago are curiously interwoven with the fading Catholicism of to-day. Nowhere in France are the ceremonies of the Church more devoutly observed; nowhere, in spite of the spread of modern education, are the people as a whole more attached to the creed of their forefathers. Here whole crowds of genuine believers can still display that fervor of religious enthusiasm which moved masses of their countrymen to such heroic self-sacrifice for a losing and hopeless cause more than four generations since. Even men who have little sympathy with either theological or social conventions of the past are stirred by the simple piety of these people, uplifted for the moment out of the sordid and monotonous surroundings of their daily toil by the collective inspiration of a common faith.

Here, too, in the Bocage of La Vendée, amid the heather and the forest, interspersed with acres of carefully tilled soil, the fays and talismans and spirits of days gone by delightedly do dwell. But below all this vesture of fancy and fable we find the least pleasing features of the life of the small proprietors and laborers on the land and fishermen by the sea. Their feelings of human sympathy are stunted, and even their family relations are, in too many instances, rendered brutal by their ever-present greed for gain. The land is a harsh taskmaster when its cultivation is carried on under such conditions as prevail in that portion of France which abuts on the Bay of Biscay. The result is a harsh people, whose narrow individualism and whole-hearted worship of property in its least attractive guise seem quite at variance with any form of sentiment, and still more remote from the ideals of poesy or the dreams of supernatural agencies which affect the imagination. But there is the contrast and such are the people of the Bocage of La Vendée.

Here, on September 28th, 1841, at the village of Mouilleron-en-Pareds, near Fontenay le Comte, on the Bay of Biscay, Georges Benjamin Clemenceau was born. His family came of an old stock of La Vendée who had owned land in the province for generations. His father was a doctor as well as a landowner; but his practice, I judge, from what his son told me, was confined to gratuitous services rendered to the peasants of the neighborhood. M. le Dr. Clemenceau, however, was scarcely the sort of man whom one would expect to find in a remote village of such a conservative, not to say reactionary, district as La Vendée. A thorough-going materialist and convinced Republican, he was the leader of the local party of extreme Radicals.

But he seems to have been a great deal more than that. Science, which took with him the place of supernatural religion, neither hardened his heart nor cramped his appreciation of art and poetry. Philosopher and philanthropist, an amateur of painting and sculpture, inflexibly devoted to his political principles, yet ever ready to recognize ability and originality wherever they appeared, this very exceptional medical man and country squire had necessarily a great influence upon his eldest son, who inherited from his father many of the qualities and opinions which led him to high distinction throughout his career. Hatred of injustice, love of freedom and independence of every kind, brought the elder Clemenceau into conflict with the men of the Second Empire, who clapped him in prison after the *coup d'état* of December, 1851. Liberty in every shape was, in fact, an essential part of this stalwart old Jacobin's political creed, while in the domain of physiology and general science he was a convinced evolutionist long before that conception of the inevitable development of the universe became part of the common thought of the time.

With all this the young Clemenceau was brought into close contact from his earliest years. A thoroughly sound physique, strengthened by the invigorating air of the Biscayan coast, laid the foundations of that indefatigable energy and alertness of disposition which have enabled him to pass triumphantly through periods of overwork and disappointment which would have broken down the health of any man with a less sound constitution. Georges Clemenceau owed much to the begettings and surroundings, to the vigorous country life and the rarefied mental atmosphere in which his earlier years were passed. Seldom is it possible to trace the natural process of cause and effect from father to son as it is in this case. From the wilds of La Vendée and the rough sea-coast of Brittany circumstances of the home and of the family life provided France with the ablest Radical leader she has ever possessed.

At first, it appeared little likely that this would be so. Clemenceau, entering upon his father's profession, with the benefit of the paternal knowledge and full of the inculcated readiness to probe all the facts of life to the bottom, took up his medical studies as a serious business, after having gone through the ordinary curriculum of a school at Nantes. It was in the hospital of that city that he first entered as a qualified student. After a short stay there he went off to Paris, in 1860, at the age of nineteen, to "walk the hospitals," as we phrase it, in the same capacity. It was a plunge into active life taken at a period in the history of France which was much more critical than it seemed.

The year which saw Clemenceau's arrival in Paris saw also the Second Empire at the height of its fame and influence. As we look back to the great stir of 1848, which, so far as Paris and France were concerned, was brought about by the almost inconceivable fatuity of Louis Philippe, we marvel at the strange turn of events which got rid of Orleanist King Log in order to replace him by a Napoleonist King Stork. But we may wonder still more at the lack of foresight, capacity and tact of Louis Philippe himself, who had been in his youth the democrat Citoyen Egalité, and an excellent general, with all the hard experience of his family misfortune and personal sufferings in exile as a full-grown man, possessed, too, of a thorough knowledge of the world and an adequate acquaintance with modern thought in several departments of science and literature. Yet, enjoying all these qualifications for a successful ruler, Louis Philippe failed to understand that a democratic monarchy, and a democratic monarchy alone, could preserve France from a republic or a military dictatorship. This was astounding. He refused to agree to the democratic vote claimed by the people, and then ran away. So the House of Orleans joined the House of Bourbon in the array of discrowned Heads of the Blood Royal. The short-lived Republic of 1848 existed just long enough to scare the bourgeoisie by the installation of the National Workshops, which might well have succeeded but for their unintelligent opposition, and the peasantry by the fear of general Communism, into a demand for a ruler who would preserve them from those whom they considered the maniacs or plunderers of Paris.

It is one of the ironies of history that the French Revolution which promulgated ideas of Liberty, Equality and Fraternity that shook the whole civilized world should have been unable to furnish France herself with a democratic republic for well-nigh a hundred years after the overthrow of Louis XVI. For scarcely had the Republic of 1848, with Louis Blanc, Ledru Rollin, Albert, and others as its leaders, been founded than the Buonapartist intrigues were successful. Louis Napoleon, who just before had been the laughing-stock of Europe, with his tame eagle at Boulogne that would persist in perching on a post instead of on his head, with his queer theories of Imperialist democracy and his close association with the Italian Carbonari, was elected President of the French Republic.

This was the outcome of an overwhelming plébiscite in his favor. There could be no doubt about the voice of France on this occasion. Paris may possibly have been genuinely Republican at that time. The Provinces, whose antagonism to Paris and the Parisians was very marked, then and later, were undoubtedly Buonapartist. From President to Emperor was no long step. Louis Napoleon, though a man of no great capacity, did at any rate believe in himself, in his democratic Imperialism and his destiny. The set of adventurers and swindlers around him believed only in full purses and ample opportunities for gratifying their taste for luxury and debauchery. Having obtained control of the army by the bribery of some and the imprisonment of others of the Republican generals, all was ready for the infamous butchery of peaceful citizens which cowed Paris and established the Empire at the same time. Once more the plébiscite was resorted to with equal success on the part of the conspirators. The hero of the *coup d'état,* with his familiar coterie of Morny, Flahault, Persigny, Canrobert and other rogues and murderers of less degree, became Napoleon III and master of Paris and of France in December, 1852.

The French threw their votes almost solid in favor of the Empire, and thus tacitly condoned the hideous crime committed when it was established. Whenever the Emperor's right to his throne was challenged he could point triumphantly to that crushing vote of the democracy constituting him the duly elected Emperor of the French and hereditary representative—however doubtful his parentage—of that extraordinary Corsican genius who, when Chateaubriand and other detractors sneered at his origin, boldly declared, *"Moi je suis ancêtre."*

From that day to this, democrats and Republicans have had a profound distrust of the vote of the mass of the people as recorded under a plébiscite, or a referendum, of the entire male population. This lack of confidence in the judgment of the majority, when appealed to on

EARLY LIFE

political issues, though natural under the circumstances, is obviously quite illogical on the part of men who declare their belief in popular government. It amounts to a permanent claim for the highly educated and well-to-do sections of an intellectual oligarchy, on the ground that they must know better what is good for the people than the people know for themselves. This might conceivably be true, if no pecuniary interests or arrogance of social superiority were involved. But as this state of things cannot be attained until production for profit, payment of wages and private property cease to exist, democrats and Republicans place themselves in a doubtful position when they denounce a reference to the entire population as necessarily harmful. All that can be safely admitted is that so long as the mass of men and women are economically dependent, socially unfree and very imperfectly educated, the possibility of their being able to secure good government by a plébiscite is very remote. But this applies as well to universal suffrage used to obtain parliamentary elections, and the argument against reposing any trust in the mass of the people may thus be pushed to the point of abrogating the vote altogether save for a small minority. And this would land us in the position of beginning with an autocracy or aristocracy and ending there.

At the time I am speaking of it is indisputable that the overwhelming majority of intelligent and educated Frenchmen were Republicans. What they meant by a Republic comprised many different shades of organized democracy. But Republic, as Republic, in opposition and contradistinction to Monarchy or Empire, was a name to conjure with among all the most distinguished Frenchmen of the time. How did it come about, then, that this minority, which should have been able to lead the people, was distrusted and voted down by the very same populace whose rights of self-government they themselves were championing on behalf of their countrymen? There was nothing in the form of a Republic, as was shown little more than twenty years afterwards, which was of necessity at variance with the interests or the sentiments of Frenchmen. Even the antagonism between Paris and the Provinces, already referred to, was not so marked as to account for the fact that twice in succession Louis Napoleon should have obtained an overwhelming personal vote in his favor as the man to be trusted, above all other Frenchmen, to control the destinies of France.

It is by no means certain that Paris herself was hostile, before the *coup d'état,* to the Napoleonic régime with its traditions not only of military glory but of capable civic administration. For the double plébiscite was more than a vote of acquiescence: it was a vote of enthusiasm: first for Louis Napoleon as President, and then for Louis Napoleon as Emperor. It is not pleasing to have to admit this; but the truth seems to be that, as Aristotle pointed out more than two thousand years ago, great masses of men are much more easily led by a personality than they are roused by a principle. That the plébiscite had been carefully worked up by assiduous propaganda; that many of the ignorant peasants believed they were voting for the Napoleon of their childhood in spite of the impossible; that there was a great deal of bribery and not a little stuffing of the ballot boxes by officials with a keen sense of favors to come; that the army was imbued with Napoleonic sympathies and helped to spread the spurious ideals of Imperialism—all this may be perfectly true. Yet, when all is said and every allowance is made, the fact remains that, even so, the success of the Napoleonic plébiscites is imperfectly explained. The main features of the vote were obvious: The French people were sick of hereditary monarchy: the Republican leaders were out of touch with the people: the ideals of the past overshadowed the hopes of the future: Napoleon was a name to conjure with: the Republicans had no name on their side to put against it: the "blessed word" Republic had no hold upon the peasantry of rural France. So plébiscite meant one-man rule. That is not to say, as so many argue nowadays, that the complete vote of the democracy on such an issue must of necessity be wrong; but it does affirm that a thoroughly educated, responsible democracy, accustomed to be appealed to directly on all matters of importance, is a necessity before we can have any certainty that the people will go right. Even if they go wrong, as in this case of Napoleon III, it is better in the long run that they should learn by their own errors than that the blunders of the dominant classes should be forced upon them. Great social and political problems can rarely be solved even by the greatest genius. And the genius himself, supposing him to exist, cannot rely upon providing his country with a successor. On the whole, consequently, it is less dangerous to human progress that we should risk such a reactionary vote as that which seated Napoleon III at the Tuileries than give no peaceful outlet whatever to popular opinion.

But the democrats and republicans, radicals and socialists of Paris, who saw all their most cherished ideals crushed by the voice of the people whom they were anxious to lead to higher things, and beheld a travesty of Napoleonic Imperialism suppressing all freedom of political thought and writing, were not disposed to philosophize about the excuses for a popular decision which led to such unpleasant results for them. They had welcomed the abdication of Louis Philippe and the installation of the Republic as the beginning of a new era not only for Paris but for all France, after the reactionary clericalism of Louis XVIII and Charles X followed by the chilly middle-class rule of the Orleanist monarch. But now a pinchbeck Napoleonism, with much sterner repression, weighed upon all that was most progressive and brilliant in the capital city. It was a bitter disappointment, not to be softened by the reflection that France herself was still far from the economic and social stage where their aspirations could be realized.

Thus Napoleon III was master of France and, feeling that war was advisable in order to strengthen his position at home, gladly joined with Great Britain in a joint campaign against Russia. This was wholly unnecessary, as has since been clearly shown. But, by promoting a better feeling between France and England than had previously existed, some good came out of the evil brought about by the treacherous suppression of the Emperor Nicholas's agreement with the English Cabinet. The foolish bolstering up of Ottoman incapacity and corruption at Constantinople when the Western Powers could easily have enforced a more reasonable rule was a miserable result of the whole war. But that the Crimean adventure helped to consolidate the position of the Emperor there is no doubt.

When also the affair of the Orsini bomb, thrown by one of his old Carbonari fellow-conspirators, impelled Louis Napoleon into the Italian campaign which won for Italy Lombardy and for France Savoy and Nice, the French people felt that their gain in glory and in territory had made them once more the first nation in Europe. Magenta and Solferino were names to conjure with. The Army had confidence in the Emperor and his generals. So the prospect for republicans and the Republic eight years after the *coup d'état* was less promising than it had been since the great revolution. Napoleon III was generally regarded as the principal figure in Europe. He was delivering those New Year proclamations which men awaited with bated breath as deciding the question of peace or war for the ensuing twelvemonth. His Empress dominated the world of fashion as her consort did the world of politics. Every effort was made to render the Court as brilliant as possible, and to attract to it some of the old nobility, who were, as a whole, little inclined to recognize by their presence the power of the man whom they both despised and hated. But the Second Empire was for a time a success in spite of the reactionists and the republicans alike.

CHAPTER II

PARIS UNDER THE EMPIRE

PARIS of the early sixties was a very different city from the Paris of to-day. It was still in great part the Paris of the old time, on both banks of the Seine. Its Haussmannization had barely begun. The Palais Royal retained much of its ancient celebrity for the cuisine of its restaurants and the brilliancy of its shops. But to get to it direct from what is now the Place de l'Opéra was a voyage of discovery. You went upstairs and downstairs, through narrow, dirty streets, until, after missing your way several times, you at last found yourself in the garden dear to the orators of the French Revolution, and since devoted to nursemaids and their babes. Much of Central Paris was in the same unregenerate state. Even portions of famous streets not far from the Grands Boulevards, which were then still French, could scarcely be described as models of cleanliness. The smells that arose from below and the water of doubtful origin that might descend upon the unwary passer-by from above suggested a general lack of sanitary control which was fully confirmed in more remote districts.

Napoleon III was a man of mediocre ability. His *entourage* was extravagantly disreputable. But he and his did clear out and clean up Paris. The new quarters since built up owe their existence in the first instance to the initiative of the Emperor's chief edile, Baron Haussmann, and his compeers. The great broad streets which now traverse the slums of old time were due to the same energetic impulse. Whether such spacious avenues and boulevards were constructed in order to facilitate the operations of artillery and enable the new mitrailleurs more conveniently to massacre the "mob," whether the architecture is artistic or monotonous, Clemenceau the doctor must for once be at variance with Clemenceau the man of politics, and admit that the monarch who, as will be seen, imprisoned him in 1862, did some good work for Paris during his reign of repression. At any rate, Napoleonic rule at this period represented general prosperity. Business was good and the profiteers were doing well. The bourgeoisie felt secure and international financiers enjoyed a good time. Nearly all the great banking and financial institutions of Paris had their origin in the decade 1860-1870. Law and order, in short, was based upon comfort and accumulation for the well-to-do.

But the peasantry and the workers of the cities were also considered in some degree, and the reconstruction of the capital provided, directly and indirectly, both then and later, for what were looked upon as "the dangerous classes"—men and women, that is to say, who thought that the wage-slave epoch meant little better for them and their children than penal servitude for life. Constant work and decent pay softened the class antagonism, conciliating the proletariat without upsetting the middle class or bourgeoisie. Such a policy, following upon two fairly successful wars, was not devoid of dexterity. A curbed or satisfied Paris meant internal peace for all France. Neither the miserable fiasco in Mexico nor the idiotic abandonment of Austria to Prussia had yet shaken the external stability of the Empire. Napoleon III and his

Vice-Emperor Rouher were still great statesmen. There was little or nothing to show on the surface that the whole edifice was even then tottering to its fall. The keen satire of Rochefort, the Duc d'Aumale, and the full-blooded denunciations of Victor Hugo failed to produce much effect. Some genuine and capable opponents were beguiled into serving the Government under the impression that the Empire might be permanent, and in this way alone could they also serve their country. Nor can we wonder at such backsliding.

Such was the Paris, such the France that saw the young medical student, Georges Clemenceau, enter upon his preparation for active life as doctor and physiologist. He devoted himself earnestly to his studies in the libraries, to his work in the hospitals, and to careful observation of the social maladies he saw around him, which made a deep and permanent impression on his mind. But, determined as he was to master the principles and practice of his profession, the bright, active and vivacious republican from La Vendée brought with him to Paris too clear a conception of his rights and duties as a democrat to be able to avoid the coteries of revolt who maintained the traditions of radicalism in spite of systematic espionage and police persecution. Clemenceau shared his father's opinions in favor of free speech and a free press.

That was dangerous in those days. *La Ville Lumière* was obliged to hide its light under a bushel. Friends of democracy and anti-Imperialistic speakers and writers were compelled, in order to reach their public, to adopt a style of suppressed irony not at all to the taste of the vivacious republican recruit from Mouilleron-en-Pareds. Then, as ever thereafter, he spoke the truth that was in him, regardless of consequences. In this course he had the approbation and support of his father's friend, Etienne Arago, brother of the famous astronomer. Arago the politician was also a playwright, an ardent republican who had taken his full share in all the agitations of the previous period, an active and useful member of the Republican Government of 1848 as Postmaster-General, and a vigorous opponent of the policy of Louis Napoleon. He was sent into exile prior to the *coup d'état*. Both then and nearly a generation later this stalwart anti-Imperialist was exceedingly popular with the Parisians, and having returned to Paris was able to aid Clemenceau in forming a correct judgment of the situation at a time when a less clear-sighted observer might have striven to cool his young friend's enthusiasm.

As it was, Clemenceau contributed to some of the Radical fly-sheets and then fêted the 24th of February. No date dear to the memory of Republicans could be publicly toasted without conveying a reflection upon the Empire, and as all important events in French history, from July 14th onwards, are duly calendared according to the month and day of the month, Clemenceau's crime in celebrating February 24th by speech and writing was obvious. He therefore fell foul of the Imperial police. The magistrate could admit no point in his favor, and there was in fact no defense. Consequently George Clemenceau, *interne de l'hôpital,* had the opportunity given him of reflecting for two months upon the advantages and drawbacks of his political creed, during a period of Buonapartist supremacy, in the prison of Mazas. This was in 1862.

Three years later he took his doctor's degree. His formal essay on this occasion gained him considerable reputation. It was entitled *De la Génération des Élé-*

ments Anatomiques, and proved not only that he had worked hard on the lines of his profession but that he was capable of taking an original view of the subjects he had mastered. This work has been throughout the basis of Clemenceau's medical, social, political and literary career. I got the book not long ago from the London Library, and on the title-page of this first edition I read in the author's own bold handwriting, "*A Monsieur J. Stuart Mill hommage respectueux de l'auteur G. Clemenceau*": a tribute to that eclectic philosopher and thinker which he followed up shortly afterwards by translating Mill's study of Auguste Comte and Positivism into French. Clemenceau was no great admirer of Comte, and specially disapproved of the attempt of some of that author's pupils and followers to limit investigation and cultivate agnosticism on matters which they considered fell without the bounds of their master's theories and categories.

"We are not of those," writes Clemenceau, "who admit with the positivist that science can give us no information on the enigma of things." This seems scarcely just to the modern Positivists, for although Comte himself wished to restrict mankind from the study of astronomy, for example, outside of the solar system, they have been as ready as the rest of the world to take advantage of discoveries beyond that system which throw light upon some of the difficult material problems nearer at hand. And Clemenceau, too, appears to fall into the line of reasoning with which he reproaches Comte; for, as will be seen later, he views nature as a mass of matter evolving and differentiating and organizing and vivifying itself with the interminable antagonisms and mutual devourings of the various forms of existence on this planet, and possibly on other worlds of the infinitely little, and then, when the great suns die out, disappearing and beginning all over again as two of these huge extinguished luminaries collide in space. This material philosophy when carried to its ultimate issue still answers no question and furnishes no clew to the strange inexplicable movement of the universe in which man is but a sentient and partially intelligent automaton. What explanation does this give of any of the problems of social or individual ethic, or of the impulse which led Clemenceau the doctor to treat his patients in Montmartre gratuitously, instead of building up a valuable practice in a rich quarter? and urged Clemenceau the politician to pass the greater part of his life in an uphill fight against the domination of the sordid minority and the timid acquiescence of the apathetic masses rather than accept the high positions which were pressed upon him time after time?

Such reflections would be out of place at this point but for the fact that Clemenceau has invariably contended that his career has been all of a piece, maintaining that the vigorous young physiologist and doctor of twenty-four and twenty-five held the same opinions and was moved by the same aspirations that have guided the mature man throughout. Whether heredity and surroundings fully account in every particular for all that he has said, done and achieved is a question which Clemenceau also might decline to answer with the definiteness he considers desirable in general philosophy. But that his doctor's thesis of 1865 did in the main give the scientific basis of his material creed can scarcely be disputed.

The following year, 1866, was the year of the Prusso-Italian war against Austria. The success of Prussia, which would quite probably have been a failure but for the incredible fatuity of the Imperial clique at Vienna, was one of the chief causes, unnoted at the time, of the downfall of Napoleon III. Few now care to recall the manner in which the Austrian Commander-in-Chief, Marshal Benedek, was compelled to abandon his entire strategy in deference to the pusillanimous orders of the Emperor, or how Benedek, with a loyalty to the House of Hapsburg which it has never at any period deserved, took upon himself the blame of defeats for which Francis Joseph, not himself, was responsible. But Louis Napoleon was equally blind to his own interests and those of France when he stood aside and allowed the most ambitious and most unscrupulous power in the world to become the virtual master of Central Europe. It was a strange choice of evils that lay before the Radical and Republican parties in all countries during this war. None could wish to see upheld, still less strengthened, the wretched rule of reactionary, tyrannous and priest-ridden Austria; yet none could look favorably on the growth of Prussian power.

The further conquest by Italy of her own territory and the annexation of Venice to the Italian crown were therefore universally acclaimed. But those who knew Prussia and its military system, and watched the nefarious policy which had crushed Denmark as a stage on the road to the crushing of Austria, even thus early began to doubt whether the substitution of Prussia for Austria in the leadership of the old Germanic Bund might not speedily lead to a still more dangerous situation. Either this did not suggest itself to Napoleon III and his advisers, or they thought that Austria might win, or, at the worst, that a bitterly contested campaign would enable France to interpose at the critical moment as a decisive arbiter in the struggle. Probably the last was the real calculation. It was falsified by the rapid and smashing Prussian victories of Königgratz and Sadowa, and Napoleon could do nothing but accept the decisions of the battlefield. But from this moment the Second Empire was in serious danger, and any far-seeing statesman would have set to work immediately to bring the French army up to the highest possible point of efficiency and prepare the way for alliances that might help the Empire, should help be needed in the near future. Neither Louis Napoleon nor his councilors and generals, however, understood what the overthrow of Austria meant for France. They turned a deaf ear then and afterwards to the warnings of their ablest agents abroad, and thus drifted into the crisis which four years later found them without an ally and overwhelmed them.

CHAPTER III

DOWNFALL AND RECONSTRUCTION

EARLY in 1866, Clemenceau, after a visit to England, crossed the Atlantic for a somewhat prolonged stay in the United States. He could scarcely have chosen a better time for making acquaintance with America and the Americans. The United States had but just emerged from the Civil War, which, notwithstanding the furious bitterness evoked on both sides during the struggle, eventually consolidated the Great Republic as nothing else could; though, owing to the behavior of "society" in England, the tone of our leading statesmen and the action of the "Alabama," the feeling against Great Britain was naturally very strong. This animosity—it was no less—of course did not extend to the young French physician of republican views who had already suffered for his opinions in Paris, and whose sympathies were with the North against the South throughout. He was well received in the Eastern States, and wrote several letters to the *Temps* on the industrial and social conditions of America which were then of value, and still serve to show how marked is the contrast between the self-contained nation of fifty years ago and the Anglo-Saxon world power that we see beginning to try her strength in the international struggle against Germanic infamy to-day. What is not so easy to comprehend is M. le Dr. Clemenceau, as we know him, acting as professor of French in a young ladies' college at the village of Stamford, in the neighborhood of New York. His record in that capacity is amusingly described by one of his friends* in a bright little sketch of his early experiences.

"An admirable horseman, the young Frenchman accompanied the still younger American misses in their rides. There were free and delightful little tours on horseback, charming excursions along the shady roads which traverse the gay landscape of Connecticut. Such years carried with them for Clemenceau ineffaceable memories of a period during which his temperament accomplished the task of gaining strength and acquiring refinement. At the same time that he enriched his mind with solid conceptions of Anglo-Saxon philosophy, and perfected his general cultivation, he took his first lessons in the delicacies of American flirtation. It was in the course of these pleasing jaunts, where the fresh laughter of these young ladies echoed through the bright scenery, that it was his lot to become betrothed to one of them, Miss Mary Plummer. Henceforth, in consequence of the sound, independent and many-sided education which he had, so to say, imposed upon himself, Clemenceau had completed the last stage of his intellectual development. He was ripe to play great parts. For the rest, events were not destined long to delay the throwing into full relief his versatile, intrepid and powerful characteristics."

And so Clemenceau, thus prepared to meet what the future might have in store for him, returned to Paris. There are cities in the history of the human race which have taken unto themselves a personality, not only for their own inhabitants, but for succeeding ages, and for the world at large. Babylon, Athens, Jerusalem, Rome,

* M. Maurice Le Blond.

Bagdad, Florence, each and all convey to the mind a conception of civic individuality and collective achievement which brings them within the range of our own knowledge, admiration and respect, which raises them also to the level of ideals of culture for men living in far different civilizations. They are still oases of brightness and greenery amid the wilderness of unconscious growth. The wars of old time, the cruelty of long-past days, the records of brutality and lust are forgotten: only the memory of greatness or beauty remains.

> Terror by night, the flaming battle-call,
>   Fire on the roof-tree, dreadful blood and woe!—
> They cease for tears, yet joyful, knowing all
>   Is over, long ago.
>
> Knowing, the melancholy hands of Time
>   Weave a slow veil of beauty o'er the place
> Of blood-stained memory and bitter crime
>   Till horror fades in grace.
>
> The mournful grace of long-forgotten woe
>   And long-appeasèd sorrows of the dead,
> The deeper silence of those streams that flow
>   Where ancient highways led.

Among the great cities of the past which is still the present Paris takes her undisputed place. In youth, in maturity, in age, the charm of intellectual and artistic Paris ever affects not merely her own citizens, but the visitors within her gates. And the young Vendéen Clemenceau was from the first a Parisian of Parisians. The attraction of Paris for him was permanent. From his ar-

DOWNFALL AND RECONSTRUCTION 23

rival in 1860 until the present time practically his whole life has been spent in the French capital. Many years afterwards he gave expression to the influence Paris had upon him. Paris for Clemenceau is the sun of the world of science and letters, the source of light and heat from whose center art and thought radiate through space. "Intuition and suggestion spreading out in all directions awake dormant energy, sweep on from contact to contact, are passed on, dispersed, and finally exhausted in the inertia of material objects. Here is the radiance of humanity, more or less powerful, more or less durable as time and place may decree."

It is this impatience of Paris with results already achieved, this desire to reach out and to embrace new forms in all departments of human achievement, which gives the French city her position as an indispensable entity in the cosmos of modern life. "Boldness and boldness and boldness again" was Danton's prescription for the orator, and it might be taken as the motto of intellectual and artistic Paris. There is no hesitation, no contentment, no waiting by the wayside. New ideas and new conceptions must ever be replacing the old. Experience may teach what to avoid: experiment alone can teach what to attempt. And this not incidentally or as a passing phase of endeavor, but as a principle to be applied in every region of human effort. "The Rights of Man," "Liberty, Equality, Fraternity," "Property is robbery" are as thought-provoking (though they solve no problem) in the domain of sociology as Pasteur's achievements in physiology and medicine. Whatever changes the future may have in store for us, we who are not Frenchmen cannot dispense with the leadership and inspiration that come to us from Paris.

On his return to France from America Clemenceau renewed his acquaintance and friendship with those who shared his political and social opinions, especially Etienne Arago, now an old man, and practiced as a doctor in the working-class district of Montmartre. Here, by his gratuitous medical advice to the people and his steady adherence to his democratic principles, he gained an amount of popularity and personal devotion from the men and women of Montmartre which, in conjunction with Arago's advice and support, prepared the way for the positions which he afterwards attained. Meanwhile the Second Empire was going slowly downhill. The change which had already taken place was not generally recognized. Nevertheless, the failure of the ill-fated Mexican Expedition with its Catholic support, its sordid financial muddling and the degrading system of plunder carried on in Mexico itself by Marshal Bazaine, the effect on Paris of the murder of Victor Noir by a member of the Buonaparte family, and the Government's growing incapacity to handle domestic and foreign affairs all told against the prestige of Napoleon. Only a successful diplomatic stroke or a victorious war could rehabilitate the credit of the Empire. The time had gone by for either. Bismarck's disgraceful forgery at Ems was as unnecessary as it was flagitious. Sooner or later the Second Empire would have collapsed from its own incompetence. But that waiting game did not suit the grim statesman of Berlin. He knew that the French army by itself could not hold its own against the Prussian and other German forces; he felt convinced also that Austria would not move without much clearer assurances of success than Napoleon could supply; while Italy was still tied to her Ally of 1866, and England was devoted to a policy of profitable non-intervention. So Napoleon was half driven, half tricked into a hopeless campaign, and every calculation on which Bismarck relied was verified by the results. Nay, the plébiscite which Louis Napoleon risked eighteen years after the *coup d'état* went entirely in his favor, and it was in reality quite unnecessary, from the point of view of internal politics, that any risk of war should be run. The Empress, however, has always had the discredit of not having been of that opinion. Hence steps were taken which played into Bismarck's hands.

At first, as I have heard Clemenceau say himself, it was almost impossible for a patriotic Republican to desire victory for the French armies. That would only have meant a new life for the decadent Empire. Sad, therefore, as was the long succession of disasters, and terrible the devastation wrought by German ruthlessness, not until the culminating defeat of Sedan, the surrender of Napoleon and the decree of Imperial overthrow pronounced by the people of Paris, could men feel that French soldiers were really fighting for their country. Thenceforward the struggle was between democratic and progressive France and autocratic and reactionary Prussia. The Empire for whose humiliation the King of Prussia had gone to war existed no longer. A Republic was at once declared in its place. Any fair-minded enemy would directly have offered the easiest possible terms for peace to the new France. But that was not the view of Prussia. France, not merely the Second Empire, was to be defeated and crushed down, because she stood in the way of that permanent policy of aggression and aggrandizement to which the House of Hohenzollern, with its Junker supporters, has always been devoted. This was the moment when England should have interfered decisively on the side of her old rival. It was not only our interest but our duty to do so, and the whole nation would have enthusiastically supported the statesmen who had given it a vigorous lead in the right direction. Unfortunately Queen Victoria, then as ever bitterly pro-German, was utterly unscrupulous in enforcing her views upon her Government: the men then in office were essentially courtiers, who combined servility at home with pusillanimity abroad: the *laissez-faire* school of parasitical commercialism which regards the accumulation of wealth for the few as the highest aspiration of humanity held the trading classes in its grip. Consequently the monarch and the ruling class of the day thought it was cheaper, and therefore better, to leave France to her fate, and make a good cash profit out of the business, rather than courageously to withstand the beginnings of evil and uphold the French Republic against the brutality and greed of Berlin. It is sad, nearly fifty years later, to reflect upon the results of this mistaken and cowardly policy. The war was continued, owing chiefly to English indifference, until France lay at the feet of the conquerors.

No sooner did the news of the defeat and surrender of Sedan reach Paris than a general shout for the overthrow of the Empire went up from the people throughout the French capital. The collapse of the Second Empire was in fact even more sudden and dramatic than its rise. The whole imperial machinery fell with a crash. There was not a man in Paris among the friends of the Emperor in good fortune who had the courage and capacity to come to the front in the time of his distress. The bigoted Catholic Empress, against whom Parisians cherished an animosity scarcely less bitter than that which their forbears felt for Marie Antoinette, was with difficulty got safely out of the city, and Paris at once took control of her own destinies. A Republic having been proclaimed, Republicans, Radicals and Socialists, harried and proscribed the day before, rushed to the front the day after, and forthwith became masters of the city. Clemenceau as one of them was immediately chosen Mayor of Montmartre, at the instance of his old friend Etienne Arago.

It was a period for action, not for argument, or reflection, or propaganda. Clemenceau understood that. In his capacity as Mayor of Montmartre, by no means an easy district to manage, he exhibited marvelous energy, as well as sound judgment, in every department of public affairs. Everything had to be reorganized at once. There was no time to respect the inevitable details of democratic authorization and delay. Clemenceau with his natural rapidity of decision was the very man for the post. Patriotic and revolutionary excitement seethed all round him. Society seemed already to be in the melting-pot. The enthusiasm evoked by eloquent orations in favor of Socialism was accompanied by the discharges of cannon and the rumbling of ammunition-wagons. But public business had to be carried on all the same. Clemenceau was indefatigable and ubiquitous. He prevented the priests from intriguing in the municipal schools, he established purely secular education, hurried on the arming of the battalions and kept a sharp eye on the defenses of the city. Simultaneously he set on foot a series of establishments for giving warmth, food and general help to the number of people who had sought refuge on the heights. He acted throughout practically as municipal dictator, raising, arming and drilling recruits for the new republican army, as well as organizing and administering all the local services.

It was a fine piece of work. Having been so closely in touch with the bulk of the population of Montmartre, he was able to act entirely in their interests and with their concurrence throughout. They therefore warmly supported him against the reactionists and religionists who, then as always, were his most virulent enemies. It was no easy task to maintain order and carry out systematic organization at this juncture. The downfall of the Empire occurred on September 4th, the Republic, with General Trochu—the man of the undisclosed strategical "plan"—as President and Jules Favre as Vice-President, being declared the same day. On September 19th Paris was invested by the Germans. Seeing that there were then no fewer than 400,000 armed men at various stages of training in the capital, with many powerful forts at their disposal, while the Germans could spare at the beginning of the siege no more than 120,000 men for the attack, the French having still several armies in the field, successful resistance by the Republic seemed by no means hopeless. Paris might even have had her share in turning the tide of victory. Clemenceau was of that opinion.

But it was not to be. France failed to produce a great general, and the "bagman Marshal," as Bazaine was called in Mexico, by shutting himself up with 175,000 men in Metz, rendered final defeat certain; though if Marshal MacMahon's advice had been followed, and if General Trochu had later sufficiently organized the forces at his disposal in Paris to break through the German lines, a stouter fight might have been fought. As it was, one French army after another was defeated in the field, and Paris and Metz were forced to surrender by literal starvation. On January 28th, 1871, an armistice was signed between Bismarck and Jules Favre and the revict-

DOWNFALL AND RECONSTRUCTION

ualing of the famine-stricken Parisians began, the siege having lasted a little over four months. A National Assembly was summoned to decide the terms of a definite peace or in what manner it might be possible to continue the war.

So well satisfied were the voters of Montmartre with the conduct of their Mayor during all this trying time that they decided to send him as their representative to Bordeaux and polled just upon 100,000 votes in his favor. To Bordeaux, therefore, Clemenceau went, on February 12th, as deputy for one of the most radical and revolutionary districts of Paris. Though neither then nor later an avowed Socialist, no Socialist could have done more for practical democratic and Socialist measures than Clemenceau had done. That, of course, was the reason why he was elected by so advanced a constituency.

He found himself strangely out of his element when he took his seat in the National Assembly. Perhaps no more reactionary body had ever met in France. The majority of the members were thorough-going Conservatives who at heart were eager to restore the monarchy. They were royalists but slightly disguised, dug up out of their seclusion, from all parts of the country, who thought their time had come to revenge themselves not so much upon the Buonapartists who had governed France for twenty years as upon Paris and the Parisians who had chased Charles X and Louis Philippe out of France. They well knew that the capital would never consent to the restoration of the candidate of either of the Bourbon factions. These fitting champions of a worn-out Legitimism or Orleanism were old men in a hurry to resuscitate the dead and galvanize the past into fresh life. Their very heads betrayed their own antiquity. So much so that a favorite pastime of young ladies of pleasure in the Galleries, who had flocked to Bordeaux, was what was irreverently called "bald-headed loo." This consisted in betting upon the number of flies that would settle within a given period upon a devoted deputy's hairless occiput. Unfortunately these ancient gentlemen found in M. Thiers a leader who could scarcely have been surpassed for ingenuity and unscrupulousness. He deliberately traded upon prejudices, and his main political assets were the fear and distrust which he awakened in one set of his countrymen against another. In modern as in ancient society there is an economic and almost a personal antagonism between country and town.

The man of the Provinces, living always in the rural districts, the tiller, the producer, the indefatigable toiler, the parsimonious accumulator of small gains, the respecter of ancestral traditions and the devotee of old-world methods and well-tried means of gaining a poor livelihood, profoundly affected likewise by his inherited religion, has, in most cases, a deep-seated contempt, strangely enough not wholly divorced from fear, for the man of the town, and especially for the man of Paris. This animosity, which has by no means wholly disappeared today, was keenly in evidence forty and fifty years ago. There is an economic cause at the bottom of the antipathy, but this does not account for its many-sided manifestation. The countryman naturally desires to sell his produce at as high a price as possible. It is for him almost a matter of life and death to do so. The townsman, on his side, the artisan or laborer or even the *rentier* of the great cities, is naturally anxious to obtain the necessaries of life which he gets from the rural districts at as low a rate as he may be able to buy them, having regard to his wages or his income. Hence any expenditure which tends to benefit the country is regarded with suspicion by the townsman and contrariwise as between town and country, except such outlay as cheapens the cost of transportation, where both have an identical interest.

But this general divergence of economic advantage which has existed for many centuries does not wholly account for the ill-feeling which too often appears. There is a psychological side to the matter as well. Thus the peasant, even when he is getting satisfactory prices for his wares, despises his own customers when they pay too much for small luxuries which they could easily do without. Moreover, he considers the cleverness of his fellow-countrymen of the city, their readiness to change their opinions and adopt new ideas, their doubts as to the super-sanctity of that individual property, property which is the small landowner's god, as evidences of a dangerous disposition to upset all that ought to be most solemnly upheld. The townsman, on the other hand, too often looks down upon the peasant and the rural provincial generally as an ignorant, short-sighted, narrow-minded, grasping creature, full of prejudices and eaten up with superstition, who, out of sheer obstinacy, stands immovably in the way of reforms that might and in many cases certainly would benefit them both.

It is the task and the duty of the true statesman to bridge over these differences as far as possible, to try to harmonize interests and assuage feelings which under existing conditions are apt to conflict with one another. Thus only can the whole country be well and truly served. M. Thiers pursued precisely the contrary course. In order to foster reaction and to strengthen the position of the bourgeoisie, he and his supporters set to work deliberately to excite the hatred of the country-folk against their brethren of the towns. They were willing to accept the Republic only on the distinct understanding that it should be, as Zola expressed it, a bourgeoised sham. The bogey of the social revolution was stuck up daily to frighten all timid property-owners. Above all, Paris was pointed out as the danger spot of order-respecting France. Paris ought to be muzzled and kept under even more strictly by the self-respecting Republic than by the Empire. That way alone lay safety. Thus the dislike of the provincials for the capital was fanned to so fierce a heat that the very title of capital was denied to her. As a result of this unpatriotic and traitorous policy Paris herself was unfortunately forced to the conviction that the reactionists of Bordeaux were determined to deprive her of all her rights, and that the great city which founded the Republic would be made to suffer dearly for her presumption. Nearly all that followed was in reality due to this sinister policy of provocation, adoped and carried out by M. Thiers, and his bigoted followers.

Clemenceau's position was a difficult one. Knowing both peasants and Parisians intimately well, he saw clearly the very dangerous situation which must inevitably be created by such tactics of exasperation. As one of the deputies of Radical Republican Paris, he did his utmost at Bordeaux to maintain the independence of his constituents and to resist the fatal action of the majority. As the son of a landowner in La Vendée, he understood clearly the views of the provincials and how necessary it was that they should be thoroughly informed as to the aims of the Parisians. But Paris had first claim on his services. He therefore associated himself with Louis

DOWNFALL AND RECONSTRUCTION

Blanc, voted with him against the preliminaries of peace and in favor of the continuance of the war. There was a strong opinion at this time that many of the Buonapartists in high military command, as well as in important civil posts, were traitors to the Republic and had acted, as Bazaine unquestionably did, in the interest of the Imperial prisoner instead of on behalf of France. These factionists too were hostile to Paris, and a demand was made, in which Clemenceau joined, for a full investigation of the conduct of such men during the siege. Unfortunately, affairs in the capital were now becoming so critical and the probability of another revolution there seemed so great that Clemenceau felt his duties as Mayor of Montmartre were still more urgent than his votes and speeches at Bordeaux, as deputy for that district. Consequently, after less than a month's stay at Bordeaux, he returned to Paris on the evening of March 5th. The Commune of Paris was set on foot within a fortnight of that date, on March 18th, 1871.

CHAPTER IV

THE COMMUNE

UNQUESTIONABLY, the revolt was brought about by the ill-judged and arbitrary conduct of the agents of the National Assembly. To attempt to seize the guns of the National Guard as a preliminary to disarming the only Citizen force which the capital had at its disposal was as illegal as it was provocative. It was virtually a declaration of civil war by the reactionaries in control of the national forces. The people of Paris were in no humor to put up with such high-handed action on the part of men who, they knew, were opposed even to the Republic which they nominally served. They resisted the attempt and captured the generals, Lecomte and Thomas, who had ordered the step to be taken.

So far they were quite within their rights, and Clemenceau at first sympathized wholly with the Federals. The Parisians had undergone terrible privations during the siege, they were exasperated by the denunciations that poured in upon them from the provinces, they saw no hope for their recently won liberties unless they themselves were in a position to defend them, they had grave doubts whether they had not been betrayed within and without during the siege itself. It is no wonder that, under such circumstances, they should resent, by force of arms, any attempt to deprive them of the means of effective resistance to reactionary repression.

There was also nothing in the establishment of the Commune itself which was other than a perfectly legitimate effort to organize the city afresh, after the old system had proved utterly incompetent. But the attempt to disarm the population of Montmartre roused passions which it was impossible to quell. Clemenceau, as Mayor of the district, did all that one man could do to save the two generals, Lecomte and Clément Thomas, from being killed. With his sound judgment he saw at once that, whether their execution was justifiable or not, it would be regarded as murder by many Republicans whom the cooler heads in Paris desired to conciliate. As was proved afterwards, he exerted all his power to check even the semblance of injustice. But his final intervention to prevent the tragedy of the Château Rouge came too late, and Lecomte and Thomas, who had not hesitated to risk the massacre of innocent citizens on behalf of a policy of repression, were regarded as the first victims of an infuriated mob.

The outcome of Clemenceau's own endeavors to save these misguided militarists was that he himself became "suspect" to the heads of the Central Committee of the Commune sitting at the Hôtel de Ville, which had taken control of all Paris. He was the duly elected and extremely popular Radical-Socialist—to use a later designation—Mayor of perhaps the most advanced arrondissement in the capital, he had been sent to Bordeaux by a great majority of his constituents to sit on the extreme Left, and, in that capacity, had stoutly defended the rights of Paris; he was strongly in favor of most of the claims made by the leaders of the Commune. But all this went for nothing. The new Committee wanted their own man at Montmartre, and Clemenceau was not that man.

So Mayor of Montmartre he ceased to be, but earnest democrat and devoted friend of the people he remained. Unfortunately, having a wider outlook than most of those who had suddenly come to the front, he could not believe that mere possession of the capital meant attainment of the control of France by the Parisians, or the freeing of his country from German occupation. For once he advocated prudence and suggested compromise. A reasonable arrangement between the administrators of Paris with their municipal forces and the National Assembly with its regular army seemed to Clemenceau a practical necessity of the situation. He therefore urged this policy incessantly upon the Communists. It was an unlucky experience. Pyat, Vermorel and others so strongly resented his moderate counsels that they issued an order for his arrest, with a view to his hasty, if judicial, removal. Failing to lay hold upon Clemenceau himself, they captured a speaking likeness of the Radical doctor in the person of a young Brazilian. Him they were about to shoot, when they discovered that their proposed victim was the wrong man. Possibly these personal adventures in revolutionary democracy under the Commune may have influenced Clemenceau's views about Socialism in practical affairs in after life.

It is highly creditable to Clemenceau that a few years later one of his greatest speeches was delivered in the National Assembly to obtain the liberation and the recall from exile of the very same men who would gladly have silenced him for good and all when they were in power. However, he escaped their well-meant attentions, and, leaving Paris, went on a tour of vigorous Radical propaganda through the Provinces.

This was a most important self-imposed mission. Clemenceau, as he showed by his vote at Bordeaux, was strongly in favor of continuing the war and bitterly opposed to any surrender whatever. At the same time he was a thoroughgoing Republican who did not forget that the mass of Frenchmen must have voted for the Empire a few months before, or Napoleon's plébiscite, of course, could not have been so successful even with the whole of the official machinery in the hands of the Imperialists. Differing from Gambetta afterwards on many points, the coming leader of the advanced Radicals was at this period entirely at one with the man who had not despaired of France when all seemed lost. But in order to carry on the war with any hope of success and to keep the flag of the Republic flying, it was essential that the people of the provincial towns and the peasants should be kept in touch with Paris and be convinced that the only chance of safety and freedom lay in sinking all intestine differences for the sake of unity. No man, not even Gambetta himself, was better qualified for this service. Throughout his tour he kept the independence, welfare, and freedom of France as a whole high above all other considerations. But the risks he ran were not trifling. The local reactionists were by no means ready to accept his views. The police was set upon his trail, with great inconvenience to himself. But at no period of his life has Clemenceau considered his personal safety of any account. He had set himself to accomplish certain work which he deemed to be necessary, and he carried it through without reference to the dangers around him. Nor must the success of this propaganda be measured by its immediate results. The great thing in those days of defeat and despair was to keep up the national spirit and to declare that, though the French armies might be beaten again and again, the

France of the great Revolution and the Republic should never be crushed down. Believing, as Clemenceau did, in the religion of patriotism and the sacred watchwords of the eighteenth-century upheaval, he spoke with a sincerity that gave to his utterances the value of the highest oratory. The speeches produced a permanent impression on those who heard them, and their effect was felt for many years afterwards.

But this was quite as objectionable to Thiers and the case-hardened reactionists as his previous conduct had been to Pyat and the extremists of the Commune. Men of ability and judgment are apt to be caught between two fires when prejudice and passion take control on both sides. It was, in fact, little short of a miracle that the future Prime Minister of France did not complete his services to his country by dying in the ditch under the wall of Père-la-Chaise at the early age of thirty-one.

Few movements have been more grotesquely misrepresented than the Commune of Paris. For many a long year afterwards almost the whole of the propertied classes in Europe spoke of the Communists as if they had been a gang of scoundrels and incendiaries, without a single redeeming quality; while Socialists naturally enough refused to listen to virulent abuse of men most of whom they well knew were inspired by the highest ideals and sacrificed themselves for what they believed to be the good of mankind. At the beginning Paris assuredly had no intention whatever of courting a struggle with the supporters of the Republic at Bordeaux, however reactionary they might be. Such men as Delescluze, Courbet, Beslay, Jourde, Camélinat, Vaillant, Longuet, to speak only of a few, were no merely hot-headed revolutionaries regardless of all the facts around them. Paris was admirably administered under their short rule—never nearly so well, according to the testimony of two quite conservative Englishmen who were there at the time. One of these was the famous Oxford sculler and athlete, E. B. Michel, an English barrister and a French *avocat;* the other was my late brother, Hugh, a Magdalen man like Michel. They both knew Paris well, and both were of the same opinion as to the municipal management under the Commune. Michel in an article in *Fraser's Magazine,* then an important review, wrote as follows:

"It is extremely important that the serious lesson which the world may read in the history of the Revolution should not be weakened in its significance or interest by any ill-grounded contempt either for the acts of the Communal leaders or for the sincerity of their motives. We have seen that the army on which the Revolutionists relied, and by means of which they climbed to power, was not, as certain French statesmen pretended, and some English papers would have had us believe, a 'mere handful of disorderly rebels,' but a compact force, well drilled, well organized, and valiant when fighting for a cause that they really had at heart. It is equally false and unfair to regard the Communal Assembly as a crew of unintelligent and mischievous conspirators, guided by no definite or reasonable principle, and seeking only their own aggrandizement and the destruction of all the recognized laws of order. Yet it is certain that such an idea respecting the Commune is very generally entertained by ordinary English readers. It may be shown that the policy of this Government, though defaced by many gross abuses and errors, had much in it to deserve the consideration, and even to extort the admiration, of an intelligent and practical statesman. . . .

"Foreign writers have delighted to represent the purposes of the Commune as vague and unintelligible. Even in Paris and at Versailles writers and talkers affected at first to be ignorant of the real projects and principles entertained by the Revolutionists. But the Commune of 1871 has itself destroyed all possibility of mistake upon the subject. It has put to itself and answered the question in the most explicit terms. The *Journal Officiel* (of Paris) contained, on April 20th, a document worthy of the most careful perusal. It appears in the form of a declaration to the French people, and explains fully enough the main principles and the chief objects which animated the men of the Commune. Without bestowing on this address the ecstatic eulogies to which certain Utopian philosophers have deemed it entitled, we may credit it as being a straightforward, manly, and not altogether unpractical *exposé* of the ideas of modern Communists.

". . . 'It is the duty of the Commune to confirm and determine the aspirations and wishes of the people of Paris; to explain, in its true character, the movement of March 18th—a movement which has been up to this time misunderstood, misconstrued, and calumniated by the politicians at Versailles. Once more Paris labors and suffers for the whole of France, for whom she is preparing, by her battles and her devoted sacrifices, an intellectual, moral, administrative, and economic regeneration, an era of glory and prosperity.

" 'What does she demand?

" 'The recognition and consolidation of the Republic as the only form of government compatible with the rights of the people and the regular and free development of society; the absolute independence of the Commune and its extension to every locality in France; the assurance by this means to each person of his rights in their integrity, to every Frenchman the full exercise of his faculties and capacities as a man, a citizen, and an artificer. The independence of the Commune will have but one limit—the equal right of independence to be enjoyed by the other Communes who shall adhere to the contract. It is the association of these Communes that must secure the unity of France.

"'The inherent rights of the Commune are these: The right of voting the Communal budget of receipts and expenditure, of regulating and reforming the system of taxation, and of directing local services; the right to organize its own magistracy, the internal police and public education; to administer the property belonging to the Commune; the right of choosing by election or competition, with responsibility and a permanent right of control and revocation, the communal magistrates and officials of all sorts; the right of individual liberty under an absolute guarantee, liberty of conscience and liberty of labor; the right of permanent intervention by the citizens in communal affairs by means of the free manifestation of their ideas, and a free defense of their own interests, guarantees being given for such manifestations by the Commune, which is alone charged with the duty of guarding and securing the free and just right of meeting and of publicity; the right of organizing the urban defenses and the National Guard, which is to elect its own chiefs, and alone provide for the maintenance of order in the cities.

"'Paris desires no more than this, with the condition, of course, that she shall find in the Grand Central Administration, composed of delegates from the Federal

Communes, the practical recognition and realization of the same principles. To insure, however, her own independence, and as a natural result of her own freedom of action, Paris reserves to herself the liberty of effecting as she may think fit, in her own sphere, those administrative and economic reforms which her population shall demand, of creating such institutions as are proper for developing and extending education, labor, commerce, and credit; of popularizing the enjoyment of power and property in accordance with the necessities of the hour, the wish of all persons interested, and the data furnished by experience. Our enemies deceive themselves or deceive the country when they accuse Paris of desiring to impose its will or its supremacy upon the rest of the nation, and of aspiring to a Dictatorship which would amount to a veritable attack against the independence and sovereignty of other Communes. They deceive themselves or the country when they accuse Paris of seeking the destruction of French unity as established by the Revolution. The unity which has hitherto been imposed upon us by the Empire, the Monarchy, and the Parliamentary Government is nothing but a centralization, despotic, unintelligent, arbitrary, and burdensome. Political unity as desired by Paris is a voluntary association of each local initiative, a free and spontaneous coöperation of all individual energies with one common object— the well-being, liberty, and security of all. The Communal Revolution initiated by the people on the 18th of March inaugurated a new political era, experimental, positive, and scientific. It was the end of the old official and clerical world, of military and bureaucratic *régime,* of jobbing in monopolies and privileges, to which the working class owed its state of servitude, and our country its misfortunes and disasters.'"

The two Englishmen, coming straight to my house from Paris, gave me a favorable account of the administration of municipal Paris, especially at the time when Cluseret held command.

Others who were there at the same time were similarly impressed. Paris ceased even to be the Corinth of Europe, since all prostitutes had been ordered out of the city. The leaders set an example of moderation in their style of living, which was the more remarkable as they had no authority but their own sense of propriety to limit their expenditure. How little they regarded themselves as relieved from the ordinary rules of the strictest bourgeois social order is apparent, also, from the fact that Jourde and Beslay, who were responsible for the finances of the Commune, actually borrowed $200,000 from the Rothschilds in order to carry on the ordinary business of the Municipality. Yet at the time not less than $300,000,000 in gold, apart from a huge store of silver, was lying at their mercy in the Bank of France; enough, as some cynically said, if judiciously used, to have bought up all M. Thiers' Government and his army to boot. The fact that the Communists left these vast accumulations untouched proves conclusively that they were the least predatory, some might say the least effective, revolutionists who ever held subversive opinions. In all directions they showed the same spirit. Every department was managed as economically and capably as they could organize it. But always on the most approved bourgeois lines. Many of the reforms they introduced, notably those by Camélinat at the Mint, are still maintained.

How, then, did it come about that people of this character and capacity were regarded almost universally as desperate enemies of society, from the moment when they came to the front in their own city? It is the old story of the hatred of the materialist property-owner and profiteer for the idealist who is eager at once to realize the new period of public possession and coöperative well-being. The fact that such an indomitable anarchist-communist as the famous Blanqui, who spent the greater part of his life in prison, took an active part in the Commune and that others of like views were associated with the rising scared all the "respectable" classes, who regarded any attack upon the existing economic and social forms as a crime of the worst description. A tale current at the time puts the matter in a humorous shape. A number of communists, when arrested, were put in jail with a still larger number of common malefactors. These latter greatly resented this intrusion, boycotted the political prisoners, and, it is said, would have gone so far as to attack their unwelcome companions but for the intervention of the warders. Asked why they exhibited such animosity towards men who had done them no harm, the ordinary criminals took quite a conservative, bourgeois view of their relations to the newcomers. "We," they said, "have some of us taken things which belonged to other people; but we have never thought for a moment of abolishing the right of property in itself. Not having enough ourselves, we wanted more and laid hands upon what we could get. But these men would take everything and leave nothing for us." So even the jailbirds embraced the bourgeois ethic of individual ownership.

Moreover, the International Working Men's Association had been founded in London in 1864, just seven years before. Although the late Professor Beesly, certainly as far from a violent revolutionist as any man could be, took the chair at the first meeting and English trade unionists of the most sober character constituted the bulk of the members in London, the terror which this organization inspired in the dominant minority all over Europe was very far indeed in excess of the power which it could at any time exercise. But the names of Marx, the learned German-Jew philosopher, and Bakunin, the Russian peasant-anarchist, were words of dread to the comfortable classes in those days. Marx with Engels had written the celebrated "Communist Manifesto," at the last period of European disturbance, in 1848, analyzing the historic development and approaching downfall of the entire wage-earning system, with a ruthless disregard for the feelings of the bourgeoisie. Its conclusion appealing to the "Workers of the World" to unite was not unnaturally regarded as a direct incitement to combined revolt. Though, therefore, few had read the Manifesto, this appeal had echoed far and wide, and the organization of the International itself was credited with the intention to use the Commune of Paris as the starting-point for a world-wide conflagration. Thus the movement in Paris, which at first had no other object than to secure the stability of the democratic Republic, was regarded as an incendiary revolt, and the brutal outrages of M. Thiers, aided by the mistakes of the Communists themselves, gradually forced extremists to the front. Some were like Delescluze, noble enthusiasts who knew success was impossible, and courted death for their ideal as sowing the seed of success for their great cause of the universal Coöperative Commonwealth in the new future; others were such as Félix Pyat, a furious subversionist of the most ruffianly type, who mixed up personal malignity and individual hatred with his every action, and brought discredit on his own comrades. Victory for the Socialist ideals, with the Germans containing one side of Paris and the Versailles troops attacking the other, was impossible—would have been impossible even if the Communists had suppressed their truly fraternal hatreds and had developed a military genius. They did neither. Cluseret showed some inkling of the necessities of the case, but Dombrowski, Rossel and other leaders exhibited no capacity. The wonderful thing about it all was that during the crisis, which lasted two months, Paris was so well administered. The sacrifice of the hostages and the tactics of incendiarism pursued at last, not by the Communist leaders, but by the Anarchist mob broken loose from all control, have hidden from the public at large, who read only the prejudiced accounts of the capitalist press, the real truth of the Commune of Paris.

But whatever may have been done in resistance to the invasion of M. Thiers' army of reaction, nothing could possibly justify the horrible vengeance wreaked upon the people of Paris by the soldiery and their chiefs. It was a martyrdom of the great city. The *coup d'état* of Louis Napoleon was child's play to the hideous butchery ordered and rejoiced in by Thiers, Gallifet and their subordinates. There was not even a pretense of justice in the whole massacre. Thousands of unarmed and innocent men and women were slaughtered in cold blood because Paris was feared by the bloodthirsty clique who regarded her rightly as the main obstacle to their reactionary policy. It was but too clear evidence that, when the rights of property are supposed to be imperiled, all sense of decency or humanity will be outraged by the dominant minority as it was by the slave-owners of old or the nobles of the feudal times.

But the Commune itself, as matters stood, was as hopeless an attempt to "make twelve o'clock at eleven" as has ever been seen on the planet. John Brown's raid on Harper's Ferry was not more certainly foredoomed to failure than was the uprising of the Communists of Paris in 1871. But the Socialists of Europe, like the abolitionists, have celebrated the Commune and deified its martyrs for many a long year. The brave and unselfish champions of the proletariat who then laid down their lives in the hope that their deaths might hasten on the coming of a better day hold the same position in the minds of Socialists that John Brown held among the friends of the negro prior to the great American Civil War. It was an outburst of noble enthusiasm on their part to face certain failure for the "solidarity of the human race." But those who watched what happened then and afterwards can scarcely escape from the conclusion that the loss of so many of its ablest leaders, and the great discouragement engendered by the horrors of defeat, threw back Socialism itself in France fully twenty years. Recent experience in several directions has shown the world that enthusiasm and idealism for the great cause of human progress, and the coördination of social forces in the interest of the revolutionary majority of mankind, cannot of themselves change the course of events. Unless the stage in economic development has been reached where a new order has already been evolved out of the previous outworn system, it is impossible to realize the ideals of the new period by any sudden attack. Men imbued with the highest conceptions of the future and personally quite honest in their conduct may utterly fail to apply plain common sense to the facts of the present. Dublin, Petrograd and Helsingfors, nearly forty years later, did but enforce the teachings of the Commune of Paris.

CHAPTER V

CLEMENCEAU THE RADICAL

ALL this Clemenceau, though not himself a Socialist, saw by intuition. His powers of organization and capacity for inspiring confidence among the people might have been of the greatest service to Paris at that critical juncture in her history—might even have averted the crash which laid so large a portion of the buildings of the great city in ruins and led to the infamous scenes already referred to. This was not to be, and Clemenceau was fortunate to escape the fate of many who were as little guilty of terrorism or arson as himself.

The trial of the men responsible for the death of Generals Lecomte and Thomas was held on November 29, 1871. Clemenceau himself was accused of not having done enough to save their lives. He was in no wise responsible for what had occurred, was strongly opposed to their execution, and, as has been seen, did all that he could do to prevent the two assailants of his own friends and fellow-citizens from being killed. That, however, was no security that he would have escaped condemnation if the evidence in his favor had not been so conclusive that even the prejudiced court could not decide against him. He was completely cleared from the charge by the evidence of Colonel Langlois, and given full credit for his efforts on behalf of the militarists who certainly could be reckoned among his most bitter enemies.

Scarcely, however, was his life relieved from jeopardy under the law than he was compelled to risk it, or so he thought, on the dueling ground. Here Clemenceau was quite at home. He used his remarkable skill in handling the pistol with moderation and judgment, being content to wound his adversary, Commandant Poussages, in the leg. None the less, the result of his encounter was that he was fined and committed to prison for a fortnight as a lesson to him not to act in accordance with the French code of honor in future.

But the truth is, M. Thiers did not wish to make a peaceful settlement with the people of the capital of France. Conciliation itself was branded as a crime as much by the political leaders and military chiefs on his side as it was by the Communist extremists on the other. The Versaillais aimed at the conquest of Paris by force of arms: they did not desire to enter peacefully by force of agreement. And having won, Paris was treated by the Republican Government as a conquered city. All sorts of exceptional laws, such as Napoleon III himself never enacted, were registered against the liberties of her inhabitants, and she was deprived of her fair share of representation in the National Assembly. The capital of France was a criminal city.

Clemenceau on March 21st, 1871, had brought into the National Assembly at Versailles a measure which established the Municipal Council of Paris with 80 members. This was a valuable service to the capital and one of which the man himself was destined to take advantage. For, having failed to bring about a reasonable compromise between the Versailles chiefs and the leaders of the Commune, and having also lost his seat for Montmartre in the Assembly as well as the Mayoralty of that district, he gave up general politics and after the fall of the Commune accepted his election as Municipal Councilor for Clignancourt. He devoted the next five years of his life to his doctor's work, giving gratuitous advice as before to the poor around him, and to constant attendance as a Municipal Councilor, where he was the leader of the reformed section. He thus gained a knowledge of Parisian life and the needs of Parisians which no other experience could have given him.

As one of the municipal representatives he never ceased to protest against the shameful legislation which deprived Paris of its rights. But he did more. The man who is regarded by many, even to-day, as essentially a political destroyer with no idea of a constructive policy in any department made himself master of the details of municipal administration and was a most valued colleague of all who, acting on the extreme left of the Council, endeavored, while upholding the dignity of the city against the repressive policy of the Government, to improve the management of city affairs in every department. In this he was as successful as the circumstances of the time permitted. He became in turn Secretary, Vice-President and President of the Council.

Though this portion of Clemenceau's career is little known, the continuous unrecognized municipal service he rendered to Paris during those eventful years gave him a hold, not only upon Montmartre but upon the whole city, which has been of great service to him at other times. He had, in fact, become a thorough Parisian from the age of nineteen onwards, which can by no means always be said of men who have afterwards taken a leading part in French politics. It is very difficult to say what qualities are those which entitle a man to this distinguished appellation. I have myself known Frenchmen able, witty, brilliant and original, good speakers and clever writers, who somehow never seemed to be at home with Parisians and Parisian audiences. Critical and cynical, though at times enthusiastic and idealist, the Parisian crowd takes no man at his own valuation and is no less fickle than crowds in cities generally are. But Clemenceau has never failed to be on good terms with them. I attribute this to the fact that in addition to his other higher qualities, which impress all people of intelligence, Clemenceau has in him a vein of sheer humorous mischief that savors of the Parisian *gamin* rather than of the hard-working student from La Vendée. There is something in common between him and the young rogues of the Parisian streets who are not at all averse from enjoying life at the cost of poking fun at other people and even at themselves. This spirit of Paris early got hold of Clemenceau and he of it.

However this may be, on February 26th, 1876, he was again elected deputy to the National Assembly. He now began the active and continuous political life which had been broken off at its commencement by the second revolution followed by the gruesome tragedy just recounted.

That he had never lost his sympathy for the men and women of the Commune, little reason as he personally had for good feeling towards them, was proved by his delivery of his speech in favor of the Amnesty of the Communists, some of whom had been so eager to get rid of him for good and all when they had been in power for a short time themselves. The speech at once put Clemenceau among the first Parliamentary orators of the day. At this time a man of such capacity was greatly needed on the extreme Left. Others who had lost much of their energy and fervor in the long struggle against repression were little inclined to run further risks for the sake of a really democratic Republic, still less for a set of people who in their misguided efforts for complete freedom had endangered the establishment of any Republic at all. They were content with what they had done before and with the positions they occupied then. It was greatly to Clemenceau's credit that he did not hesitate a moment as to the line he should take. Popular or unpopular, fair play and freedom for all were his watchwords.

When the Amnesty question came up again in 1879 Clemenceau's speech in favor of the release of the indefatigable Communist Blanqui was, like his appeal for the amnesty of the members of the Commune generally, very creditable to him, for it was an unpopular move and gained him little useful political support from any party. Perhaps no man in the whole history of the revolutionary movement ever devoted himself so entirely and with such relentless determination to the spread of subversive doctrines as Auguste Blanqui. He began early and finished late. He was first imprisoned at the age of twenty-one and spent more than half of his seventy-six years of existence in jail or exile. He was a strong believer in organized violence as a means of bringing about the realization of his communist ideals. Insurrection against the successive French Governments he regarded as a duty. It was a duty which he faithfully fulfilled. In 1827 he was an active fighter in the insurrection of the Rue St. Denis. It was suppressed and Blanqui was wounded. He was one of the leaders of the successful rising against Charles X in 1830, in which he was again wounded. In the reign of Louis Philippe, which followed the failure to establish a Republic, he speedily went to work again. Insurrection, conspiracy, establishment of illegal societies, accumulation of weapons and explosives for organized attacks, attempts to constitute a communist republic, were followed by the usual penalties, and after his participation in the insurrection of the Montagnards, by condemnation to death, commuted to imprisonment for life. Such was Blanqui's career up to 1848. Then the revolution of that year set him free again. No sooner was he released than he began afresh, forming a revolutionary combination which led to another three days of insurrection, with the result that he was sentenced to a further ten years of imprisonment. In 1858, under the Second Empire, he returned to Paris, his birthplace, but was soon ejected and passed eight years more in exile. In 1870 and 1871 Blanqui took part in the overthrow of Napoleon III, and in the Commune which followed was captured by the Versaillais troops and sentenced to transportation to New Caledonia, after the Communards had offered to exchange for him the Archbishop of Paris, then held by them as a hostage. Instead of being shipped off to New Caledonia he was imprisoned at Clairvaux, where he remained until 1880, when he was elected, while still in jail, deputy for Bordeaux, was not allowed to take his seat but was released, and died in Paris in 1881.

This brief summary gives but a poor idea of Blanqui's activities and sufferings. At the period when Clemenceau pleaded for his release he was still, at seventy-one, the most dangerous revolutionary leader in France. From the first and throughout he was absolutely uncompromising in his adherence to his communist theories, and, being at the same time of dictatorial tendencies, he was an extremely difficult man to work with. None the less Blanqui represented the highest type of educated anarchist. He never considered himself for a moment. So long as he was able to keep the flag of revolution flying, and thus to prepare the way, by constant attempts at direct action, for the period when the people would be strong enough and well-organized enough to achieve victory for themselves, he was satisfied. A leader of his knowledge and capacity must have known and did know that his views could not possibly be accepted and acted upon, even if scientifically correct for a later date, at the stage of evolution which France had reached in his day. But, like Raspail, Delescluze, Amilcare Cipriani, Sophie Perovskaia, and more than one of the French dynamitical anarchists, he deliberately sacrificed his whole career, as he also risked his life time after time, in desperate efforts to uplift the mass of the people from their state of economic and social degradation. Nothing daunted him. His courage was of that exceptional quality which is strengthened by defeat. Even his bitterest enemies respected his devotion to his cause, his disregard of danger and the spirit he maintained, in spite of years upon years of confinement. He hated and despised the bourgeoisie, with their capitalist wage-earning, profit-making system, even more than he did monarchy and aristocracy. He revolted against the slow processes of social evolution, as he did against the inherited wrongs of class repression. No weapon of agitation came amiss to him. Journalist, pamphleteer, author, orator, organizer, conspirator, he covered in his own person the whole of the ground open to a convinced revolutionist. The suppressive order of to-day must be smashed up to give an outlet to the liberative order of to-morrow. Such a program was in direct opposition to the ideas of Clemenceau, who, individualist as he is, has always regarded political action and trade organization of a peaceful nature as the best means of attaining thorough reform and social reconstruction without running the risk of provoking monarchist or imperialist repression. Blanqui to him was an idealist who, by his very honesty and singleness of purpose, played into the hands of reaction, when he spent so much of his life as he lived outside of a prison in one broken but relentless effort to overthrow the existing society of inequality and wage-slavery by the same forcible methods that capitalist society itself uses to maintain the system in being. On the other hand, the right to freedom of person and freedom of expression was erected by the Radical leader into something not far from an intellectual religion. On this ground, therefore, he argued strongly in favor of Blanqui's release, though quite possibly, and indeed probably, Blanqui's freedom, had it been secured, would have been vigorously used against Clemenceau and his party—whom the great Anarchist-Communist would have regarded as mere trimmers—to the advantage of the reactionists themselves. But in this case as in that of the amnesty to the Communists, the Clemenceau of the Rights of Man and Liberty, Equality and Fraternity overcame Clemenceau the practical politician. That he failed to get Blanqui out of prison could only have been expected, having regard to the character of the Assembly to which his appeal is addressed.

His Amnesty speech made a fine beginning for Clemenceau's active Parliamentary life. It put him on a very different level from that occupied by the mere political adventurers and intriguers whose main objects were either to help on the reconstitution of some form of monarchy or to secure for themselves posts under the Republic of much the same kind as existed under the Empire. Men who but yesterday had been champions of a genuine Republic in which the interests of the majority of the French people should be considered first, foremost and all the time had now become mere plotters for reaction, or opportunists anxious never to find an opportunity. They were Republicans in name but not in spirit. They were convinced that the most important portion of their policy consisted henceforth not in organizing the factor of democracy for general progress but in reassuring their conservative opponents and the propertied classes generally, from the plutocrat to the peasant proprietor, that the Republic meant only a convenient form of government, in which all classes should agree harmoniously together to stand at ease for the next few generations. Their arguments in favor of such a scheme of permanent repose were unfortunately only too striking. They had but to recall the downfall of the Commune and to point to the ruins of fine public buildings to appeal effectively to the feelings of a large and influential portion of the people. Enthusiasm had become suspect, idealism the antechamber to violent mania, even Radicalism a vain thing.

Gambetta himself, regarded in England as the most eloquent and capable leader of the Republican party, invented an excuse for the existence of the Republic which he had taken an active part in creating, by the formula, "It is that which divides us the least." Indifference on every important question except colonial expansion became the highest political wisdom. It was, in fact, hesitating opportunism and cowardly compromise which then dominated France. Such tactics evoked no loyalty and solved no problem. The old became cynical, the young contemptuous. To attack such flabby consistency in doing nothing seemed as bootless an enterprise as entering into conflict with a feather-bed. The early years of the French Republic constituted a period of apathy led, with one or two exceptions, by mediocrity. Even the scathing sarcasm and biting irony of Rochefort failed to produce any serious effect upon the smug stolidity of the rest-and-be-thankful representatives of the French middle class. Hence arose "a divorce between politics and thought," and men of capacity became disgusted with the form of government itself. All this played directly into the hands of reaction and was preparing the way for a series of attempts against the Republic.

It was at this unhopeful period of stagnation, compromise and mediocrity that Clemenceau came to the front as leader of the Left in the National Assembly. He at once showed that he had every qualification for this important position—never more important than when there was a conspiracy afoot to prove to the world that there was no Radical Left at all. At the time he entered the Assembly in 1876 Clemenceau was thirty-five years of age, with an irreproachable past behind him and the full confidence of the Republicans of Paris around him. In his work in Montmartre and on the Municipal Council the people had come to know what manner of man he was. Without their steady support it would have been difficult, if not impossible, for him to carry on the uphill fight he fought for so many years. His principles upon every subject of public policy were from the first clear and well defined.

Freedom of person, of speech and of the press were cardinal points in his program. He demanded that Paris should be released from all exceptional measures of repression inflicted by the so-called Conservatives upon the whole of the inhabitants of the capital as revenge for the rash action of a small number of fanatical idealists and as a means of keeping down any agitation against their own corruption and incompetence. He claimed also that no perpetual disability, in the shape of imprisonment and exile, should attach to the members of the Commune of Paris, and called for the fullest pardon and freedom even for the irreconcilable Anarchist, Blanqui. On questions of political rights, universal secular education, the separation of Church and State, the generous treatment of the rank and file of the army, the prevention of the intrigues of the Catholics, and the expulsion of the Jesuits, Clemenceau took the line of an out-and-out democrat. So, likewise, in regard to the treatment of the working classes. Though not really a Socialist, the Radical leader recognized clearly the infinite hardships suffered by the wage-earners under the capitalist system, and proposed and supported palliative legislation to lessen and redress their wrongs. In foreign affairs he was a man of peace, never forgetting the outrages committed by the German armies in the war nor the territory seized and the huge indemnity exacted by the German Government at the peace; but hoping always that the friendly development of the peoples of both France and Germany might avert further antagonism and eventually lead to a full understanding which would assuage the hatreds of the past and lay the foundations of mutual good feeling in the future. To colonization by conquest and colonial adventures generally Clemenceau was steadfastly opposed. The entire policy of expansion he regarded as injurious to the true interests of the country, diverting to doubtful enterprises abroad resources which were required for the development of Republican France at home. Such colonial schemes also were apt to create difficulties and even to risk wars with other nations which could in nowise benefit the people, while they might strengthen the financiers whose malefic power was already too great.

Such in brief was the general policy which Clemenceau set himself to formulate and put to the front on behalf of the only party which at that moment could exercise any serious influence in the political world. The whole program was closely knit together, and for many years stood the brunt of the bitterest Parliamentary warfare conceivable. It was a conflict of ideas that Clemenceau entered upon. He conducted it throughout on the most approved principle of all warfare: Never fail to attack in order to defend. The advice of the American banker, "David Harum," might have been enunciated as the motto of Georges Clemenceau the French statesman: "Do unto others as they would do unto you, and do it *first.*"

But the main point of all, that which assured and confirmed and strengthened his leadership under the most difficult and dangerous circumstances, was his resolute opposition to compromise. This was contrary to all the ideas of political strategy and tactics which then prevailed in France. "Men became Ministers solely on condition that they refused when in power to do that which they had promised when in opposition"—quite the English method, in fact. He himself never failed to denounce nominal Republicans who set themselves stubbornly against reform and progress in every shape, as mere reactionists in disguise. They were, in fact, the staunch buttresses of that bourgeois Republic of which Clemenceau not long afterwards said to me, *"La République, mon ami, c'est l'Empire républicanisé."* It was indeed a republicanized Empire which best suited the leading French politicians of that day. For at first bourgeois domination of the narrowest and meanest kind, leading, so the reactionaries hoped, to the restoration of the monarchy, had its will of Paris and all that Paris at its best stood for. As we look back upon that period of pettifoggery in high places, the wonder is that the Royalists were not successful. If they had had a king worth fighting for they might have been; for more than one President was certainly not unfavorable to the monarchy or empire. Prime Ministers were similarly tainted with reaction, and the army was none too loyal to the Republic.

CHAPTER VI

FROM GAMBETTA TO CLEMENCEAU

MEDICI, Mazarin, Riquetti-Mirabeau, Buonaparte, Gambetta—these names recall the great influence which Italians have had upon French affairs. Few, if any, nations have allowed persons of foreign extraction to lead them as France permitted the men recorded above. Much, too, as these Italians were affected by their French surroundings, there is something in them all quite different from what we regard as distinctively French intelligence and general capacity. Possibly that gave them their power of control. They had that faculty of detachment, of looking at the situation from without which is so invaluable to any man who has to play a great part in the world. Some of them could so far survey as well as enter into the peculiarities of the French mind that they could play upon its weaknesses as well as call forth its strength. Yet, with all their genius, the four men named failed to accomplish what they set out to achieve, and none left behind him and amid his own immediate followers those who were capable of carrying on his work.

Léon Gambetta had but fourteen years of active political life, and during only eleven of those years was he in a position to make himself seriously felt. But what an amazing career this was of the grocer's boy of Cahors who stirred all France to enthusiastic support or ferocious denunciation between 1871 and 1882! When William

Morris died, the doctor who attended him was asked what he died of. "He died of being William Morris," was the reply. Although Gambetta's death was due to a pistol-shot received under circumstances never fully explained, it may be said that he also died of being Léon Gambetta. For his inner fires had burnt the man out. He crowded all the excitement and passions of a long lifetime into those stormy eleven years, and without some account of him and his efforts for the foundation of the Republic the story of Clemenceau is not complete.

Born in 1848 and enabled to come to Paris by the touching self-sacrifice of a maiden aunt who believed that her nephew's confidence in his destiny to do great things would be realized, Gambetta was soon regarded as a leader among the young men of the Quartier Latin, who were in full revolt against the Empire. He distinguished himself by his easy-going, rough-and-tumble mode of life, his carelessness about study of the law which was to be his means of earning a livelihood, and his perfervid eloquence in the political circles which he frequented. Lawyer, journalist, bohemian orator of the clubs, strongly anti-Imperialist, he had much personal magnetism, but was not generally recognized as a man of exceptional ability. The few cases he had had in the Courts did not give him any considerable standing. Such was Gambetta when a number of Republican journalists were arrested on November 12th, 1868, for starting a subscription to erect a monument to M. Baudin, the Republican deputy who had been shot down in cold blood during Louis Napoleon's massacre of the people of Paris on December 2nd, 1851—seventeen years before. Among these prisoners was the famous Delescluze, then editor of the *Réveil*. His counsel was Léon Gambetta. Gambetta's speech was not merely a defense of his client, it was a scathing indictment of the Empire, from its foundation on the ruin of the Republic of 1848 by the *coup d'état* onwards. "Who," the advocate asked, "were the men who 'saved' France at the cost of the death or transportation or exile of all her most eminent citizens? They were, to quote Corneille, *'un tas d'hommes perdus de dettes et de crimes.'* These are the sort of people who for centuries have slashed down institutions and laws. Against them the human conscience is powerless, in spite of the sublime march-past of the martyrs who protest in the name of religion destroyed, of morality outraged, of equity crushed under the jackboot of the soldier. This is not salvation: it is assassination." And this was no longer a press prosecution, it was the Emperor and his set of scoundrels who were now on their trial before the people of France and Europe.

The speech gave Gambetta great popularity and the opening into public life he desired. The cause itself was lost before the trial began. Delescluze was fined and imprisoned. "You may condemn us, but you can neither dishonor us nor overthrow us," cried Gambetta. From that time forward he was regarded as a new force on the side of the Republic. His behavior in the Corps Législatif, to which he was soon afterwards elected, justified this opinion. When the disasters of the Empire came Gambetta was one of the first to cry for Napoleon's abdication and the establishment of the Republic, taking an active part in the foundation of the new order in Paris. It may be said that he worked side by side, though never hand in hand, with Clemenceau.

But those scenes of the downfall of the Empire in the capital, dramatic and exciting as they were, could bear no comparison with his bold escape from beleaguered Paris in a balloon and the magnificent effort he made to rouse the Provinces against the invaders. He failed to turn the tide of German victories, but he prevented the shameful surrender without a fight for the French Republic which many would have been glad to accept, and he, more than any other man, kept the flag flying, when Legitimists, Orleanists and Buonapartists were all doing their utmost to set on foot a reactionary government against the best interests of France. All this is part of the common history of the time. But we are apt, in looking back over that period of his activities, to underrate the almost superhuman energy he displayed, to attach too much importance to the mistakes he inevitably made, and to forget that his own countrymen were among his worst enemies in the work he undertook. Also, if the Empire had left the Republic one single really first-rate general at the disposal of France, the result might have been very different from what it was. There is such a thing as luck in human affairs, and luck was dead against Gambetta. All the more credit to him for never losing heart even in the face of continuous disasters and even betrayals. First as leading member of the Government of Defense, and then as virtual Dictator of France, Gambetta bridged over for the time being the bitter antagonism which separated Paris, the besieged seat of government, from the rest of France. Immediately on his arrival at Tours he created a new National Government out of the unpromising elements gathered together almost accidentally there. The fall of Metz and the threatened starvation of Paris, which might lead to surrender at any moment, made Gambetta's own position desperate. The Paris Government, which apparently looked only to Paris, had failed to make a resolute effort to break through the lines of the German investment before Metz fell, and had lost heart altogether, refusing even to listen to any remonstrance from outside against a humiliating peace. Gambetta never gave way. Arrived at Bordeaux, he stuck to his text of carrying on the war, having in the meantime vigorously denounced the Government in Paris for its weakness. He and his fellow-delegates were deaf to the counsels of despair brought red-hot by members of the Government, but at last, overwhelmed by circumstances he could not control, the young Dictator resigned. After Paris had surrendered there was really no further hope, and those who voted in the new Assembly, as did Louis Blanc, Clemenceau and others, for the continuance of the war, did so more by way of protest against the apathy which pervaded the whole Assembly and because foreign intervention in favor of France and against Germany seemed possible even thus late in the day, than because they saw at the moment any prospect of success.

Thus France lay prostrate at the feet of Germany, but at least Gambetta and the Republicans who acted with him showed their confidence that she would rise again. They were not responsible for the collapse of the French nation: undismayed by defeat they believed in Republican France of the near future.

Gambetta had created new armies out of disarray and disorder, and he had also aroused a fresh spirit which rose superior to disaster. The victory of the Republic in years to come over all the forces of reaction was largely due to the work done during Gambetta's four months of dictatorship.

Universal Suffrage, General Secular Education, No Second Chamber, the Republican form of Government:

those were the principal measures advocated by the extreme Left of the National Assembly, and these were advocated by Gambetta both at Bordeaux and when he took his seat at Versailles as one of the Deputies for Paris. But the Royalists were still in a majority, and were determined to take every advantage of their position while power still remained in their hands. Their object was to render Republicanism hateful. The object of their opponents was to show that no other form of government was possible and to prevent any other form from being established. Now that the Republic has been maintained for more than forty-seven years, under all sorts of difficult and dangerous circumstances, the obstacles which stood in its way at the start are sometimes under-estimated. Continuous agitation was needed to keep the country fully alive to the intrigues of the Royalists and Catholics. It was essential to put the misdeeds of the Empire and the real objects of the monarchists constantly before the public. No man in France was better qualified for this work than Gambetta, and he did it well, so well that the whole reactionary party was infuriated against him. There was no opportunism about him at this period, beyond the necessary adaptation of means to ends under circumstances which rendered immediate success impossible.

M. Thiers, in consequence of his horrible suppression of the Commune, was by far the most powerful public man in the country. He was acting, though a Constitutional Monarchist, as trustee for a provisional form of government which could not be distinguished from a conservative Republic. The longer this continued the better the chance of obtaining a Government which would not be conservative. It was of great importance, therefore, to keep M. Thiers on the Republican side, and this was made easier by the action of M. Thiers' own old friends. So antagonistic was their attitude to the former Minister of Louis Philippe that, even when Gambetta supported the ex-Mayor of Lyons, a fervid Radical, M. Barodet, against M. Thiers' eminent friend and coadjutor M. de Rémusat, as representative of Paris, and the former won by 40,000 votes, Thiers never wavered in his decision to keep away from any direct connection with the monarchists. They therefore determined to upset the President, did so by a majority of 26 votes in the Assembly, and elected a President of their own in the person of Marshal MacMahon. This was on May 24th, 1873.

Reaction had won at Versailles. It remained to be seen whether it would win in the country. A "Ministry of Combat" for reaction, headed by the Duc de Broglie, was formed, and a Ministry of Combat it certainly proved to be. They were allowed no peace by their opponents, who never ceased to attack them all round, and they met these persistent assaults by attempts secretly to cajole and suborn public opinion. So the great combat went on. The majority remained a majority and rejected the Republic. It was useless. But in his anxiety to win speedily in conjunction with M. Thiers, Gambetta himself and his followers practiced that very opportunism which he had previously denounced. A non-democratic Senate, which had always been opposed by Republicans, was enacted as an essential part of the Republican Constitution, and on February 25th, 1875, the French Republic was firmly established as the legal form of government by the very same majority that, in the hope of rendering any such disaster to monarchy impossible, had made Marshal MacMahon President and the Duc de Broglie Premier.

But it was a truncated Republic that Gambetta had thus obtained. What he had gained by political compromise he had lost in the enthusiasm of principle. A leader who desires to achieve great reforms must always keep in close touch with the fanatics of his party. They alone can be relied upon in periods of crisis, they alone refuse to regard politics merely as a remunerative profession. The compromise—for men of principle compromise spells surrender—of February 25th, 1875, was destined to be fatal to the democratic parliamentary dictatorship which Gambetta might have achieved by common consent of his party, had he pursued his original policy of democratic Republicanism through and through. He stunted the growth of his own progeny by helping to establish a Republicanized Empire. No doubt this averted friction for the time being, but it slackened the rule of progress, placed obstacles in the path of democracy and destroyed public enthusiasm. By one of the strange ironies of political life, however, it so chanced that nearly thirty years later Clemenceau himself owed his return to Parliament to the institution of that same Senate the creation of which he had always resolutely opposed.

But during these years of reconstruction from 1871 to 1875 Clemenceau had been excluded from the Assembly and actively engaged in the work of the Municipal Council of Paris. There he did admirable service in consolidating the organization of Parisian municipal life to which he had been instrumental in giving expression in legal shape as Deputy for Montmartre. Paris had become the bugbear of all the reactionists and law-and-order men. The capital was constantly referred to by them as if the last acts of despair of the irresponsible extremists of the Commune were the habitual diversions of the Parisian populace when allowed free play for the realization of their own aspirations. The Parisians, in fact, according to these persons, were burning with the desire to destroy their own city in order to avenge themselves upon their provincial detractors and enemies. It was important to show, therefore, not only that Paris could manage her own affairs coolly and capably, but also that she could take a progressive line of her own which might give the lead to other French cities in more than one direction. This was precisely what the Municipal Council did, and Clemenceau, by his constant attendance and the continuous pressure he exerted as an active member of the Left of that body, prevented the Council from being used at any time as a center of reactionist intrigue. By this means also he strengthened his personal influence in his own democratic district as well as in Paris as a whole. He took care likewise all the world should know that on the matter of the full restitution of Parisian rights and the return of the Assembly to the capital he was as determined as ever, and that in the affairs of general politics he was and always would be a thoroughgoing Radical Republican. Thus he was building up for himself outside the Chamber a reputation as a capable municipal administrator as well as a fearless champion of the public rights of the great city he had made his home. At the same time his local popularity, due to his thorough knowledge of social conditions and his advocacy of municipal improvements of every kind, added to his gratuitous service as doctor of the poor, gave him an indisputable claim upon the votes of the people when, after having become

FROM GAMBETTA TO CLEMENCEAU 71

President of the Municipal Council, he should decide to offer himself for reëlection to the Assembly.

And from February 25th, 1875, onwards, matters were taking such a turn that the presence of a thoroughly well-informed, determined, active and fearless representative of Paris became necessary. A leader was wanted on the extreme Left who should loyally support the moderate Republicans when they were going forward and have the courage to attack them when they seemed inclined to hesitate or go back. The success of the conservative compromise in the constitution of the Republic had strengthened the belief of the reactionary majority in the Assembly in their own power under the new conditions. Gambetta's own moderation deceived them as to the real position in the country. They began to think that the Republicans were afraid not only of how they would fare in the elections to the newly constituted Senate, but that the result of the General Elections which must shortly be held would be unfavorable to their cause. The Prime Minister, M. Buffet, aided and abetted by the President, MacMahon, who never forgot that the members of the Right were his real friends, made full use of the Exceptional Laws and the State of Siege which was still in force to show the Republicans plainly what a reactionary majority would mean. The Conservatives and Imperialists had things all their own way. Democracy became a byword and Radicalism a vain thing.

With the ministry at their command and the President in their hands, they needed only to obtain the control of the Senate to have the people of France entirely at their mercy. Then, with the army favorable, with whole cohorts of anti-Republican officials at their service, they might postpone the General Elections, maintain the state of siege permanently and prepare everything for a monarchical restoration or a Buonapartist plébiscite. *L'Empire républicanisé* indeed!

M. Buffet, within a few months of the declaration of the Republic as the real form of government of France, spoke quite in this sense. Happily the forces of reaction fell out among themselves. They could not trust one another in any sharing of the booty which might fall to the general lot. Therefore, when the time came for nomination and election of the seventy-five members of the Senate to be elected by the Assembly, their intestine differences lost them the battle: one portion of their motley group even went over to the enemy. So the Republicans actually obtained a majority by the votes of their opponents. In this way the danger of the Senate as a whole being used against the Republic was averted and the Radicals had secured the first point in the political game. Yet, in spite of this preliminary success, the reactionists had a majority of the Senate of 300 when the limited votes of the country had been polled. But the Republicans in revenge gained a surprising majority at the General Elections for the National Assembly, such a majority that it might have been thought any further serious effort on the part of the anti-Republicans would be impossible and even that Gambetta's previous policy of opportunism was unnecessary.

It was at this election of 1876 that Clemenceau was returned again for the 18th Electoral District of Paris to the National Assembly as a thoroughgoing Radical Republican, and took his seat on the extreme Left under the leadership of Gambetta.

Marshal MacMahon, the President, was a good honest soldier who served his country as well as he knew how, but was quite incapable of understanding the new forces that were coming into action around him. The Parisians were never tired of inventing humorous scenes in which he invariably figured as the well-meaning pantaloon. Everybody trusted his honor, but all the world doubted his intelligence. He was by nature, upbringing and surroundings a conservative in the widest sense of the word. Radical Republicanism was to him the accursed thing which would bring about another Commune of Paris, if its partisans were given free rein. Although, therefore, incapable of plotting directly for the overthrow of the Constitution he had pledged himself to uphold, he was liable to yield to influences the full tendency of which he did not discern. Thus it happened that he allowed himself unconsciously to become the tool of the highly educated and clever Duc de Broglie, who was undoubtedly a monarchist and, what was still worse, a statesman imbued with the ideals of clericalism and of the Jesuits—precisely those powers which the growing spirit of democracy and Republicanism most feared. It was this growing spirit and its expression in the National Assembly that the Prime Minister, M. Jules Simon, who succeeded de Broglie, had to recognize and deal with. Gambetta was still the leader of the Republican Party, and with him for this struggle were all the more advanced men, including Clemenceau, who afterwards stoutly opposed his policy of opportunism and compromise. M. Jules Simon, finding the majority of the Assembly in favor of steady progress towards the Left, was quite unable to check the movement in this direction or to refuse the legislation to which the Republican demands of necessity impelled him. The President could not see that an extremely moderate man, such as Jules Simon undoubtedly was, would not have taken this course unless he had been convinced that the Republic had to be in some degree republicanized if serious trouble were to be averted. In short, Marshal MacMahon felt that the floodgates of revolution were being opened, and forthwith knocked down the lock-keeper. In other words, he sent for M. Jules Simon and talked to him in such a manner as gave the Premier no option but to resign. Resign he did. Thereupon France was thrown into that turmoil of peaceful civil war ever afterwards known as the *Coup du Seize Mai*. The Duc de Broglie, with a trusty phalanx of seasoned reactionaries and devotees of priestcraft, again took office, regardless of the fact that the majority of the Chamber was solid against them all. Even with the most strenuous support of the President of the Republic, the de Broglie Ministry never had a chance from the first. They were in a hopeless minority, and their attempt to govern on the basis of MacMahon's reputation and the support of the priests could not but result in failure unless the Marshal himself were prepared to risk a *coup d'état*. This the Duc de Broglie and his followers were ready to attempt, but it was useless to embark upon anything of the kind so long as the President held back.

Then came the famous division, following up a most violent discussion, which for many a long year formed a landmark in the history of the Republic. Three hundred and sixty-three Republicans declared against the President's Ministry of reaction and all its works. But Marshal MacMahon still would not understand that in his mistaken attempt to override the National Assembly in order to save France from what he believed would be an Anarchist revolution, he himself, with his group of monarchists and clericals, was steadily impelling the country into civil war. The action taken against Gambetta, then at the height of his vigor and influence, for declaring in his famous phrase that, in view of the attitude of the Chamber, the President must either "submit or resign," made matters still worse. The President's manifestoes to the Assembly and the country also only confirmed the growing impression that a sinister plot was afoot against the Republic itself in the interest of the Orleanists.

This was a much more serious matter than appeared on the surface. In the six years which had passed since the withdrawal of the German armies and the suppression of the Commune, France had become accustomed to the Republic and to the use of universal suffrage as a democratic instrument of organization. Great as were its drawbacks in many respects, the Republic was, as Gambetta phrased it, the form of government which divided Frenchmen the least. The people, who comprised not only the enlightened Radical Republicans of the cities, but the easily frightened small bourgeoisie and the peasantry, could now make the Assembly and the Senate do what they pleased. They were not as yet prepared to push those institutions very fast or very far, but they were unquestionably moving forward and were in no mind whatever to go back either to Napoleonism, Orleanism or Legitimism. France as a Republic was becoming the France of them all.

When, therefore, the 363 deputies who voted against the Duc de Broglie's rococo restoration policy and Marshal MacMahon's constitutional autocracy stood firmly together, sinking all differences in the one determination to safeguard and consolidate the Republic, there could be no real doubt as to the result. Those 363 stalwarts issued a vigorous appeal to the country, and the issue was joined in earnest at the General Elections. Gambetta meanwhile was the hero of the hour, straining every nerve for victory, exhausting himself by his furious eloquence, and the other advanced leaders did their full share of the fighting. In all this political warfare Clemenceau was as active and energetic as the fiery tribune himself, and as one of the framers and signatories of the great Republican appeal identified himself permanently with the document that recorded, as events proved, the decision of France to be and to remain a Republic.

Although it did not seem so at the time, the President played completely into the hands of the Republicans by the Message he sent to the Assembly and the Senate just before the prorogation he had so autocratically decreed. Here is a portion of it:—

"Frenchmen,—You are about to vote. The violence of the opposition has dispelled all illusions. . . . The conflict is between order and disorder. You have already announced you will not by hostile elections plunge the country into an unknown future of crises and conflicts. You will vote for the candidates whom I recommend to your suffrages. Go without fear to the poll.
"(Signed) MARÉCHAL MACMAHON."

The elections followed. It is difficult to exaggerate the advantage which is given in a French General Election to the party in power at the time. An unscrupulous Minister of the Interior has at his disposal all sorts of devices and machinery for helping his own side to victory. He can bring pressure of every kind to bear upon individuals directly or indirectly dependent on the Government of the day, and the whole official caste may be enlisted on behalf of the administration in control. This is the case ordinarily and in quiet times. But here was a direct stand-up fight between Reaction and Clericalism on the one side and Republicanism and Secularism—for that was at stake too—on the other. Both Marshal MacMahon and the Duc de Broglie honestly believed that they were doing their very utmost to preserve France from rapine and ruin. Every Radical Republican of the old school or the new was to them a bloody-minded Communard in disguise, veiling his instincts for plunder with eloquent appeals for patriotism and humanity. It is easy for the fanatics of conservatism and reaction thus to delude themselves. And once self-deceived they lose no chance of imposing their own wise and sober views upon the misguided people! So it happened in this case. Never were the powers of the Government in office strained to the same extent as in these elections of 1877 —the elections which followed on the *"Seize Mai"* stroke of MacMahon. Not an opportunity for coercing, cajoling and intimidating the voters was missed. In every urban district and rural village throughout France the State, the Church, the Municipality, the Commune were used to the fullest extent possible to obtain a vote favorable to the de Broglie Ministry. Swarms of priests and Jesuits buzzed around the constituencies, and promises of an easy time of it in this life and the next if things went the right way were made in profusion. If the Republic could be beaten by the forces of reaction it would be beaten now! Gambetta had predicted that the 363 would return to the Assembly as 400. This was not to be. But in view of the tremendous efforts made to stem the tide of progress, not only by promises, but by serious threats wherever threats might tell, the wonder is the Republicans were so successful as they proved to be. In spite of all that the President and the Prime Minister and the Catholic Church and the Jesuits—who were fighting for the right to remain in France—and the curés and the State functionaries, and all that the agencies of aristocratic, monarchist and Buonapartist—more particularly Buonapartist—corruption could do, the Republicans returned to the Chamber with a substantial majority of upwards of 100 votes. This victory was universally recognized not only in France but throughout Europe as irrefragable evidence that the French people had finally decided for a Republic, and had dealt at the same time a serious blow to the Church.

But, obvious as this was to everybody else, the respectable old soldier who had been a party to all this reactionary turmoil was still unconvinced of the error of his ways! He repeated the formula of the Malakoff fortress: *J'y suis, j'y reste.* But the Republicans were more tenacious than the Russians. They resolved to dislodge him, political Marshal though he was. A resolution was passed by the Assembly to inquire into corrupt practices during the election. It was a challenge to battle, and signed by such men as Albert Grévy, H. Brisson, Jules Ferry, Léon Gambetta, Floquet, Louis Blanc and Clemenceau.

A great debate, lasting several days, followed, in which de Broglie defended himself in a high-handed manner against the fervid denunciations of Gambetta. A Committee of Inquiry was nominated and the arena of the struggle changed to the Senate, which presently, as might have been expected from its reactionary character, gave a small vote of confidence in the Marshal and his Ministers. Nevertheless the feeling in the country was such that even MacMahon could not hold on. De Broglie resigned, and the Marshal evolved—almost from the depths of his inner consciousness—an "extra-Parliamentary Cabinet" which might have been called "The Cabinet of Men of No Account." But these were so unknown and so incompetent that all France made fun of them; and the will of the old Marshal, which nothing else could conquer, was broken by ridicule. In December, 1877, the President of the Republic saw that unless he appealed to the army, as the Buonapartists vigorously incited him to do, an appeal which more than probably the army itself would have rejected, there was no course open to him but the alternative which Gambetta had pointed out as being the Marshal's inevitable destiny if he kept within the limits of law and order—to submit or to resign. The old soldier of the Empire submitted, and did his country a service by accepting the rebuff which he had courted: a moderate Republican Ministry under the Premiership of M. Dufaure took office. MacMahon himself remained President of the Republic until January, 1879 (when he was succeeded by Jules Grévy), but his reactionary power was broken and France entered on a moderately peaceful era of recognized Republicanism. Gambetta was the acknowledged leader of the Republican majority; and Clemenceau, after this first taste of victory, now began that fine career of destructive, anti-opportunist Radicalism and semi-Socialist democracy which made him for many years the most redoubtable politician and orator in the Republic. The Radical-Socialist Clemenceau stood next in succession to the Opportunist Gambetta.

CHAPTER VII

THE TIGER

WHEN a political leader in the course of some fifteen years of Parliamentary life has upset, or has helped to upset, no fewer than eighteen administrations and has always refused to take office himself, that leader is likely to have created a few enemies. When, in addition to these feats of destruction, he has during the same period secured the nomination and election of three Presidents of the Republic and has thus proved an insuperable obstacle to the realization of the legitimate ambitions of the most important public men in France who were not elected, it is clear that personal popularity was not the object he had in view. It is impossible for the ordinary politician or journalist to judge fairly a man of this sort. Politics in modern Europe is an interesting game and, quite frequently, a remunerative profession. Party interests sap all principle and the attainment of personal aims and ambitions in and out of Parliament is, as a rule, quite incompatible with common honesty. Instead of Court intrigues and backstair cabals there are nowadays lobby "transactions" and convenient sales of titles and positions arranged, for value received, at private meetings. That is as far as democracy has got yet. It is all an understood business, often complicated with more flagitious pecuniary dealings outside.

Republican Government, or Constitutional Government, means, therefore, the success or failure of vote-catching and advantage-grabbing schemes, quite irrespective, from the public point of view, of the merits of the proposals which are put forward. Honest enthusiasts, who really wish to get something done for the benefit of the present or the coming generation, are only useful in so far as they act as stokers-up of public opinion for the profit of the political promoter of this or that faction. Steam is needed to drive the machine of State. Men of real convictions furnish that steam. But they are fools for their pains, all the same. Half the amount of energy used in the right direction would gain for them place, pelf, and possibly power, which is all that any man of common sense goes into politics for. Anybody who carries high principle and serious endeavor into political life is not playing the game. Everybody around him wants to know what on earth he is driving at. The only conceivable object of turning a Ministry out is to get in. To turn a Government out in order to keep out yourself is an unintelligible and therefore dangerous form of political mania, or a persistent manifestation of original sin.

Clemenceau was found guilty on both counts. But he was the ablest public man in all France. Moreover, he was successful in the diabolical combinations he set on foot. The thing was uncanny. That he should begin by overthrowing other politicians was all in the way of business. But that he should go on at it, time after time, for year after year, while other and inferior men took the posts he had opened for them, was not to be explained by any known theory of human motives. If he had been a cranky religionist, now, that would conceivably have met the case. He might have been "possessed" from on high or from below. But Clemenceau was and is a free-thinker of free-thinkers: neither Heaven nor Hell has anything to say to him. Clearly it is a case of malignant atavism: Clemenceau has thrown back to his animal ancestry. What is the totem of the tribe which has entered into him, whose instinct of depredation pervades his every political action? We have it! He is of the jungle, jungly. His spring is terrific. His crashing attack fatal. He looks as formidable as he is. In short, he is a Tiger, and there you are. That accounts for everything!

When Clemenceau was reëlected Deputy for the 18th Arrondissement to the National Assembly, on October 14th, 1877, and took the active part in the renewed struggle with Marshal MacMahon already spoken of, Gambetta was the leader at the height of his power and influence, with a solid Republican majority of more than a hundred votes. But from this period he became steadily more and more Opportunist, which gained him great credit in Great Britain, and Clemenceau was thenceforth the recognized leader of the advanced Left. MacMahon having resigned, M. Grévy was elected President with the support of Gambetta.

From the first Clemenceau had vigorously opposed the establishment of a Second Chamber in the shape of a Senate divorced from a direct popular vote. This was a step calculated to hamper progress at every turn, and at critical moments to intensify those very antagonisms which it was Gambetta's intention, no doubt, to compose entirely, or at any rate to mitigate. Clemenceau did not view the matter from Gambetta's point of view. The Monarchists and Buonapartists were the domestic enemy, as the Germans had been and might be again the foreign enemy. The only sound policy for strengthening the

Republic to resist both was to favor those measures political and social which would make that Republic, which they had established with so much difficulty and at such great cost, a genuinely democratic Republic. Any surrender to the reactionists and the clericals must inevitably dishearten those parties, now shown to be the majority of the whole French people, who were for the Republic and the Republic alone. Opportunism also gave the antidemocrats and intriguers a false notion of their own power, virtually helped them to carry on their underground agitations for a change of the new constitution, and provided them in the undemocratic Senate with a political force that might be turned to their own purpose.

It was more important all through, thought Clemenceau, to inspire your own side with confidence than to placate your opponents by half-measures. It was, in fact, not enough to eject officials who were known to be hostile to the Republic; it was still more essential to give such shape to the political forms and so vivify political opinion that even the most unscrupulous officials could not turn them to the account of reaction. Both steps were necessary to carry out a thorough democratic program. In fact, the whole scheme of administration in France could not be permanently improved merely by substituting one set of bureaucrats for another. Much more drastic measures of a peaceful character were indispensable, and these Opportunism thwarted. Gambetta may not have given up his desire to carry these Radical measures in 1877 and 1878: he still retained and expressed his old opinions upon clericalism and its sinister influence. But he was no longer the vehement champion of the advanced party at Versailles, and the position which he had abandoned Clemenceau took up and pushed further to the front.

There was no matter on which the lines of cleavage between the Republicans and the reactionists were more definitely and clearly drawn than on the question of the amnesty of the Communists. No man in the Assembly was stronger in favor of their complete amnesty by law than Clemenceau. This he showed in 1876, and in his powerful advocacy of the release of the great agitator and conspirator Blanqui in 1879. Every reactionary and trimming man of moderate views was bitterly opposed to a policy of justice towards the victims of the wholesale measures of repression formulated by M. Thiers and so frightfully carried out by General Gallifet and the Versailles troops in 1871. Even when measures of partial amnesty were passed, their application was nullified as far as possible by Ministers. It was part of an organized policy to frighten the bourgeoisie and peasants into another Empire. The reprisals of the Bloody Week and the transportations to Cayenne and New Caledonia had not by any means fully satisfied the enemies alike of the Commune and the Republic. So Clemenceau and his friends never ceased their attacks upon M. Waddington and others who took the rancorous conservative view of unceasing persecution of the men and women who, after all, were the first to declare the Republic. M. Waddington, as Premier, got a resolution passed by the Chamber in his favor. But this did not silence either Clemenceau's friends or himself. Here, in fact, was a crucial case of his power of getting rid of an obnoxious Ministry even in the face of a Ministerial majority. The Tiger showed his claws and made ready to spring. But first he gave fair warning of his intentions. Nothing could be plainer than this: "Why has the Minister of Justice demanded a partial amnesty? Because he is anxious that the country should not forget the horrors of the Commune. But then, if you do not wish it to forget the horrors of the Commune, why do you desire that those who have been condemned should forget the horrors of its repression? Because for eight long years we have kept under cover the abominable facts at our disposal, you have thought yourselves in a position to trample on us! You say: We shall not forget the hostages and the conflagrations. Very well. I who speak here tell you: If you forget nothing, your opponents will remember too."

The speech from which that passage is an excerpt was regarded as a distinct menace on Clemenceau's part. It was followed up by the extreme Left with a series of interruptions, interrogations and denunciations which ended in the retirement of M. Waddington. He had his majority but he had no Clemenceau. So out went Waddington and his colleagues. In came M. Freycinet—"the white mouse." "We have had," said Clemenceau's organ, *La Justice,* "in the Waddington cabinet a Dufaure cabinet without M. Dufaure. To-day we have a Waddington cabinet without M. Waddington. It is a botch upon a botch." A nice welcome for M. Freycinet! A pleasing congratulation for the President, M. Grévy! The administration was regarded as a political monstrosity. It had two heads, M. Freycinet and M. Jules Ferry, one looking to the right and the other to the left. The friends of Freycinet could not stand Ferry: the friends of Ferry abhorred Freycinet. This new political marriage not only began but went on with mutual aversion. It stood at the mercy, therefore, of Clemenceau, who was less inclined to be merciful since the Premier declared himself bitterly hostile to the plenary amnesty proposed by the famous old Republican, M. Louis Blanc. Also on account of clerical tendencies. Out goes Freycinet, therefore, in his turn, and in comes M. Jules Ferry, with various clerical, educational and other troubles of his own hatching to clear up. Ministries, in short, were going in and out on the dial of Presidential favor like the figures of a Dutch clock. Clemenceau was getting his claws well into the various political personages all the time. As none of them had any blood to lose in the shape of principles there was no great harm done—except to the Republic! It was the perpetual immolation of a sawdust brigade. A keen critic of the period said of the Ferry Ministry—which was beaten on its proposal to postpone on behalf of education the reform of the magistracy and all that this carried with it in regard to the amnesty—that it wished to die before it lived. Down it went for the moment, and returned to place out of breath and half-ruined. But there the Ministry still was, and that by itself was something in those days of political topsy-turveydom, with Clemenceau and his party ever ready to assert themselves.

Thus the Republic stumbled rather than marched on, from the date of Marshal MacMahon's resignation and the installation of M. Grévy as President up to the period of the declaration of July 14th, in remembrance of July 14th, 1789, and the Fall of the Bastille, as the fête day of the Republic after the passage of a practically complete amnesty. This was really a great triumph for all Republicans, as it put the Republic in its true historic relation to the past, the present and the future. With such a national fête day, with the certainty that Republicans, if they chose to keep united, could always command a large majority in the Assembly, the elections of 1881 might well have been a first step towards a thorough political and social reorganization of the Republic. Unfortunately there were several causes of disunion. President of the Assembly though he was, and therefore excluded by his position as well as by M. Grévy's prejudice against him from coming into immediate competition with M. Ferry for the Premiership, Gambetta was actively supporting the *scrutin de liste,* or political appeal to the whole country, against *scrutin d'arrondissement,* or local elections. This was regarded as a bid on his part for a clear Parliamentary dictatorship. Already on October 20th, 1880, Clemenceau had denounced the hero of the dictatorship of despair of 1871, fine as his effort had then been, as aiming at personal power ten years later. A victory at the polls gained through *scrutin de liste* would probably ensure him success in this venture.

Nevertheless, in spite of open and secret opposition, Gambetta had sufficient influence to carry the *scrutin de liste* through the National Assembly. But with the curious irony of fate he was defeated by a majority of 32 in the Senate which he himself had been so largely instrumental in forcing upon the Republic! This was on June 9th, 1881. Three months before, M. Barodet had brought forward a resolution backed by 64 deputies which, if carried, would have abolished the equality of rights between the Senate and the National Assembly, would have withdrawn the right of the former to dissolve Parliament, would have made the Chamber permanent like the Senate, would have modified the system of election of the second House; would have prevented the reënactment of the *scrutin de liste* by again making the electoral law for the Deputies part of the Constitution; and lastly would have summoned a Constituent Assembly in order to carry out these reforms. This whole project was discussed in the Assembly on May 31st. There was no mistake about Clemenceau's attitude. He formulated a vigorous indictment against the Constitution of 1875 and attacked the Senate with great violence. The Constitution of 1875 was, he declared, a powerful weapon of war expressly forged for use against the Republic. The Senate with its anti-democratic method of election was a permanent danger to the State. It was not in any sense an element of stability but an element of resistance. "What is the use of talking of a brake on the machine or a weight to counterbalance popular opinion? Does not universal suffrage provide its own brake, its own regulator?" This time, however, Clemenceau missed his *coup*. M. Barodet's motion was rejected and the conservative Republic rumbled on comfortably, though Clemenceau shortly afterwards very nearly toppled M. Ferry's Cabinet over, the Ministers only securing a vote in their favor by a majority of 13 by their own votes.

Looking back to that period when the whole Constitution seemed almost certain to go into the melting-pot and come out again in a thoroughly democratic shape, it is remarkable to notice how, in spite of the efforts of Clemenceau, M. Naquet and other democrats, the Republic of compromise has steadily adhered to its old machinery. Why the cumbrous and often reactionary Senate, elected in such wise as to exclude democratic influence, should have been maintained for more than forty years is difficult to explain. But nations, as our own belated and unmanageable Constitution proves, when once they have become accustomed to a form of government, are very slow indeed to adapt it to rapidly changing economic and social developments. This, it may be said, suits the English turn of mind with its queer addiction to perpetual compromise. But the French are logical and apparently restless. Yet their Constitution remains an unintelligible muddle. Their real conservatism overrides their revolutionary tendencies except in periods of great perturbation. Thus the Opportunist Republic of Gambetta, which ought to have been a mere makeshift, has held on, with partial revision, for more than forty years. Fear of the monarchists on one side and of the Communists, afterwards the Socialists, on the other has kept Humpty-Dumpty up on his wall.

The elections of 1881, conducted as they were amid much excitement, gave the Republicans of all parties a crushing majority—a majority in the Assembly greatly out of proportion even to the total vote. There were five millions of votes for Republicans against 1,700,000 for the various sections of monarchists. The Republican deputies in the Chamber, however, numbered 467 to only 90 "conservatives." According to the returns, this was a victory for the Government and its chief, M. Jules Ferry, especially as the Prime Minister had arrived at some understanding with Gambetta, who at this time had become extremely unpopular with the democracy of Paris. But those who were of this opinion reckoned without the question of Tunis and, above all, without taking account of the difficulty of facing the criticisms of the irreconcilable Clemenceau. Clemenceau had always opposed a policy of colonial adventure. This of Tunis was from his point of view not only adventurous but dangerous. Tunis had been offered to France in an indefinite way at the Peace-with-Honor Congress of Berlin in 1878.

But the policy of expansion pushed on by financial intrigues did not take shape at once. When it did it was serious enough, for France not only had to deal with troubles in Algeria itself, with the natural opposition of the Bey of Tunis to French interference and annexation, but Italy took umbrage at the advance, regarding Tunis as specially her business, Turkey was by no means favorable, and there was even a possibility that Germany might stir up trouble for purposes of her own. Moreover the whole business had been extremely ill-managed, not only by the Government itself but by M. Albert Grévy, the brother of the President, who was the Governor-General of Algeria. This personage, on account of his Presidential connections, could neither be censured nor replaced. So credits were asked for, troops were moved, a railway concession granted—everything as usual, in short, when annexation is being prepared.

Clemenceau quite rightly denounced the whole mischievous business as the policy of intriguers and plutocrats, and demanded an inquiry into the affair from the first. He did not measure his phrases at all. French blood and French money, sadly needed at home, were being wasted abroad. M. Ferry, to do him justice, fought hard for his policy of colonization by force of arms. His attacks upon the extremists who criticized him did not lack point or bitterness. Discharged officials from the Ministry of Foreign Affairs and returned Communards from Noumea who composed the public meetings and irregular assizes that condemned him, M. Ferry, "as is fitting, kicked aside with his boot." As to Clemenceau, if he had allowed matters to take their own course in Tunis, what a tornado of malediction would have raged around them from that orator! "I can hear even now the philippics of the honorable M. Clemenceau." Clemenceau did not get the inquiry he demanded. But on November 10th M. Ferry retired, so badly had he been mauled in the fray. It was a win, that is to say, for Clemenceau, who by his speech on November 9th again overthrew the Government in spite of the cordial support of Gambetta. What made this victory of Clemenceau and the extreme Left the more astounding was the fact that the Treaty concluding the "first pacification" of Tunis had been confirmed on May 23rd by a majority of 430 to 1. Clemenceau was that one. Six months later, therefore, he had his revenge. The *expédition de vacances,* which had developed into a *guerre de conquête,* cost M. Jules Ferry his Premiership, notwithstanding this unheard-of majority. The Tiger at work indeed!

So now at last, in spite of M. Grévy's ungrateful conduct towards him, in spite likewise of the rejection of the *scrutin de liste,* Gambetta became President of the Council instead of President of the Chamber. He was still at this time in the eyes of all foreigners the most eminent living French statesman. In England particularly his accession to office was received with jubilation in official circles. It meant, so said Liberals like Sir Charles Dilke, who were then in power, a permanently close understanding between France and England, a joint settlement of the troublesome and at times even threatening Egyptian question, as well as a fair probability of the arrangement of other thorny problems between the two countries. But in order to accomplish all this Gambetta must carry the Assembly, the Senate and the bulk of his countrymen with him, and control a solid Republican party, even if Clemenceau and his squadrons still hung upon his flank. Gambetta, however, had shaken the confidence of the country.

It was no longer Clemenceau and his friends only who accused him of aiming at supreme dictatorial power. The public in general suspected him too. Nor did his immediate friends, either old or young, do much to destroy this unfortunate impression.

Truth to tell, Gambetta was not the man he had been a few years before. He looked fat, even bloated, unhealthy and sensual. His magnificent frame had undergone deterioration. A brilliant French journalist cruelly comparing him to Vitellius, as a man of gluttony and debauchery combined, summed up his career against that of the extraordinary Roman general and Emperor who had played so many parts successfully, as soldier in the field and as courtier in the palace, and wound up in derision of Gambetta with the terrible phrase, *"Je te demande pardon, César!"* And over against this self-indulgent and fiery man of genius was a very different personage, who had taken up the rôle which had once been that of the great tribune of the French people. Spare, alert, vigorous, always in training, despising ease and never taken by surprise; equal, as he had just shown, to fighting a lone hand victoriously, yet never despising help in his battles even from the most unexpected quarters—what chance had Gambetta against such a terrible opponent as Clemenceau? None whatever. Down he went, after a Premiership of but sixty-six days. Many believe that, finding the situation too complicated, and relying still upon obtaining the *scrutin de liste* later—as indeed came about some time after his death—Gambetta deliberately rode for a fall. Certain it is that M. Spüller, who had Gambetta's complete confidence, gave this explanation of his intentions three weeks before his defeat in the Assembly.

Gambetta, with all his great reputation, being overthrown, straightway his old Secretary of 1871, de Freycinet, came again to the front. The affairs of Egypt, always with Clemenceau's genial assistance, made short work of him. The Anglo-French Condominium having fallen through and England having thought proper to suppress a people "rightly struggling to be free," de Freycinet was anxious to reassert the claims of France in Egypt after a fashion which threatened unpleasantness with Great Britain. Whatever Clemenceau may have thought privately of English policy at this juncture, he would have none of that. His arguments convinced the Assembly that French intervention in Egypt against England would be dangerous and unsuccessful. France, said Clemenceau, had neither England's advantages nor England's direct interests in Egypt. France is a continental, not a great sea power. Her apprehensions are from the East. Do nothing which may drive England into the arms of Germany.

What was much worse, the same colonial expansion which had been carried out in Tunis was now followed up in Tonquin, Annam and Madagascar, at great expense and to little or no advantage. Clemenceau still opposed this entire policy on principle. Ferry thought France would recompense herself for the disasters of 1870-71 by these adventures: Clemenceau was absolutely convinced to the contrary. "Why risk $100,000,000 on remote expeditions when we have our entire industrial mechanism to create, when we lack schools and country roads? To build up vanquished France again we must not waste her blood and treasure on useless enterprises. But there are much higher reasons even than these for abstaining from such wars of depredation. It is all an abuse, pure and simple, of the power which scientific civilization has over primitive civilization to lay hold upon man as man, to torture him, to squeeze everything he has in him out of him for the profit of a civilization which itself is a sham." There could be no sounder sense, no higher morality, no truer statesmanship than that. Clemenceau had aspirations that France should lead the world, not by unjustifiable conquests over semi-civilized populations, but by displaying at home those great qualities which she undoubtedly possesses. His attacks were inspired, therefore, not by personal animosity against Jules Ferry or any other politician, but against a megalomania that was harmful to his country and the world. Unfortunately, Clemenceau could not this time persuade the Assembly or his countrymen to recognize the dangers and disadvantages of expansion by conquest in the Far East, until the disaster of Lang Sen and the demand for additional credits enabled him to push the perils of such a policy right home. Then M. Ferry was once more discharged, practically at Clemenceau's behest.

So matters went on, Clemenceau striving his utmost, in opposition, to enforce the genuine democratic policy of abstention from Imperialism abroad and strengthening of the forces of the Republic at home which the successive Opportunist Administrations in power refused to accept. In each and every case, Tunis, Tonquin, Annam, Madagascar and Egypt, he considered first, foremost and all the time what would most benefit Frenchmen in France, and refused to be led astray by any will-o'-the-wisps of Eastern origin, however gloriously they might disport themselves under the sun of finance. But now came a still more awkward matter close at home. There are not the same facilities for shutting down inquiries into the financial peccadilloes or corrupt malversations of public men in France as there are in England. Monetary scandals will out, though political blunderings may be glossed over, as in the cases of the Duc de Broglie, M. Jules Ferry and M. Albert Grévy. The President, M. Grévy, was very unfortunate in his relations. His brother, the Governor-General of Algeria, had shown himself dreadfully incompetent in that capacity. But M. de Freycinet, M. Jules Ferry and the whole Ministerial set had entered into a conspiracy of silence and misrepresentation, throwing the blame of his mistakes upon anybody but the Governor-General himself, in order to uphold the dignity of the President quite uninjured. Now, however, the President's son-in-law, M. Wilson, was found out in very ignoble transactions. He was actually detected in the flagitious practice of trading in decorations, the Legion of Honor and the like, not for what are considered on this side of the Channel as perfectly legitimate purposes, the furtherance, namely, of Party gains or Ministerial advantages, but in order to increase his own income. The thing became a public scandal. Those who could not afford to buy the envied distinctions were specially incensed. But out of regard for the President, out of consideration for their personal advancement in the future, because when you start this sort of thing you must know how far it will go, because other Ministers in and out of office had had relations of their own addicted to similar trading in other directions—for all these reasons, good and bad, nobody cared to take the matter up seriously.

Nobody, that is to say, except that tiger Clemenceau. He actually thought that the honor of the Republic was at stake in the business: was of opinion that a President should be more careful than other people in keeping the doubtful characters of men and women of his own household under restraint. And he not only thought but spoke and acted. M. Rouvier, who was then Premier, felt himself bound to stand by the President and exculpated him from any share in the affair. This made matters worse. For M. Grévy, when the whole transaction was fully debated, could not withstand the pressure of public opinion against him; Clemenceau carried his point and the President resigned. Thereupon M. Rouvier thought it incumbent upon him to retire too, though Clemenceau took pains to tell him that this was a concern purely personal to the President and not a political issue at all. There were consequently a Presidential Election and a new Ministry at the same time. So great was Clemenceau's influence at this juncture that although three of the most prominent politicians in the Republic were eager for the post, he, out of fear of the election of the irrepressible expansionist M. Ferry, persuaded the electors to favor the appointment of the able and cool but popularly almost unknown M. Sadi-Carnot—who turned out, it may be said, quite an admirable President up to his outrageous assassination.

By this time Clemenceau had fully justified his claim to the distinction of being the most formidable and relentless political antagonist known in French public life since the great Revolution. As he would never take office himself and was moved by few personal animosities, he stood outside the lists of competers for place. He had definite Radical Republican principles and during all these years he acted up to them. He was throughout opposed, as I have said, to compromise. He fought it continuously all along the line. Moreover, he had a profound contempt for politicians who were merely politicians. "I have combated," he said, "ideas, not persons. In my fight against Republicans I have always respected my party. In the heat of the conflict I have never lost sight of the objects we had in common, and I have appealed for the solidarity of the whole against the common enemy of all."

As, also, he triumphantly declared in a famous oration against those who were engaged in sneering at Parliamentary Government and the tyranny of words, he was ever in favor of the greatest freedom of speech, and even stood up for the commonplace debates which often must have terribly bored him. "Well, then, since I must tell you so, these discussions which astonish you are an honor to us all. They prove conclusively our ardor in defense of ideas which we think right and beneficial. These discussions have their drawbacks: silence has more. Yes, glory to the country where men speak, shame on the country where men hold their tongues! If you think to ban under the name of parliamentarism the rule of open discussion, mind this, it is the representative system, it is the Republic itself against whom you are raising your hand."

A great Parliamentarian, a great political Radical was Clemenceau the Tiger of 1877 to 1893. He, more than any other man, prevented the Republic from altogether deteriorating and kept alive the spirit of the great French Revolution in the minds and in the hearts of men.

CHAPTER VIII

THE RISE AND FALL OF BOULANGER

THE relations of Clemenceau to General Boulanger form an important though comparatively brief episode in the career of the French statesman. Boulanger was Clemenceau's cousin, and in his dealings with this ambitious man he did not show that remarkable skill and judgment of character which distinguished him in regard to Carnot and Loubet, whose high qualities Clemenceau was the first to recognize and make use of in the interest of the Republic. Boulanger was a good soldier in the lower grades of his profession, and owed his first important promotion to the Duc d'Aumale. This patronage he acknowledged with profound gratitude and even servility at the time; but repaid later, when he turned Radical, by what was nothing short of treacherous persecution of the Orleanist Prince. Boulanger went even so far as to deny that he had ever expressed his obligations to the Duke for aid in his profession, a statement to which the publication of his own letters at once gave the lie.

The General was, in fact, vain, ostentatious and unscrupulous. But having gained popularity among the rank and file of the French army by his good management of the men under his command and his sympathy with their grievances, he was appointed Director of Infantry, and in that capacity introduced several measures

THE RISE AND FALL OF BOULANGER

of military reform and suggested more. A little later, circumstances led him into close political harmony with the Radicals and their leader. At this juncture Clemenceau seemed to have convinced himself that good use could be made of the General, who owed his first great advance to Orleanist favor, without any danger to the Republic. Having, as usual, upset another short-lived Cabinet, he therefore exercised his influence to secure his relation the post of War Minister in the new Administration of M. de Freycinet. This was in January, 1886. At first Boulanger was true to his Radical friends and carried out the program of army reforms agreed upon between himself and Clemenceau, thus justifying that statesman's choice and support. The general treatment of the French conscript was taken in hand. His food was improved, his barrack discipline rendered less harsh, his relations to his officers made more human, his spirit raised by better prospects of a future career. All this was good service to the country at a critical time and should have redounded to the credit of the Radical Party far more than to Boulanger's own glorification. This, however, was not the case. All the credit was given to the General himself. Hence immense personal influence from one end of the country to the other.

Practically every family in France was beneficially affected, directly or indirectly, by Boulanger's measures of military reform, and thanked the brave General for what had been done. Not a young man in the army, or out of it, but felt that his lot, when drawn for service, or actually serving, had been made better by the War Minister himself. So it ever is and always has been. The individual who gives practical expression to the ideas which are forced upon him by others is the one who is regarded as the real benefactor: the real workers, as in this instance Clemenceau and his friends, are forgotten.

One of the incidents which helped to enhance Boulanger's great popularity was what was known as the Schnäbele affair. This person was a French commissary who crossed the French frontier into Alsace-Lorraine to carry out some local business with a similar German official which concerned both countries. He was arrested by the German military authorities as not being in possession of a passport. This action may possibly have been technically justifiable, but certainly was a high-handed proceeding conducted in a high-handed way. At that time France was constantly feeling that she was in an inferior position to Germany, and her statesmen were slow to resent small injuries, knowing well that France was still in no position to make head against the great German military power, still less to avenge the crushing defeats of 1870-71. When, therefore, Boulanger took a firm stand in the matter and upheld in a very proper way the dignity of France, the whole country felt a sense of relief. France, then, was no longer a negligible quantity in Europe. M. de Bismarck could not always have his way, and Boulanger stood forth as the man who understood the real spirit of his countrymen. That was the sentiment which did much to strengthen the General against his opponents when he began to carry out a purely personal policy. He had inspired the whole nation with a sense of its own greatness.

He was then the most popular man in the country. He stood out to the people at large as a patriotic figure with sound democratic sympathies and an eminent soldier who might lead to victory the armies of France.

Thenceforth Boulanger gradually became a personage

round whom every kind of social and reactionary influence and intrigues of every sort were concentrated. To capture the imposing figure on the black horse, to fill him with grandiose ideas of the splendid part he could play, if only he would look at the real greatness and glory of his country through glasses less tinted with red than those of his Radical associates, to inspire him with conceptions of national unity and sanctified religious patriotism which should bring France, the France of the grand old days, once more into being, with himself as its noble leader—this was the work which the fine ladies of the Boulevard St. Germain, hand in hand with the Catholic Church, its priests and the cultivated reactionaries generally, set themselves to accomplish. From this time onwards the *mot d'ordre* to back Boulanger went round the *salons*. Legitimists, Orleanists and Buonapartists were, on this matter, temporarily at one. Each section hoped at the proper moment to use the possible dictator for the attainment of its own ends. Thus Boulanger was diverted from the Radical camp and weaned from Radical ideas even during his period as War Minister in M. de Freycinet's Cabinet. So subtle is the influence of "society" and ecclesiastical surroundings upon some natures, so powerful the effect of refined and charming conversation and genial flattery delicately conveyed, that men of far stronger character than Boulanger have now and then succumbed to it. Only devotion to principle or ruthless personal ambition can hold its own against such a combination of insidious forces dexterously employed—and women of the world and Jesuits are both very dexterous—when once the individual to be artistically trepanned permits himself to be experimented upon. Boulanger, though not devoid of cleverness, was at bottom that dangerous description of designing good fellow who all the time means well; and he fell a victim to the delightful women and clever adventurers around him. He himself was probably not aware that he had passed over to the enemy until the irresistible logic of events and his changed relations with his old friends proved to him how far he had gone.

M. Rouvier, a shrewd and cynical politician of the financial school, saw through the General, understood how dangerous he might become, and refused to accept the ex-Minister of War into the Cabinet he formed on the fall of Freycinet. But Boulanger had now so far established himself personally that neither a political check nor even general ridicule affected his career. Even his duel with M. Floquet, a farce in which General Boulanger made himself the clown, could not shake him. Floquet was a well-known Radical of those days, who had been a fellow-member of the League of the Rights of Man with Clemenceau at the time of the Commune. Boulanger was a soldier, accustomed to the use of arms all his life, and reported to be a good fencer. Floquet, quite unlike his old friend of years before, scarcely knew which end of his weapon to present to his opponent, so inexperienced was he in this sort of lethal exercise. When, therefore, the duel between the two men was arranged, the only point discussed was how small an injury would Boulanger, in his generosity, deign to inflict upon his Radical antagonist, in order that the seconds might declare that "honor is satisfied." No doubt Clemenceau himself, who acted as one of Floquet's seconds on this occasion, took that view of the matter.

What actually occurred was quite ludicrous. Floquet, duly instructed thereto by his own friends, stood, good harmless bourgeois as he was, like a waxwork figure, with his rapier stuck out at arm's length straight in front of him. No science there. But there was still less on the other side. Boulanger, to the amazement of Clemenceau and everybody on the ground, in what appeared to be a sudden stroke of madness, immediately rushed at Floquet and his rigid skewer and, without any such elaborate foolishness as the laws of fence enjoin, carefully spitted his own throat on the point of Floquet's weapon. Honor was thus satisfied and ridicule began. But ridicule did not kill.

No sooner was Boulanger cured of his self-inflicted wound than he went on much as he did before. Having ceased to be Minister for War, he was sent down to command an army corps at Clermont-Ferrand. According to all discipline, and regulations duly to be observed by generals at large, this kept the man appointed out of Paris. Not so Boulanger. He visited the capital at least twice. Thereupon, he was deprived of his command and his name was removed from the Army List. That, by the rules of war and politics, ought to have finished him. But it didn't. The Radicals and Republicans had still no idea what an ugly Frankenstein they had created for themselves. True, Clemenceau had declared definitely against his own protégé the moment he saw the line he was taking; but he underrated entirely the position to which Boulanger had attained, not only among the reactionaries but in the hearts and minds of the French people. For Boulanger, now gifted with a free hand, went into the political arena at once, and was a candidate simultaneously for the Nord and the Dordogne: provincial districts with, of course, a totally different sort of electorate from that of the capital, where the *brav' Général* with his fine figure on horseback was already the hero of the Parisians. He was elected and sat for the Nord.

Still Clemenceau, far-seeing and sagacious as he generally is in his judgment of political events and personal character, failed to appreciate what his cousin had drifted into rather than had deliberately worked for. Nor perhaps did he estimate highly enough either the cleverness or the unscrupulousness of the men and women who were backing him. Certain it is that, although Boulangism was now becoming a powerful political cult, Clemenceau and other advanced men, such as my old friend Paul Brousse, President of the Paris Municipal Council, were still of opinion that Boulanger was going down rather than up. It was a mistake that might have cost not only the Radicals but the French Republic as a whole very dear. For the General had the qualities of his defects. Agreeable, good-natured, frank, accessible and friendly to all who approached him, with enough ability to gauge fairly well what was going on around him, loving display for its own sake, and ever ready to pose in dignified and pleasing attitude before a populace by no means averse from well-managed advertisement, while not apparently bent upon forcing his own will or dictatorship upon the country—Boulanger, both before and after his election for the Nord, was much more formidable than he looked to those who only measured his power from the standpoint of wide intelligence. This the rather because there was no lack of money to push his pretensions to high place.

Boulanger came to the front also at a time when the bourgeois Republic—owing to the weakness, incapacity and instability of the bourgeois politicians themselves—was discredited and was believed to be tottering. Clemenceau's own unceasing campaign against widespread abuses and incapable Ministers was largely responsible for this. There was a general sense of insecurity and unsettlement, engendered by the fall of Administration after Administration, due to political or financial proceedings of doubtful character, exposed and denounced by Clemenceau and the Radicals themselves. Some of the Radicals and intellectuals even now supported Boulanger as an alternative to perpetual upsets. Disgusted with lawyers, professional politicians and place-hunters of high and low degree, the people likewise were again on the look-out for a savior of France who should secure for them democracy without corruption, and honest leadership devoid of Socialism. The old story, in fact.

At this particular moment, too, the organized forces in Paris, the army and the gendarmerie, were Boulangists almost to a man. The danger, therefore, of the Boulangist agitation now being carried on alike in Paris and in the Departments seemed to a looker-on to be growing more serious every day. This, however, continued not to be the view of Clemenceau and his party. They thought, in spite of the voting in the Nord and the Dordogne and the apparent popularity of the General in Paris, that the whole thing would prove a mere flash in the pan; that the good sense and Republican conservatism of the French people would display itself when peril really threatened the Republic; and that Boulanger would be even less successful than the Duc de Broglie. Then came the General Elections. Boulanger was candidate for Paris. Once more the obvious evidence of his great popularity was overlooked by the Clemenceau group, the Boulangist fervor went on unrecognized, and it seemed that it might depend upon the General himself at any moment—as indeed proved to be the case—whether he should follow in the footsteps of Louis Napoleon and accomplish a successful *coup d'état,* or fall permanently into the background. But up to the last moment his opponents could not believe that a general with no great military career behind him, a citizen with no great name to conjure with, a politician with no great program to attract voters, could win Paris or become master of France.

The crisis really was the more acute since there was no rival personality, no Republican of admitted ability and distinction ready to stake his reputation against Boulanger. Though Clemenceau, as the preparations for the election proceeded and Boulanger's growing strength became manifest, now did his utmost to stem the tide, there was no doubt that, failing a really powerful opponent, Boulanger would hold the winning place at the close of the poll. He took up a bold position. He was the hero of the hour. The whole contest was admirably stage-managed and advertised on his side. He rode through the city on his black horse, a fine figure of a man, full of confidence of victory, the halo of a coming well-earned triumph around him. It was universally felt that the previous votes of the provinces would be quite eclipsed by the vote of the capital. Parisians, peasants and miners, small owners and proletariat would for once be together.

This was the unshaken opinion of his friends and followers, who seemed in those exciting days to have with them the great majority of the people. On the other side a wave of incapacity seemed to be flooding the intelligence of his opponents. Instead of putting forward a really representative man, either Republican or Socialist, with a fine democratic record behind him, they made an absolutely contemptible choice for their champion. One Jacques, an obscure liquor-dealer, whom nobody ever heard of before the election or gave a thought to after it, was chosen to fight for Paris against the General. This man had never done or said or written anything that anybody could remember, or would remember if he could. If no Radical Republican was ready to stand, Joffrin, an old member of the Commune and a skilled artisan most loyal to his principles, always returning at once to his trade when he failed to be elected for the National Assembly, would have been a far better and more worthy candidate in every way. The election then would have been a conflict between the enthusiasm of social revolution and the fervor of chauvinist reaction. As it was, the Boulangists could say and did say with truth that the General would represent the citizens of Paris much more genuinely than Jacques. The result of this error of tactics could have been foreseen from the first. General Boulanger won by a heavy majority.

That evening saw the crisis of the whole Boulangist agitation. Such a victory at such a time called for immediate and decisive action. That was the universal opinion. A political triumph so dramatic and so conclusive could only find a fitting climax in the victor proclaiming himself to be a Cromwell, a Monk or a Napoleon. Nothing less was hoped for by the reactionists: nothing less was feared by the Republicans. The figures of the poll were welcomed with enthusiastic cheering all along the boulevards, and the Boulangist anthem, *"En revenant de la Revue,"* was played from one end of Paris to the other. The ball was at the General's feet. He might have failed to win his goal, but all Paris expected he would make a good try for it. This meant that the very same night he should either go straight to the Elysée himself or make some bold stroke for which he had prepared beforehand, which would fire the imagination of the people. Such was the prevailing impression. The General celebrated his election for the City of Paris at dinner at Durand's famous restaurant, surrounded by his intimate supporters. The excitement outside was tremendous. Hour after hour passed. Nothing was done, nothing apparently had been made ready. The strain of waiting became almost unbearable. The crowd gradually got weary of anticipating the opening of a drama whose prologue had so roused their expectations. At last, instead of staying to watch the first scenes of a revolution, they took themselves off quietly to bed. Boulanger's chance of obtaining supremacy was gone.

It was always said that, backed by the Radicals, and supported by the President, the Minister of the Interior, M. Constans, a most resolute and unscrupulous man, who was himself in the crowd outside the restaurant, was the main cause of this miserable fiasco. Strong precautions had been taken against any attempt at violence. Powerful forces whose loyalty to the Republic was beyond question had been substituted for brigades of known Boulangist tendencies. That M. Constans would not, under the conditions, have stuck at trifles was well known. He was kept at a distance from France for years afterwards, on account of his ugly character, in the capacity of French Ambassador at Constantinople, a city where at that time such a trifling peccadillo as murder was scarcely noticed. So Boulanger knew what to expect. Moreover, Clemenceau and the Radical Republicans, as well as Jaurès and Socialists of every shade of opinion, had become thoroughly alarmed by what they had heard and seen during the election, and would not have given way without a fight to the death. The jubilant group at Durand's, intimidated by these assumed facts, and Boulanger with his lack of determination and easy self-indulgence, let the opportunity slip.

All sorts of excuses and explanations were made for the hesitation of the General to provoke civil war. But on that one night he should have made his position secure or have died in the attempt. Success was, so far as a foreigner on the spot could judge, quite possible. It might even have been achieved without any forcible action. There was no certainty that, when the move decided upon was actually made, either troops or the people would have sided against the hero of the day. But that hero failed to rise to the level of the occasion, and the result was fatal to the immediate prospects of himself and his followers. A warrant was issued for his arrest and he ran away from Paris. He now became an object of pity rather than of alarm. He was condemned in his absence, and not long afterwards his suicide on the grave of his mistress, in Brussels, ended his career. Thus the estimate which Clemenceau had formed of his permanent influence was justified. But it was a narrow escape. The three pretenders who had come to France to watch the final development soon found their way across the frontier. Nevertheless, General Boulanger, with all his weakness and hesitation, was for many months the most dangerous enemy the Republic ever faced. His downfall helped also to add to the number of Clemenceau's bitter enemies, and was partly instrumental in bringing about the political disaster which befell him later. For the Radicals who had been deceived by Boulanger cherished animosity against the Radical leader for reasons which, though quite incompatible, were decisive for them.

CHAPTER IX

PANAMA AND DRAGUIGNAN

THE great Panama Canal Affair was only one of many financial scandals which seriously damaged the good fame of the French Republic, founded upon the fall of the Empire, and consecrated by the collapse of the Commune of Paris. But this Panama scandal was by far the most important and most nefarious, alike in respect to the amount of money involved, the position and character of the people mixed up in it, and the wide ramifications of wholesale corruption throughout the political world that were in the end revealed.

M. Ferdinand de Lesseps, the originator and organizer of the Suez Canal, was a man of quite exceptional ability, energy and force of character. He carried through his great project in the face of obstacles, political and financial, that would certainly have broken the heart and frustrated the purpose of a weaker personality. At no period did he show any disposition to keep the canal under harmful restrictions, and the Khedive Ismail Pasha, though a Turk of no scruples, who backed him throughout, also took a very wide view of the services which the canal would render to the world at large. It was to be neutral and open under the same conditions to the ships of all nations. Unfortunately, England, whose commerce has chiefly benefited by the canal, bitterly opposed its construction, going so far at one time as actually to prohibit the Khedive from carrying on the canal works in his own territory, thus occasioning considerable delay. As it happened, however, this delay itself was turned by de Lesseps to the advantage of the Canal Company, as he used the time to create new engines for excavation which in the end expedited the completion of the waterway.

The result of this ignorant British opposition was that the finance of the great enterprise was chiefly provided in France, and when the canal was first opened in 1869 it was considered, as in fact it was, a triumph of French sagacity and foresight over the obstructionist jealousy of England. This view was accompanied also by natural jubilation at the consequent increase of French influence in Egypt itself. Count Ferdinand de Lesseps, therefore, became a great French hero who, by his capacity, persistence and diplomacy, had not only gained glory for France and extended her power, but had also furnished his countrymen with an excellent investment for their savings on which British commerce was paying the interest. His popularity in France was well earned and unbounded. The work of de Lesseps was, in fact, regarded as the one great and indisputable success of the French Empire. Anything which he took in hand thereafter was certain to prove of great value to the country and an assured benefit to those who followed his financial lead. He was also a lucky man. He and his set had won against heavy odds.

It is true the cost of the Suez Canal had been more than double his original estimate, even up to the time when it was first opened, and many millions sterling had been expended since; it was likewise the fact that his great idea had taken fully ten years to realize in the shape of a completed enterprise. But this was the larger tribute to his foresight, and power of overcoming obstacles, due either to natural causes or to the malignity of enemies. Thus Ferdinand de Lesseps, ten years after the Suez Canal had been made available for shipping between the Mediterranean and the Red Sea, held an unequaled position in the eyes of French engineers, French bankers and, what was more important, French investors.

Early in the year 1879 M. de Lesseps, following the course adopted by him in the case of the Isthmus of Suez, called a Congress of the nations to consider the entire project of a Panama Canal. There was nothing new in the matter. The line of the canal had been surveyed by a capable French engineer nearly forty years before. The Congress estimated the actual cost of the construction of the canal at about $125,000,000, or a little more than the highest sum thought sufficient by the English engineer of the Panama Railroad. But the mere figures are of little importance. That they were quite insufficient, as the business was managed, has since been abundantly proved. But at first there is no reason to believe that de Lesseps was other than quite straightforward. He had bought the concession for the canal from Mr. Buonaparte Wyse, who had acquired it from the United States of Colombia, through whose territory the canal as surveyed ran. That this concession itself had previously been found very difficult to finance in any shape was a matter of common knowledge; that also the canal, when constructed, might prove far less valuable in every way than was calculated for world commerce was the opinion of many skilled engineers. But then the same things had been said about Suez. So the French public rushed in to subscribe the money required for the French Company immediately formed by M. de Lesseps to exploit the concession.

The great name of de Lesseps covered the whole risk and rendered criticism quite useless. But the management of the excavation was wildly incapable and inconceivably extravagant. It was very soon discovered that the original estimates were absurdly at variance with the cost of the real work to be done. The entire enterprise, as undertaken in 1884, was entered upon possibly in good faith, but in a wholly irresponsible and ignorant manner. In spite of warnings as to the certainty of encountering exceptional obstacles, no steps were taken to provide against contingencies, to inform the shareholders as to the position, or to revise the plans in accordance with the facts. The canal was inspected by M. Rousseau at the end of 1885. This engineer gave a most unfavorable report in regard to the excavations and constructions already carried out at vast expense, and the enormous additional sum needed to give any chance of completing the works. Instead of honestly facing this most unpromising situation and disclosing to the shareholders the real state of the case, or declaring that at least three times the amount would be required to bring the project to a satisfactory conclusion, and calling for this huge sum at once, the directors resorted to all the worst tactics of the unscrupulous promoter. This part of the matter went into the hands of M. Jacques Reinach and M. Cornelius Herz, names and persons afterwards covered with obloquy in connection with the whole affair. They set to work systematically, and were restrained by no inconvenient scruples. Strong political influence in both Chambers was needed in order to obtain the passing of the

Panama Lottery Bill. Strong political influence was bought, though the Bill itself was not carried. From 1885-86 onwards this wholesale bribery was continued on an enormous scale.

The company was as careless of men's lives as it was of shareholders' money. Laborers from all parts of the world had been gathered together in what was then a deadly climate, without proper sanitation or reasonable medical attendance. Some time prior to the financial troubles it was known that such anarchy and horrors prevailed on the Isthmus that intervention by the French Government, or even by an international commission, was called for. Nothing but the great reputation of de Lesseps could possibly have upheld such a state of things, or have obtained more and still more money to perpetuate the chaos. Even when the truth as to the frightful mortality of the men employed and the incredible waste due to incompetence and corruption must have been known to the President of the Company (M. de Lesseps himself) and his fellow-directors, when, likewise, they must have been convinced that the company was drifting into a hopeless position, they still appealed to their countrymen for more and more and more money to throw into the bottomless quagmire at Panama, and sink of French savings in Paris, to which the whole company had been reduced.

By the year 1888 no less than 1,400,000,000 francs had been expended in one way or another, while not one-third of the necessary work had been done. Of that $280,000,000 nominal amount not a few millions found their way into the pockets of deputies, senators, and even Academicians, to say nothing of commissions and brokerages of more or less legitimate character.

Politicians in France are no worse than politicians in other countries. But the proportion of well-to-do men among them is less than elsewhere. There was consequently a margin of them always on the look-out for an opportunity of adding to their income, and this margin was much larger in the National Assembly before payment of members than it is to-day. For such men the Panama finance was a glorious opportunity. Nobody could suspect de Lesseps of being consciously a party to a fraud. To make a French venture like the Panama a great success, in spite of all difficulties, was a patriotic service. To receive good pay for doing good work was a happy combination of circumstances none the less gratifying that, the work being honestly done, remuneration followed or preceded in hard cash. The extent to which this form of corruption was carried and the high level in the political world to which streams from the Panama Pactolus were forced up is only partially known even now. But so wide was the flow and so deep the stream that, when the outcry against the Company began in earnest, statesmen whose personal honor had never been challenged were afflicted with such alarm, on the facts being laid before them, that they did their very utmost to suppress full investigation.

This, however, was not easy to accomplish. For there were no fewer than 800,000 French investors in the Panama Company. All of these were voters and all had friends. It became a question, therefore, whether it was more dangerous to the Republic and its statesmen—for personal as well as political considerations came in—to compel full publicity, or to hush the whole thing up as far as possible. Meanwhile, the public, and important journals not suspected of Panamism, took the whole thing down from the Cabinet and the Bureaux into the street.

For the opponents of the Republic it was a fine opening. That enormous sums out of the $280,000,000 subscribed had been paid away to senators, deputies and Academicians for services rendered was certain. Who had got the money, and under what conditions? Imputations of the most sinister character were made all round. Paris rang with accusations of fraud. That more than a hundred deputies were concerned in Panama corruptions is a matter of common knowledge. One who was in a position to know all the facts declared that more than a hundred were mixed up in other nefarious transactions who used Panama to divert attention from their own malfeasances. However that may be, public opinion, excited by the clamor and denunciations of eight hundred thousand shareholders and electors, clove to Panama. It became an instrument of political warfare as well as of personal delation. The obvious determination of Presidents Carnot and Loubet to prevent a clear statement from being issued and the Directors prosecuted only rendered the sufferers more determined to get at the facts and wreak vengeance on somebody.

There were two views as to Count de Lesseps—to give him his title, which had its value in the Affair—and his conduct in the Panama Canal Company. There were those who held that de Lesseps, beginning as an enthusiast, and perhaps believing himself to be inspired in everything he undertook, no sooner found that his carelessness, in disregarding real natural difficulties and in organizing the excavations on the spot, must result in failure unless he could obtain unlimited resources, and doubtful of ultimate success even then, began at once to display the worst side of his character. The successful adventurer became, by degrees, the desperate gambler with the savings of his countrymen. Instead of regarding himself as the trustee of the people who, on the strength of his reputation and character, had risked their money, he deliberately shut his eyes to the real facts. He resorted to all the tricks of an unscrupulous charlatan, misrepresented the truth in every respect and had no thought for any other consideration than to get in more funds. For this purpose he paraded the country, making the utmost use of his personal and social advantages, and losing no opportunity for unworthy advertisement. All this time he knew perfectly well that his enterprise was doomed. Consequently, there was little to choose between de Lesseps and Reinach, Herz and the rest of them, except that he was perhaps the greatest criminal of all. Such was the view taken of the promoter-in-chief by lawyers and men of business who looked upon the whole matter as a venture standing by itself, to be judged by the ordinary rules of financial probity.

On the other side a capable and influential minority regarded de Lesseps as an enthusiast, a man of high character and noble conceptions, quite devoid of the power of strict analysis of any matter presented to him, and destitute of common sense. His financial methods and commercial obliquities were due to his overweening confidence in his own judgment and faith in his good fortune to pull him through against all probabilities. The one great success he had achieved rendered him a man not to be argued with or considered on the plane of ordinary mortals. He saw the object he was aiming at, felt convinced he would accomplish it, regarded all who differed from him as ignorant or malignant, and went straight ahead to get money—not for his own purposes but in order to carry out the second magnificent scheme to which he had committed himself. Corruption and malversation by others were no concern of his.

President Sadi-Carnot, a cold, silent, upright man, little given to allow his feelings to inflame him at any time, warmly took this view of de Lesseps' character. M. Carnot had been brought into close contact with de Lesseps on another of his vast projects. The President, like many others, refused to look at the Panama matter from the point of view of fraud or imposture. Money was for de Lesseps always a means, never an end. When the whole matter was brought before him, and one of the legal personages whose duty it was to investigate the whole of the facts came to a very harsh conclusion as to de Lesseps' responsibility for the waste, corruption and malversation, M. Carnot said with some vivacity: "No, no; M. de Lesseps is not a man of bad faith. I should rather consider him punctilious. Only his natural vehemence carries him away; he is a bad reasoner, and has no power of calculation. Hence many regrettable acts on his part, done without any intention of injuring anybody. I knew him well, having seen him very close, when his imagination suggested to him the scheme for excavating an inland sea in Africa. A commission of engineers, of whom I was one, was appointed to hear him and study his proposal. We had no difficulty in showing that the whole thing was a pure chimera. He seemed very much astonished, and we saw that we had not convinced him. Take it from me as a certainty that he would have spent millions upon millions to create his sea, and that with the best of good faith in the world."

This was probably the truth, so far as de Lesseps himself was personally concerned. Promoters, discoverers and inventors of genius are men of mighty faith in their respective enterprises. As a great anarchist once said of his own special nostrum for regenerating humanity at a blow: "All is moral that helps it, all is immoral that hinders it." So with de Lesseps. All was moral that got in money to construct his canal: all was immoral that checked the flow of cash to the Isthmus. But an enthusiast of this temper, "without power of calculation," is a very dangerous man, not only to the subscribers to his shares, but to the Republican politicians who confined their enthusiasm to the acquisition of hard cash for use not in Panama but in Paris.

In 1888 the Panama Canal Company collapsed, and the thing was put into liquidation. But that was not the end of it. All sorts of schemes were afoot for carrying on the works and completing the canal before the concession expired in 1893. Although, however, from the date of the breakdown onwards—when it was stated that fully $350,000,000 would be needed in addition to the amount already expended or frittered away to carry out the canal—most virulent attacks were continually made upon prominent politicians and financiers, as well as upon the Directors of the Company, neither the political nor the legal consequences of the disaster were felt to the full extent until four years later. Judicial investigations, it is true, were going on. But it was an open secret that, in spite of the losses and complaints of the shareholders, and the strong desire of the public that the whole vast transaction should be exposed in every detail, the anxiety of men in high place was to calm down natural feeling in the matter. What made this attitude more suspicious was the fact that the Government had certainly not shown itself unfavorable to the scheme, but on the contrary had helped it, even when the gravest doubts had been thrown upon its practicability, at a cost vastly exceeding anything contemplated by the Company. In fact, an atmosphere of general distrust pervaded Paris and the whole of France. Yet Panama still had its friends, and it was believed that somehow or other the affair would be tided over.

But there was a good deal more to come. Things, in fact, now took that dramatic turn which seems the rule in France with affairs which directly or indirectly influence high politics and high finance. There were people who believed that the entire enterprise could be set on its legs, although parts of the recent excavations were deteriorating and some of them had been covered already with luxuriant tropical growths which one imaginative critic spoke of as "forests." Either the Government, they thought, could be forced to take up the enterprise itself, or at any rate would think it best, in view of what had already been done, to support de Lesseps in a fresh scheme, should the concession be renewed. This, no doubt, was the opinion of M. Gauthier, who urged the Government in the Assembly to appoint a commission to prepare plans for the completion of the canal. This, he declared, was the only means of safeguarding the interests of the shareholders and the many hundreds of millions of francs sunk by poor French investors in this great enterprise.

Such a daring proposal necessarily raised the whole question of the responsibility for the serious engineering and financial fiasco. The Government was at once charged from several quarters, not as being answerable for past mistakes in supporting the Panama Company, but with present obliquity in screening and protecting delinquents who should long since have been brought to justice. One deputy vehemently declared that the only reason why no adequate action was taken was that "men possessed of great names and high positions" checked any attempt to handle the scandal boldly. Other deputies declaimed with equal warmth against throwing good money after bad. Meanwhile rumors floated round the Chamber as to the number of deputies who had put their services at the disposal of the Company for money received. Later, this accusation took definite shape as a formal accusation that fifty deputies had received among them the sum of $600,000. Senators and Academicians were in the same galley. Exaggeration was imputed, but the figures were proved afterwards to be less than the truth. Then everybody concerning whose position there could be the slightest doubt was accused of having "touched."

Even MM. Rouvier and Floquet were taunted with having accepted large sums. The Chamber passed a resolution "calling for prompt and vigorous action against all who have incurred responsibilities in the Panama affair." This might mean anything or nothing. It was pointed out, however, by a high authority that a judicial inquiry was proceeding all the time. But the public became impatient because nothing was done to stop the campaign of vilification on the one hand or to prosecute the Directors on the other; though de Lesseps was being denounced daily in the press as a fraudulent adventurer. Excitement ran very high. The shareholders and some of the deputies cried aloud for justice.

Matters being thus exceptionally perturbed, Baron Jacques Reinach, the chief agent in the manipulation of political corruption, committed suicide by apoplexy. That was the gruesome explanation given in the press of this financier's sudden death. His fellow Semite, Cornelius Herz, survived the tragedy. Just at this moment, when everybody thought that something must be done, the Panama Concession was extended for a year. The Panamists took heart again and believed all would blow over. So the ups and downs of public expectation went on.

Then, quite suddenly and without any general notification, all the Directors of the Panama Canal Company, Count Ferdinand de Lesseps, M. C. de Lesseps, M. Fontane, M. Eiffel and M. Cottu, were formally charged in court with having resorted to fraudulent methods in order to engender confidence in chimerical schemes, and with obtaining credits on imaginary facts, squandering the money of the shareholders and lending themselves to most nefarious practices. A terrible indictment!

By this time all who cherished a political or personal grudge against any public man of note had no better or surer means of discrediting him than by imputing to him some connection with the Panama affair. Mud of that sort was warranted to stick. Never was there a greater scandal. Never were people more credulous. Never did political feeling run higher, and never certainly was there a keener anxiety to connect leading Republicans with the seamy side of the concern. The more that could be done in this way the better for the Conservatives and anti-Republicans who still constituted a very formidable combination in Parliament and in the press. It was not likely, therefore, that Clemenceau would be able to escape criticism and calumny if he had been in any way connected with men some of whom were then rightly regarded as malefactors.

In a time of so much excitement it was easy to mix up

truth and fiction to an extent which would render it extremely difficult for Clemenceau to clear the public mind of allegations made against him, however false they might be. All Clemenceau's enemies, and he had not a few, took advantage of the situation to try and overwhelm him with obloquy. Now was the opportunity to pay off many old scores; and they set to work to do it with whole-souled zest and vitriolic acrimony. Circumstances aided them. They did not stick at trifles in their efforts to crush the Radical leader who had fought the good fight against reaction and Imperialism with such vigor and success for so many long years. M. Clemenceau was at this time editor of *La Justice,* a journal founded by himself and written by men of ability, most of whom are still his friends. The tone of the paper and the style of the contributions were no more calculated to bring over recruits from his adversaries than were his speeches and tactics in the Assembly. He was ever a fighter with tongue and with pen. Though he wrote little, if anything, in *La Justice* himself, the inspiration came from its editor. One thing he lacked, and always has lacked—money. If now they could only get hold of evidence that Clemenceau was contaminated with Panama, the worst foe of French obscurantism would be put out of action and his influence permanently destroyed. So they calculated. And not without good reason, as afterwards appeared.

Cornelius Herz, the co-corrupter of political impeccables, with Jacques Reinach, his "apoplectic" fellow-Jew, had subscribed $5,000 to *La Justice* in its early days. What could be better? A Semite of Semites, a Panamist of Panamists, he it was who with sinister features and corrupt record stood forth as the dexterous wire-puller of the malignant marionette, Georges Clemenceau. If *La Justice* had been tainted with the accursed thing, Clemenceau had had his share, and the lion's share, too, in this wretched swindle. Did anybody really care what a journal of small circulation like *La Justice* published or stood for? Certainly not. But Clemenceau, the terrible leader of the Left, the upsetter of Ministries, the creator of Presidents, the overthrower of the Church and the enemy of all religion, here was a man worth buying; and beyond all question Clemenceau had been bought—bought by Reinach and Herz, whose tool, therefore, he was and had been! The calumnies were credible; for if Senators and Academicians had succumbed to the wiles of the serpents of Old Jewry, why should not the Aristides of Draguignan have fallen a victim to the astute de Lesseps and his *"entourage du Ghetto"*? Nor did this wind up the indictment. There was more to come. A group of rascals of the Titus Oates type were set to work to put incriminating facts on record in writing behind the scenes. They forged the endorsement as well as the bill. Documents of this character proved to the complete satisfaction of all who wished to believe it that Clemenceau was corrupt. The very fact that he was known not to be well-off strengthened the case against him. The empty sack could not stand upright! The *Petit Journal,* a paper of great circulation, was foremost in all this business, and its editor, M. Judet, distinguished himself by his exquisite malignity amid the crowd of Clemenceau's detractors.

It was an ugly experience. Panama was dinned into Clemenceau's ears daily. And there was enough to go upon to make the attacks most galling. Herz had been a large subscriber to the funds of Clemenceau's organ.

Moreover, Reinach and Herz had called upon him, though not he upon them. That was quite enough. The assailants did not stop to inquire when Herz ceased to have anything to do with *La Justice,* neither did they investigate who sent Reinach and Herz to the Radical leader, nor what passed between Clemenceau and the two Jewish financiers. They were only too glad to be able to take the whole thing for granted and to strengthen any weak links in the chain of evidence by the suborned perjuries of M. Norton and his colleagues.

So it went on. The fact that first the murdered President Carnot, who could not believe that de Lesseps was worse than a misguided enthusiast, and then President Loubet, who wished to deal with the entire matter in a thoroughly judicial fashion, had owed their positions to Clemenceau's nomination and support rendered the hunting down of their political friend a delightful pastime for the whole reactionary combination. Things had come to such a pass that the common opinion grew that there was "something in it." People actually believed that Clemenceau really had wrecked his entire career and ruled himself out of public life by taking bribes like the hundred other deputies, when he had refused to accept time after time positions which would have given him control of the national treasury and of France.

Clemenceau was quite unmoved by the storm of detraction which raged around him. He bided his time with a coolness that could scarcely have been expected from a man of his character. At length his chance came. The whole affair was brought up again before the National Assembly. Clemenceau rose to defend himself against this long campaign of successful misrepresentation. So great had been the effect of the attacks upon him that rarely, if ever, has a favorite orator stood up to address a more hostile audience. It seemed as if he had not a single friend in the whole House. Not a sound of greeting was heard. He was met with cold and obviously hostile silence. Clemenceau dealt in his most telling manner with his own personal conduct throughout. He completely immolated his accusers and dissipated their calumnies. When he sat down, the whole Assembly, which had received him as if persuaded of his guilt, cheered him enthusiastically as a much wronged man. A greater triumph could hardly be. The condemnation in open court of the forgers, whose nefarious malpractices had built up the edifice of calumny and misrepresentation upon which Clemenceau's enemies relied for the proof of their case, cleared the atmosphere so far as his personal integrity was concerned.

But, unfortunately for Clemenceau, there were other charges against him from which he could not hope to clear himself, and would not have cleared himself if he could. Now all his political crimes were recited against him at once. He had been the means of bringing to naught M. Jules Ferry's great schemes of colonial expansion in the East. He had opposed running the risk of war for the sake of Egypt. He had been largely instrumental in causing the failure of General Boulanger, whom not only reactionists but many vigorous Radicals admired and believed in. He had never lost a chance of pointing to the danger of priestly influence and the anti-Republican attitude of the heads of the Catholic Church. By his action in favor of the strikers at Carmaux, whom he went down himself specially to encourage and support, he had alienated a large section of the bourgeoisie.

Not the least weighty of the charges brought against

him, and one which perhaps had as much effect as any in bringing about the crushing result of the poll, was that Clemenceau had steadily opposed the alliance with Russia. This was regarded as still further and more conclusive evidence of downright treachery to France. Those were the days when France felt the need for an ally who could give her powerful military support, and her people were not disposed to inquire too closely into the character of the Czar's Government. Clemenceau regarded the connection as immoral, injurious, calculated to reduce France's democratic influence and to lessen the probability of a close *Entente* with England. But Clemenceau's adversaries had no concern whatever with the Radical leader's reasons for his action, which all democrats and Socialists, at any rate, must have cordially approved. All they wanted was another ugly weapon wherewith to discredit and defeat the man who, though he had not gone so far as the extreme Socialists desired, had done enough to hinder and rout reactionists with their monarchist or Buonapartist restorations. At the moment Clemenceau's anti-Czarist policy injured him as a politician, but it certainly did him great credit as a man.

But, worse than all, he had steadily pursued his policy of a lifetime as a close and constant friend of England and of the English *Entente*. That was still more criminal than Panamism or anti-Imperialism. For England at that time was, and to a large extent naturally, very unpopular in France. Clemenceau, therefore, was overwhelmed with charges of being in the pay of Great Britain and working for Great Britain as well as for Panama. Broken English was used to hurl insults at him, which lost none of their fervor by being uttered in a foreign tongue. He had escaped from the obloquy of

Panama, but it should go hard if one or other of these counts did not ruin him. The political warfare became more bitter than ever. His persecutors were relentless: *la politique n'a pas d'entrailles.*

It was at this time that I begged Clemenceau to make some terms with the Socialists, who were gaining ground rapidly and appeared to be the coming party in France. His recent tactics had been decidedly favorable to Socialist views. And again I express my surprise that Clemenceau, while holding fast to his opinions as to the necessity for maintaining "law and order" in every sense, should never have seen his way to adopting the definite Socialist view as to the necessary and indeed inevitable policy of a collective social progress. But his strong personal individualism has prevented him from embracing our principles.

The statesman may quite honestly accept the theories of economists and sociologists, while compelled to adapt their application to the circumstances of his time. No really capable Socialist who has taken an active part in public life has ever attempted to do anything else. In France the Guesdists, who are certainly the most thoroughgoing Marxists in the country, have always proceeded on these lines in their municipal, and not unfrequently in their State, policy. Jaurès was a specially fine example of the opportunist in public affairs; so much so that he was taunted by more extreme men with being a Ministerialist before he was a Minister. Vaillant the Blanquist, in theory at least an advocate of a physical force revolution where possible, was in favor of an eight-hour law, compensation for injury to workmen, and so on. One and all, that is to say, were ready to use the social and political forms of to-day in order to prepare the way for the complete revolution to-morrow. All Clemenceau's speeches and writings, before and after the Panama crash and its consequences to him, contain many passages which every convinced Socialist would accept. I always felt, nevertheless, that I was arguing with a man deaf of both ears when I put forward my well-meant suggestions. Socialism, Clemenceau then declared—this, of course, was now nearly a generation ago—would never become an effective political power in France. France, and above all rural France, which is the real France, constituting the bulk of Frenchmen, is and will always remain steadfastly individualist—"founded on property, property, property." That was their guiding principle in every relation in life, and, he added, "I have seen them close at every stage of existence from birth to death. It is as useless to base any practical policy upon Socialist principles as it is chimerical to repose any confidence in Socialist votes." "But," I urged, "extremes meet: the Catholics and Socialists, both of whom are your opponents, may combine with the men whose minds have been poisoned by the Panamist and Anglophobe imputations of the *Petit Journal* and turn you out of your constituency in the Var for which you now sit as deputy." He laughed at the very idea of such a defeat.

But the persistence and malignity of monarchists and men of God of the Catholic persuasion are hard to beat. Socialists with an anarchist twist in their mental conceptions are not far behind them. So the fight for the constituency of Draguignan, which Clemenceau had chosen in preference to a Paris district at the previous election, developed into a personal tussle unequaled in bitterness at that period. Every incident of the candidate's life was turned to his discredit. The Panama scandal and his relations with Semitic masters of corrupt practices were only a portion of an atheist record unparalleled for infamy. All the Ministries he had destroyed, all the true lovers of France whom he had gibbeted, all the patriotic colonial policies he had frustrated were brought up against him, embroidered with every flaming design the modern votaries of the Inquisition could invent! He had been guilty, in fact, of the unpardonable offense of making too many enemies at once. What might have been counted to him for righteousness by one faction was blazoned forth as the blackest iniquity by another. His anti-Imperialism with his friendly attitude to the strikers incensed the reactionaries. His refusal to make common cause with them in an out-and-out program against bourgeois Republicanism infuriated the extremists. All his energy, all his oratory, all his genuine love for and services to France in days gone by went for nothing. The friends of Jules Ferry, too, were eager for their revenge. Clemenceau had thought his loss of the seat was impossible. Nevertheless the impossible occurred. He was thrown out of Draguignan at this General Election of 1893, and after more than seventeen years of arduous and extremely useful service was compelled to retire from Parliamentary life. It was a complete break in his career.

Clemenceau at this period was fifty-two, and still in the prime of a vigorous life. He looked what he was, active, alert, capable and highly intelligent. His face was an index to his character. It gave an impression of almost barbarous energy, which induced his Socialist detractors, long afterwards, to speak and write of him as "The Kalmuck." But this was merely caricature. Refinement, mental brilliancy, deep reflection and high cultivation shone out from his animated features. A teetotaler, abstemious in his habits, and always in training, Clemenceau, with his rapidity of perception, quickness of retort and mastery of irony combined with trenchant wit, was a formidable opponent indeed. Add to this that he was invariably well-informed—*très bien documenté*—in the matters of which he treated. It is quite inconceivable that he should refer to or deal with any speech, or convention, or treaty which he had not thoroughly studied. It was hopeless to catch Clemenceau tripping on any matter of fact or political engagement. Moreover, as remarked before, his rule in politics was based upon the soundest principle in all warfare: Never fail to attack in order to defend.

As an orator he was and is destitute of those telling gestures, modifications of tone and carefully turned phrases which we associate with the highest class of French public speaking. His voice rarely rises above the conversational level and, as a rule, he is quiet and unemotional in his manner. But the directness of his assaults and the dynamitical force of his short periods gain rather than lose on that account; while his power of logical, connected argument, marshaling with ease such facts and quotations as he needs, has never been surpassed. His famous Parliamentary encounter with my friend and comrade Jean Jaurès was a remarkable example of his controversial ability. My sympathies were, of course, entirely with the eloquent and able champion of Socialism, whose power of holding even a hostile audience was extraordinary, as was shown in that same National Assembly many a time. I was of opinion then, and I believe now, that Jaurès had much the stronger case. He spoke as he always did, with eloquence, fervor and sincerity. As an oratorical display it was admirable. But I am bound to admit that, as a mere question of immediate political dialectics, the Radical Premier got the better of the fray. It is possible, of course, that had Jaurès followed Clemenceau instead of having preceded him, that might have made a difference. But Jaurès's style, with its poetic elevation and long and imposing periods, was not so well suited as that of Clemenceau to a personal debate on immediate practical issues before such an audience as the French National Assembly.

In private conversation Clemenceau is the most delightful yet unartificial talker I ever had the pleasure of listening to. Others who possess great gifts in this direction are apt to work up their effects so that you can hear, as it were, the clank of the machinery as their pyrotechnic monologues appeal to your sense of cleverness while they balk your desire for spontaneity. There is none of this with Clemenceau. He takes his fair share in any discussion and leaves nothing unsaid which, from his point of view, can elucidate or brighten up the friendly discussion. Never was any man less of a brilliant bore.

Another quality he possesses, which proved exceedingly useful to him at more than one stage of his adventurous career. Clemenceau was, and possibly is even to-day, at the age of seventy-seven, the most dangerous duelist in France. A left-handed swordsman and a perfect pistol-shot, no one who valued the integrity of his carcass was disposed to encounter with either rapier or pistol the leader of the extreme Left. Even the reactionary fire-eater, Paul de Cassagnac, who himself had killed three men, shrank from meeting his quietus from Clemenceau. His power of work also is extraordinary. In this he was only equaled by Jaurès. Even an English barrister of exceptional physique, striving to make his mark or endeavoring to keep the place already won, could scarcely surpass the inexhaustible energy and endurance of either of these great Frenchmen. It is doubtful whether the generation of younger men keep abreast with the pace set by their elders in this respect. Both Jaurès and Vaillant complained to me more than once that, to use an English expression, the younger deputies did not "last over the course," and thus frequently lost in the Committees what they had gained in the set debates. Certainly, few of the French politicians of to-day, at half Clemenceau's age, would care to attempt to do the work which he is doing now, day after day, with all the anxiety and responsibility which now rest upon his shoulders.

What perhaps is still more noteworthy, especially from the English point of view, Clemenceau has never at any period of his career been a well-to-do man. His complete independence of monetary considerations, at a time when place-hunting had been brought to a fine art in French politics, gave him an influence all the greater by consequence of its rarity. Politicians whom he could have easily eclipsed in the race for well-paid positions or the acquisition of wealth became Prime Ministers and rich people, while Clemenceau remained what he had always been, the leader of the most difficult party to control, without the means which have usually been considered indispensable for such a thankless post. Only once did he offer himself as the candidate for a well-paid office—the Presidentship of the Chamber—to which his experience and services fully entitled him. He was then beaten by one vote. Honorable and dignified as is the chairmanship of such an Assembly, it was well for

France, in the long run, that the recorder of that single vote should have allowed what he believed to be a personal grievance to influence his natural inclination to support Clemenceau.

CHAPTER X

PHILOSOPHER AND JOURNALIST

RARELY has a politician received a heavier blow than this which fell upon Clemenceau in 1893. Ordinarily, a man of his intellectual eminence and remarkable political faculties has no difficulty, if he loses one seat in the National Assembly of any country, in speedily getting another. Not so with Clemenceau. His very success as leader of the advanced Left and the proof that, though always a comparatively poor man, he had remained thoroughly honest amid all the intrigues and financial scandals around him told against him. He interfered with too many ambitions, was a stumbling-block in the way of too many high policies, to be able to command his return for another constituency. The same interests and jealousies which had combined against him at Draguignan would have attacked him with redoubled fury elsewhere. Persistent determination to carry really thorough democratic reforms in every department, combined with very high ability, relentless disregard of personal claims, complete indifference to mere party considerations and perfect honesty are qualities so inconvenient to modern politicians of every shade of opinion that the wonder is Clemenceau had held his position so long as he did. To have destroyed no fewer than eighteen more or less reactionary administrations, while always refusing to form a Cabinet himself, was a title to the highest esteem from the mass of his countrymen: it was a diabolical record from the point of view of the Ministers whom he had displaced and the cliques by whom they had been surrounded. Not a French statesman but felt that his reputation and his hold upon office were more secure now that Clemenceau's masterly combinations and dynamitical oratory were safely excluded from the National Assembly. So Clemenceau, at this critical period of his life and career, could rely upon no organized political force strong enough to encounter and overcome the persistent hostility of his enemies.

A weaker man would have felt this exclusion less and have been discouraged more. After seventeen years of such valuable work as Clemenceau had done, to be, to all appearance, boycotted from the Assembly for an indefinite period was a strange experience. I wrote him myself a letter of sympathy, and in his reply he expressed his special bitterness at the attitude of the Socialists towards him. This hostility might have been easily averted without any sacrifice of principle on Clemenceau's part. But Clemenceau, defeated and driven out of his rightful place in active French politics, did not hesitate for a moment as to the course he would pursue. He had left the National Assembly as the first Parliamentarian in France: he at once turned round and at the age of fifty-two became her first journalist. Nothing in his long life of stress and strain is more remarkable than the success he then achieved and the vigor with which he devoted himself to his new vocation.

It is no easy matter, especially in France, for a publicist and journalist to discover a fresh method of bringing his opinions to bear upon the public. Yet this is what Clemenceau did. He applied his humanist-materialist philosophy to the everyday incidents of French life. That philosophy is a strange compound of physical determinism and the ethical revolt against universal cruelty involved in the unregulated struggle for existence. The fight for life is inevitable. So far, throughout historic times it has been a long campaign in which the usurping minority have always won. Wholesale butchery and cannibalism by conquering tribes have been transformed first into slavery, then into serfdom, lastly into the wage-earning system of our own time. In each and every case the many have been at the mercy of the dominating few. There is little or no effective attempt made to remedy the evils arising out of such a state of things. The struggle for mere subsistence still goes on below, and those who revolt against it or endeavor seriously to ameliorate it by strikes or combinations are treated as misdemeanants or criminals. Mining capitalists, industrial capitalists, railway capitalists, landowners large and small have the law, the judges, the magistrates, the police and all the reactionary forces on their side. Hence the grossest injustice and the most abominable oppression of the poor.

Therefore the State ought to intervene, not in order to repress the aspirations and punish the attempts of the wage-earning class to obtain better conditions of life for themselves and their children, but to protect this most important portion of the community in every possible way: to secure for them shorter hours of labor, thorough education, full opportunity for legitimate combination, boards of arbitration to avert strikes, fair play at the hands of the courts and the police. The State, in fact, is to act as a national conscience and perpetual trustee for the poor. Note that the struggle for existence, the fight for subsistence must go on—Clemenceau has never contemplated the possibility of a human scheme of co-operation by which competition would be largely eliminated—but its harsher features ought to be reduced. There is no complete overthrow of mutual destruction, and no condition of universal fellowship is in view. Only the mind and heart of the community must be changed; men must survey modern society from the point of view of humane guidance and prepare the material development and economic arrangements which shall by degrees render individual injustice and cruelty as unheard-of as now is anthropophagy.

At the back of all this lies a picturesque pessimism and what nowadays is frequently spoken of as a philosophy of despair. No sooner has this planet, its solar system, its galaxy of suns and worlds reached its full development than they all begin to traverse the downward path which leads slowly and inevitably to decay and eventual destruction, until the entire process unconsciously and inevitably begins over again. Infinity oppresses us all: the cosmos with its interminable repetitions eludes conception by the human intelligence. Yet we live and strive and feel and hope and have our conceptions of justice and sympathy and duty which come we know not whence and pass onwards we know not whither. Man as a highly organized individual entity becomes superior to the mere matter of which his mind is a function, because as an individual he can rise up out of himself and criticise and reflect upon that which, without any such power of conception, surrounds, upholds and then immolates him. "The universe crushes me," wrote Pascal, "yet I am superior to the universe, because I know that it is crushing me and the universe knows nothing about it at all." Strange to find Clemenceau quoting and agreeing with an intelligence so wholly different from his own as Pascal's!

Then, fate, necessity, the Nemesis of Monism working on to its foreseen but uncontrollable destiny, dominates the cosmos and through the cosmos that infinitesimally small but sentient and critical microbe man, who creates an individual ethic out of this determinist material evolution. Francis Newman, the brother of the famous John Henry the Cardinal, said that it is as impossible for man to comprehend matter developing and reproducing itself from all time as it is for him to conceive of an omnipotent deity superintending the matter he has created in its evolution from all time. We are therefore driven back, whether we like it or not, upon the ancient and never-ending discussion of free-will and predestination in a non-theological form which leaves in the main all the psychologic phenomena untouched, including Clemenceau's own social morality which impels him to champion the cause of the oppressed. Beyond the demand for justice in the abstract and freedom in the abstract applied as a test to each special case as it arises, there is no guiding theory in Clemenceau's philosophy. The recognition of the struggle for existence among human beings, as among plants and animals, does not imply any conscious coördination of effort arising out of the growth of society in order to do away with the antagonism engendered by life itself. So with all his humanism Clemenceau will not accept the theories of scientific Socialism which could give an unshakable foundation to his own views of life. That is the weakness which runs through all his books and articles. His own individuality is so powerful that he simply cannot grasp the possibility of anything but individual effort, personal suasion and isolated measures of reform.

Nevertheless, we come upon a passage which, written obviously in perfect good faith, would, within its limits, be accepted as a fair statement of Socialism from an outsider: "Socialism is social beneficence in action, it is the intervention of all on behalf of the victim of the murderous vitality of the few. To contend, as the economists do, that we ought to oppose social altruism in its efforts is to misrepresent and seriously calumniate mankind. To complain that collective action will degrade the individual by some limitation of liberty is to argue in favor of the liberty of the stronger which is called oppressive. Is it not, on the contrary, to strengthen the individual by restraining and controlling every man who injures another man as does the employer of to-day when left to the bare exigencies of competition? . . . Follow the *laissez-faire* policy for the individual, says the antisocial economist, and speedily a whole regiment of devotees will rush to the succor of the vanquished. We always wait, but see nothing save the terrible condition of humanity which ever remains. . . . Against this anarchy it is man's glory to revolt. He claims the right to soften, to control fatality if he cannot escape from it. How?"

And then Clemenceau, whom in active life none would accuse of undue sentiment, goes off into a series of moral reflections and the need for perpetual moral preachments which really lead us nowhither; though, some pages further on, he quotes Karl Marx, who speaks of the unemployed as the inevitable "army of reserve" due not to human immorality but to the necessary functioning of the unregulated competitive capitalism of our period. Yet the great French Radical shrinks from the organized social collective action and revolution needed to lift us out of this anarchy of oppression. He turns to the individual himself and his hard lot under the domination of fate. He has a justifiable tilt at free-will and personal responsibility. Thus:—

"But what is absurd, contradictory, idiotic is the responsibility of the creature before the creator. I say to God, 'If you are not satisfied with me, you had only to make me otherwise,' and I defy him to answer me." And then, quoting from "Lucian's Dialogues of the Dead," he cites Minos as discussing with a new-comer who is brought before him for punishment:

"All that I did in life," says Sostrates, "was it done by me voluntarily, or was not my destiny registered beforehand by Fate?"

"Evidently by Fate," answers Minos.

"Punish Fate, then," is the reply.

"Let him go free," says Minos to Mercury, "and see to it that he teaches the other dead to question us in like manner."

"Substitute Fate for Jehovah or 'by the laws of the Universe,' and tell me," puts in Clemenceau, "when the pot owes his bill to the potter." All this and the farewell benediction which the author vouchsafes to the human plaything of all these preordered decisions of society do not get us much further, even though after so many mischances he may live on only to appreciate more thoroughly "the sublime indifference of things eternal." That is not very consolatory by way of a materialist viaticum. But it is the best Clemenceau can give.

None the less it is easy to comprehend why this sort of philosophy, illustrated and punctuated by the keenest criticism and sarcasm on the wrongs and injustice of our existing society, produced a great effect. The commonest incidents of everyday life were made the text for vitriolic sermonizing on the shortcomings of statesmen and judges, priests and police, industrial capitalists and mine-owners. Here and there, also, a description of working-class life is given, so accurate, so vivid, so telling that administrators of the easiest conscience were led to feel uncomfortable at the kind of social system with which they had been hitherto satisfied. With no phase of French life is Clemenceau better acquainted than with the habits and customs of the French peasantry. Thus we have a description of the peasant tacked on to a nice little story of a poor fellow who, strolling along the highway on a hot day and feeling thirsty, plucks a few cherries from the branch of a cherry-tree which overhangs the road. The small proprietor is on the look-out for such petty depredations and at once kills the atrocious malefactor who had thus plundered him. The cherry-eater "had despoiled him of two-ha'porth of fruit!" It justified prompt execution of the thief by the owner. That such small robbery did not at once give the latter the power of life and death over the thief is a point of view that the peasant can never take. Why? Because of the penal servitude for life to which he is condemned by the very conditions of his existence, and the greed for property driven into him from birth to death. It is the outcome of private ownership: the result of the fatal saying, "This is mine."

"The peasant is the man of one idea, of a sole and solitary love. Bowed, he knows only the earth. His activity has but one end and object: the soil. To acquire it, to own it, that is his life, harsh and rapacious. He speaks of *my* land, *my* field, *my* stones, *my* thistles. To till, to manure, to sow the land, to mow, to uproot, to prune, to cut what comes from the land, that is the eternal object of his entire physical or intellectual effort. Amusement for him: not a bit of it. He has no other resource than to console himself for the disappointment of to-day with the hope of to-morrow. He is at war with the seasons, the elements, the sun, rain, hail, wind, frost. He fights against the neighboring intruder, the invading cattle, the birds, the caterpillars, the parasites, the thousand-and-one unknown phenomena which, without any apparent reason, bring down upon him all sorts of unlooked-for ills.

"Then has he risen at dawn for nothing, badly fed, badly clothed, sweating in the sun, shivering in the wind and the rain, exhausting his energies against things which resist his utmost efforts? Do sowing, manuring, labor and the pouring out of life all, too, go for nothing, without rest, without leisure, without any thought but this: I toiled and suffered yesterday, I shall toil and suffer to-morrow? And all this is balanced by no pleasures but drunkenness and lust. No theatres, no books, no shows, no enjoyments of any kind. Hard to others, hard to himself, everything is hard around him."

Such is the peasant of Western France. Though the peasant of the South is of a livelier and happier disposition on the surface, both are at bottom the same. And France is still in the main rural France as Clemenceau himself impressed upon me many years ago. That is the influence which holds in check the advanced proletariat of the towns and mining districts. They can see nothing outside private property, property, property: yet it is this very unregulated individual ownership which forces them to fight out their existence against the hardships of nature with inefficient tools, insufficient manure and no adequate arrangements for marketing the produce they have for sale. High prices and a few advantages gained have somewhat ameliorated the lot of the peasant, but it is still a hard, depressing existence which cannot be made really human and happy for the great majority under the conditions of to-day. The only boon the peasant has is that he is not under the direct sway of the capitalist exploiter. What that means in the mines Clemenceau had an opportunity of seeing very close, as a member of the Commission appointed to examine into the coal-mines of Anzin in 1884. He tells of his experience ten years later in one of the pits he descended. "Never go down a coal-mine," wrote Lord Chesterfield to his son. "You can always say you have been below, and nobody can contradict you." Clemenceau did not follow this cynical advice. He went down, "and after having waded through water, bent double, for hundreds upon hundreds of yards through dripping scales which hang from the upper stratum, I crawled on hands and knees to a nice little vein *twenty inches thick.* On this seam human beings were at work, lying on their side, bringing down coal which fell on their faces and replacing it continuously by timber in order not to be crushed by the upper surface. You must not neglect this part of the work!" He was not allowed to talk with the men themselves, and when they came to interview him secretly they implored him not to let the manager or the employers know, or they would be discharged at once! The old story of miners in every country which even the strongest Trade Unions are as yet scarcely able to cope with, though the tyranny in French mines has been checked since the time Clemenceau wrote. These and similar cases of oppression on the part of the capitalist class caused Clemenceau to support Socialists more and more in their demands for limitation of the then unrestricted powers of individual employers and "anonymous" companies. So, too, individualist as he was, he wrote article after article in defense of the right of the men to strike against grievous oppression, holding that the combination of the workers was more than sufficiently handicapped by the fact that they were bound to imperil their own subsistence as well as the maintenance of their wives and children by going on strike at all. This argument he applied to all strikes in organized industries.

But Clemenceau naturally found himself drawn into bitter antagonism to the doctrine of *laissez-faire* and the law of supply and demand. "You say all must bow down to them. I contend all must revolt against them." "The individual struggle for existence is only a great *laissez-faire!* Far from being liberty, it is the triumph of violence, it is barbarism itself. The man who mastered the first slave founded a new system . . . so completely that after some ages of this rule a physiocrat overlooking it all would have sagely pronounced: Slavery is the law of human societies. This with the same amount of truth as he says to-day: The law of supply and demand is an immutable ordinance. And, for all that, the supreme irony of fate has decreed that the first slave-driver was at the same time the first sower of the seed of liberty, of justice. For by enslaving men he created a social relation, a relation different from that enjoined by the primitive form of the struggle for existence: kill, eat, destroy. Henceforth man was bound to man. The social body was formed." Man had to discover the law governing the new relation, and he found it at last in the first flashes of justice and liberty. "What, then, is this your *laissez-faire,* your law of supply and demand, but the pure and simple expression of force? Right overcomes force: that is the principle of civilization. Your law once formulated, let us set to work against barbarism!"

All that is telling criticism; though to-day it reads a bit antiquated in view of the revolt everywhere against both these catch-phrases and the anarchist chaos which they connote. But here again Clemenceau, with all his acuteness and brilliancy, displays the need for a guiding historic and economic theory—the sociologic theory which scientific Socialism supplies. It was not justice or liberty which created slavery, or destroyed slavery, but economic development and social necessity. The cult of abstraction leads to social revolt but not to material revolution.

Holding the opinions he did, it was inevitable that Clemenceau should put the case of the Anarchists such as Vaillant, Henry, Ravachol. They were the victims of a system. They could not rise as a portion of a collective attack against the unjust class dominion and economic servitude which crushed them and their fellows down into interminable toil with no reward for their lifelong sufferings. So they made war as individuals for anarchy. *Vive l'Anarchie!* were the last words of Henry. The man was a fanatic. "The crime seems to me odious. I make no excuse for it," says Clemenceau, but he objects to the capital penalty. "Henry's crime was that of a savage. The deed of society seems to me a loathsome vengeance." Clemenceau compares, too, the anarchists of dynamite to the would-be assassin Damien, so hideously tortured before death. "My motive," said he, "was the misery which exists in three-quarters of the kingdom. I acted alone, because I thought alone." The anarchist, asked by his mother why he had become an anarchist, answered, "Because I saw the suffering of the great majority of human beings." Vaillant, Henry, Caserio and their like are overmastered by the same idea as Damien. They kill members of the king caste of our society of to-day in order to scare the bourgeoisie into justice. There is no arguing with honest fanatics of this type. Whether society is justified in guillotining or hanging them is another matter. That their method is futile, as all history shows, gives society the right if it so chooses to regard it also as criminal.

The above is all argument and criticism put with almost savage vigor. But Clemenceau used likewise the lighter touch of French irony. Thus a wretched family of father, mother and six children, tramping along the high road near Paris, find some coal which has dropped from a wagon long since out of sight. They pick up these bits of chance fuel as a godsend. They have gleaned after the reapers. Straightway, the story of Boaz and Ruth occurs to Clemenceau, of Boaz and his descendant of Nazareth, who is the God of Europe to-day. The Hebrew Boaz, the landowner of old, gladly left the wheat-ears to be gleaned by Ruth and married her into the bargain. The Christian Boaz, the coal-owner of our time, gets the males of the distressed family of coal-gleaners six days' imprisonment. Such is progress through the centuries! The moral of the whole story is brilliantly touched in.

So again in his comment on the catastrophe at the Charity Bazaar. It was the rank and religiosity of the persons burnt alive which rendered the tragedy so much more terrible than if the crowd thus incinerated had only consisted of common people! It was the cream of French piety that was there sacrificed. Quite an ecclesiastical and political propaganda was developed from their ashes. The spirit of class made these accidental victims of gross carelessness martyrs of Christian heroism. Yet "if I go to dance at a charity ball, paying twenty francs for my ticket, and expire on the spot, I am not on that account a hero. . . . These gatherings are not exactly places of torture. People laugh, flirt, and amuse themselves, it is an opportunity to display fine dresses, and the charity sale has supplemented the Opéra Comique for marriage-provoking interviews superintended by good grandmothers. . . . Here is class distinction in action. Observe these aristocratic young gentlemen beating with their canes and kicking their frightened womenkind in their cowardly attempt to get out of danger. Then see the servants rushing in to save them! Look also at the workmen by chance on the spot risking their lives with true heroism, the plumber Piquet, who saved twenty people and, though much burnt himself, went back to his workshop without a word." The contrast is striking. It is not drawn by a Socialist.

Then the criticism on the German fête in commemoration of the victory of Sedan. "William II is obliged to keep his people in training, to militarize them unceasingly, body and soul. . . . In spite of the handsome protests of most of the Socialist leaders, we may be sure that it is in very truth the soul of Germany whose innermost exultation is manifested in these numberless jubilations which have beflagged every village in the Empire. . . . It is the curse of the triumphs of brute force to leave room in the soul of the conqueror for nothing but a blind faith in settlement by violence." Then follows a prophetic summary of what must be the inevitable consequence of this consecration of brutal dominion inspired by the hateful instincts of barbarism, which together prepare to use in Central Europe the most efficient means of murder at the disposal of scientific civilization. The ethics of the nation are being deliberately corrupted for the realization of the Imperial policy!

Thus Clemenceau, like others of us who knew the old Germany well, and had watched its sad hypnotization by the spirit of ruthless militarism, foresaw what was coming more than twenty-five years ago. And thus anticipating and reflecting, he chanced to see on one of the monuments of Paris illumined by the sun, "The German Empire falls." It was dated 1805! "Short years pass. What remains of these follies? If law and right outraged, reason flouted, wisdom contemned must blight our hopes, as your warlike demonstrations too clearly prognosticate, then for you, men of Germany, the inscription of the Carrousel is patient and bides its time."

"And yet two great rival peoples worthy to understand one another could nobly make ready a nobler destiny."

There you have the statesman and idealist as well as the clear-sighted journalist. Clemenceau saw the storm-cloud ever menacing and ready to break upon France. He warned his countrymen of their danger, bade them prepare to meet it, but hoped continuously that his forecasts might prove wholly erroneous. Jaurès unfortunately, with all his vast ability, was too idealist and far too credulous. Hence his great influence was thrown against the due preparation of his own country; he did his utmost to support the anti-navy men even in Great Britain, and only began to recognize how completely mistaken he had been just before he was assassinated by the modern Ravaillac of religionist reaction. To anticipate fraternity in a world of conflict is to help the aggressor and to court disaster. This Clemenceau the Radical knew; to this the French Socialists shut their minds.

It was natural that the Vendéen by birth, the Parisian by adoption, should feel himself drawn rather to the ideals of the French capital, which in matters of intelligence and art is also the capital of Europe, rather than to the narrow spirit of the Breton countryside which he has so vigorously sketched. In his writings as in his political activities this preference, this admiration find forcible expression. From the days of Julian the great Pagan Emperor down to the French Revolution and thence onwards, Clemenceau briefly traces the development of the City by the Seine, the French Renaissance and the University of Paris, by the influence of the writings of Montaigne—"this city in right of which I am a Frenchman" —and Rabelais: this meeting-place of Europe, this Central Commune of the planet proposed by Clootz, the Prussian idealist, becomes in the words of the same foreign enthusiast "a magnificent Assembly of the peoples of the West." We may forgive the French statesman his unbounded enthusiasm for the Paris where he has spent the whole of his active life. "One phrase alone, 'The Rights of Man,' has uplifted all heads. Lafayette brings back from America the victory that France sent thither and straightway the great battle is joined between Paris of the French Revolution and the coalition of things of the past. True, we have measured

'A la hauteur des bonds la profondeur des chutes,'

but at least we have striven, and we abate not a jot of our generous ambitions. Thus decrees the tradition of Paris . . . that Paris which now as ever holds in her hands the key to supreme victory."

CHAPTER XI

CLEMENCEAU AS A WRITER

M. CLEMENCEAU had a ready pen as well as a very bitter one, and he did not confine himself to articles on politics and sociology. Besides *La Mêlée Sociale*, of which I have given some account in the previous chapter, he published the following books in order within eight years: *Le Grand Pan*, a volume of descriptive essays; *Les Plus Forts*, a novel; *Au Fil des Jours*, and *Les Embuscades de la Vie*, which were, in the main, collections of sketches and tales. At the same time he did a great deal of ordinary journalism, including his articles on the Dreyfus case, which make in themselves four good-sized volumes.

Le Grand Pan followed close upon *La Mêlée Sociale*, and came as a delightful surprise to M. Clemenceau's readers, a piece of pure literature. In this book he no longer writes as a citizen of Paris, a man of the boulevards and pavements, but as one country-born and bred, knowing the hills and the sea. Although he describes his own Vendéen scenery with loving familiarity, making the "*Marais*," the "*Bocage*" and the "*Plaine*" live before us, he does not cling to them with the monotonous affection of some French writers, who are, as it were, dyed in their own local color. Without elaboration, without the detailed building-up of a scene which is the careful habit of some others, he conveys in two or three lines the *feel-*

ing of a countryside and that elusive but immutable thing, the character of a landscape. This belongs really to the poet's art, and gives, I cannot tell why, a deeper impression, a far more lasting pleasure than all the abundance and detail of prose. Clemenceau's neighbor, and almost fellow-countryman, Renan, had this gift. All the gray waters of the rocky Armorican shore seem to sweep through the first lines of his essay on the Celtic Spirit; and the influence of Renan is marked in *Le Grand Pan*. The first article, which gives the book its title, sets the reader's fancy sailing among the Greek Isles, steered by poetry and tradition, in the light of the golden and the silver age. Clemenceau, like Heine, mourns for the overthrow of the Greek gods in the welter of quarreling priesthoods and fierce Asian ugliness that flooded the Mediterranean world. "Pan, Pan is dead!" But in the Renaissance—"the tumultuous pageant of Art hurrying to meet the classic gods reborn"—he welcomes the magnificent restoration of the ancient and eternal Powers. And he claims for the nineteenth century the honor of beholding another re-birth of the gods of Nature in the development of science, and the labor that has brought some of the secrets of earth within our ken.

But science, as we know, has revealed the horrors as well as the wonders of earth. It troubles us; man has shed rivers of needless blood, but we shrink from recognizing Nature as she is, "red in tooth and claw." It did not trouble the ancient Greeks; their gods, developing from the rough deities of place or tribe into the embodiments of the natural forces of matter or of mind, were outside human ethic, although they were cast in human form. They might take the shape of mortals, but only Euripides and a few other hypersensitive moralists thought of blaming the gods when, as often happened, they fell below the standards of human conduct. But we are creatures of another era; and man, criticising and even condemning the Powers that rule his little day, has, for good or ill, reached out to a level that is above the gods, whose plaything he still remains.

And there is another change. Man—*some* men, that is to say—have taken the animals into their protection and fellowship: and M. Clemenceau is truly one of these. Not only those charming, kindly essays, *La Main et la Patte* and *Les Parents Pauvres,* in *Le Grand Pan,* but the history of the two pigeons in the *Embuscades de la Vie,* and a hundred little touches and incidents throughout Clemenceau's books show him to be a man of most generous sympathies, looking at animal life from a far higher and finer point of view than the majority of his countrymen.

There is much else in *Le Grand Pan* that it would be pleasant to dwell upon: a delicate classic spirit, a certain ironic grace, humor and mockery, but everywhere and above all keen indignation at needless human suffering and a sympathy which is poles apart from sentiment, for human pain. M. Clemenceau might well be called "a soldier of pity," as, in one of the Near Eastern languages, the members of his first profession, the doctors, are termed. But I must pass on. *Le Grand Pan* is, as it deserves to be, the best known of M. Clemenceau's books, and no one who has overlooked it can form a complete idea of this remarkable man.

It is said that any one who has the power of setting down his impressions on paper can write at least one good novel, if he tries, for he will draw with varying degrees of truth or malice the individuals he has met, liked, or suffered from, and the main circumstances of his life. What a Homeric novel M. Clemenceau might have written if he had followed these lines! But *Les Plus Forts* is unfortunately no such overflow of personal impressions and memories; it is merely what used to be called "a novel with a purpose." That is to say, it is one of the many works of fiction which not only record the adventures of certain imaginary yet typical characters, but also contain severe criticism of contemporary social conditions and life. Such novels were much more common in England during the nineteenth century than in France. In English fiction the sequence is unbroken from *Sandford and Merton* to the earlier works of Mrs. Humphry Ward's venerable pen. But in 1898 there were still not many French novels concerned with the serious discussion of social conditions, and M. Clemenceau's early work stands out among these for sincerity and simplicity of intent. However, in spite of the excellent irony of some passages—notably the description of the Vicomtesse de Fourchamps' career—*Les Plus Forts* is to modern readers a trifle tedious and a little naïve. It is of the same caliber as Mr. Shaw's two first novels, but less eccentric and not so amusing. M. Clemenceau himself would probably write upon it *"Péché de jeunesse,"* and pass on. Yet it deserves more attention than that; for *Les Plus Forts* unconsciously reveals the central weakness of its author's criticism of modern life. The situation is a good one, although the actors are not so much characters as types.

Henri de Puymaufray, a ruined French gentleman, who has lost the world and found a kind of Radicalism, and Dominique Harlé, a rich paper manufacturer, live side by side in the country as friendly enemies or, rather, close but inimical friends. Their views of life are as the poles asunder, but for the purposes of the story they must be constantly meeting in conversational intimacy; and they have each an almost superhuman power of expressing themselves and their attitude towards the world they live in. The chief link between them is Harlé's supposed daughter and only child, Claude, whose real father is Puymaufray. Both these elderly gentlemen are deeply concerned about Claude's future; each wishing, as parents and guardians often do, to make the child's career the completion of their own ambitions and hopes. Here Harlé has the advantage; he knows what he wants, that is, money and power, and he means his daughter to have plenty of both. He is the ordinary capitalist, with a strain of politician and Cabinet-maker, who ends by founding a popular journal that outdoes Harmsworth in expressing the "Lowest Common Factor of the mind." Society, the Church, and a particularly offensive form of charity all serve him to increase his own power and the stability of his class. All is for the best in the best of bourgeois worlds. Such is the theory of life which he puts before his supposed daughter, together with a *prétendant* who will carry out his aims. Unhappily, Puymaufray has nothing positive to set against this very solid and prosperous creed. He and Dechars, the young traveler whom he wishes to give Claude for a husband, can only talk pages of Radicalism in which the words "pity" and "love" would recur even more frequently if M. Clemenceau's fine sense of fitness did not prevail. What do they really want Claude to do? The best they can offer her appears to be a life of retired and gentle philanthropy, inspired by a dim sense of human brotherhood, which might, under very favorable circumstances, deepen into a sort of Socialist mood.

But "mere emotional Socialism cuts no ice." This has often been said, and means that a vague fraternal purpose and a perception of the deep injustice of our present social system, even when sharpened with the most destructive satire, will never change this world for the better, unless they lead up to some theory of construction that is based on economic facts. Pity and brotherhood may move individuals to acts of benevolence, but they cannot alone recast the fabric of society, or even bring about fundamental collective reforms. Besides, when young people are asked to give up certain definite things, such as money, pleasure and power, they must see something more than mere renouncement ahead. They must be shown the fiery vision of an immortal city whose foundations they may hope to build. Clemenceau's own knowledge of human nature works against his two heroes, and he says:

"Deschars was the child of his time. He had gone about the world as a disinterested beholder, and he returned from voyaging without any keen desire for noble action. . . . Perhaps, if he had been living and working for some great human object, Deschars would have carried Claude away by the very authority of his purpose, without a word. . . ."

And Madame de Fourchamps observes:

"It is very lucky for the poor that there are rich people to give them bread."

To which Claude replies:

"My father's factory provides these workmen with a livelihood; where would they be without him?"

Then, instead of a few plain words on labor-value, Puymaufray can only reply:

"Well, they give him something in exchange, don't they?"

The old capitalist fallacies here uttered in their crudest form cannot be refuted by mere injunctions to pity and goodwill; and even the magnificent words Libery, Equality, Fraternity are no adequate reply. To the successful profiteer and all who acquiesce in his domination they mean, Liberty of Enterprise, Equality of Opportunity, and Fraternity among Exploiters. Facts and the march of events alone can persuade Dominique Harlé and his like to use their ingenuity in serving their fellow-creatures, and not in profiting by them. And only collective action, guided by some knowledge of the direction in which our civilization is tending, can hasten the march of events.

It is remarkable how greatly the "novel with a purpose" has developed during the last twenty years in England and, to a less extent, in France. The characters are creatures of their conditions; and it is these conditions, not the characters, that do the talking. Some novels to-day are such careful and withal highly interesting guides to the sociology of England towards the end of the black Industrial Age that we cannot wonder if their authors take themselves too seriously as politicians and reformers. Yet these works show, after all, the same defect as *Les Plus Forts,* they have no constructive theory of life to set against the very well-defined, solid, and still apparently effective system which they criticize. All their most ironic descriptions, their most penetrating satire are negative, and, in the end, the utterances of men "wandering between two worlds, one dead, one powerless to be born."

Au Fil des Jours is an interesting collection of pieces in which the author has not made up his mind whether he will write short stories or articles upon social conditions. There is no harm in that; some people may even say that M. Clemenceau has produced a new variety of readable matter; but, curiously enough, the substance of the story is often so telling that one quarrels with the writer for not having put it into the best shape. Take one of the pieces in *Au Fil des Jours—La Roulotte*. Briefly, a weary old gypsy drives in a covered donkey-cart into a country hamlet, and stops by the riverside, where all the gossips are washing. He is received with hostile and watchful silence, because gypsies are always the scapegoats in a peasant district, and anything and everything that may be lost, stolen or strayed—even if it turns up again—is always laid to their account. In the night he dies, unnoticed; and, after some further time has passed, the villagers inspect his cart. Finding him there, dead, with a very small grandson living, they fetch the local constable and the mayor. The arm of the Law begins to function, the child is sent to the workhouse, the moribund donkey is "taken care of" by one of the villagers, and the dilapidated old cart, which only contained a few rags, is left by the riverside.

But the French peasant knows how to turn every little thing to profit: nothing is useless in his eyes. Gradually handy fragments of the donkey-cart begin to disappear. Bits of the iron fittings vanish, the tilt-props go, a shaft follows, one wheel after another slips away and is no more seen. In fact, the donkey-cart, as such, disappears from mortal sight. Then, one fine day, a gypsy-woman comes swinging along the road, where she had followed the traces of the donkey-cart, and asks for news of her old father and her little boy. The authorities of the village tell her of the old gypsy's death and burial: they do not require her to pay for his obsequies only because they see it would be no use. She goes to fetch the child from the workhouse, and then asks for the donkey and cart. The former, they tell her, died in the hands of the villager who "took care of him" (and sold his skin for a fair sum). She accepts this loss with resignation; but the cart, as she says, cannot have died: where is her father's *"roulotte"?*—Ah, well, nobody in the village knows anything about *that!* It *was* here, no doubt, since the old gypsy died in it—but since then—— The Law, once more represented by mayor and constables, can only shrug its shoulders in the finest French manner and disclaim all responsibility for a vagabond's goods. But the gypsy-woman persists: she begins even to clamor for her rights. *"Rights, indeed!"* The village, hitherto indifferent, becomes hostile; and the old cry that meets the gypsy everywhere is raised, for some one on the edge of the crowd calls out, "Thief!" It is a mere expression of disapproval, not a direct accusation, but the whole village takes it up joyfully: "Thief! Thief!" So the gypsy-woman, who, as it chanced, has stolen nothing, is hounded out of the commune with sticks and stones and objurgations by those who had themselves appropriated her old donkey-cart piecemeal. "A bit of rusty iron whizzed past her as she crossed the bridge. It may once have served as her donkey's shoe."

Such is the tale: a sample of many in *Au Fil des Jours*. Irony and realism are not wanting, nor yet the grimly picturesque, but the reader is left thinking: "What a little gem this would be if it were told by Maupassant, or some other master of the *conte!*" Certainly M. Clemenceau has something else to do than tell *contes!* But h* literary material is so fine that it is his own fault if we expect the very best of him. As it is, he does not take the trouble to cut the story out clearly from the matrix of thought and memories which enfolded it in his own mind. The effect on the reader is, one might say, a little vague and murmurous, like some tale half-heard in a crowd.

It is a strange thing that the countryside, Nature, the pure and never-failing spring of inspiration for poetry and human delight, should turn so different a countenance towards those who live with her, year out and year in, winning sustenance for us all from her broad and often ungenial breast. Our Mother Earth is an iron taskmaster to the tillers of the soil grinding out their youth and strength, bowing their eyes to their labor, so that all her beauty passes them by unseen. Either Nature keeps her charms jealously for the untroubled mind and the leisured eye, or else all the beauty that we see in her is borrowed, a glamor lent by some immaterial force—not ours, perhaps, but certainly not her own. Be this as it may, in the *Embuscades de la Vie* M. Clemenceau can see and describe the careless, endless, natural beauty amid which the peasant-lives that he sketches for us are set; but these themselves are often as ugly as bare stone, and the men and women are hard and close-fisted with one another mainly because the earth is so grudging to them. These stories are the most clear-cut of all Clemenceau's essays in fiction. They are not exactly *contes,* either: they are the discoveries, one might say, of Clemenceau in his ancestral character as the descendant of a line of doctors and landowners who worked for generations among the small bourgeois and the tillers of the soil. How he knows them! and—if French fiction is to be believed—how unchangeable they are! Since the bourgeois gained his freedom in the great Revolution by using the arm of the sansculotte, what a grip he has kept upon his possession! and how much dearer to him his property is than anything else in the world! Clemenceau does but take up the theme of Balzac and others when he describes provincial France and its twin gods, money and the land—money which compels loveless marriages, envy, fawning, bitterness, perpetual small cheating or endless insect-like toil; and the land, in whose service men work themselves and their kindred to the bone, and grudge a pittance to old age.

The bourgeoisie and their customs vary with their nationality, but peasant life is much the same all over Europe. Clemenceau found similar traits of life and character in Galicia to those of La Vendée; and others will tell us that from Ireland to Russia, from the Baltic to the Black Sea, the peasant and the small farmer conduct their lives upon the same lines: hard work, dependence upon the seasons, family authority, tribal feuds, and a meticulous social system of comment and convention, under which the individual finds himself far less free than in the unhampered, unnoticed life of the towns.

Yet many of the "ambushes of life" are to be found in the cities; and about a third of these tales are laid in the towns and among the well-to-do middle class. M. Clemenceau's satire plays freely upon the "marriage of convention," by which two families agree, after a certain amount of haggling and mutual sharp practice, to bind two young strangers together in the closest of relationship, for time (and also, we are told, for eternity), in the interest of property alone. Still human nature adapts itself to anything, and even such marriages have their compensations, as our author lightly and ironically points out. Being a genuine sociologist, he does not handle these tales of the bourgeoisie and their vagaries within what is, after all, an artificial and exclusive form of existence, as seriously as he does the great plain outlines of peasant life.

Whether he writes of town or country, of *Fleur de Froment* and *Six Sous,* or of a *Ménage à trois;* whether he calls up a Greek courtesan to theorize about her profession, or describes a long-standing, bitter and motiveless peasant feud, his style is always fluent and charming, vivid with irony, and graceful with poetic thought. Yet the defect as well as the merit of M. Clemenceau's fiction and essay-writing is just this admirable, unvarying ease and fluency. One feels that he writes with perfect unconsciousness, as the thoughts come into his head. And, after a while, the ungrateful reader is inclined to ask for some kind of selection in the feast before him, where all is good, very good, even, but nothing is *excellent.* Like a far greater writer, Clemenceau—on paper at least—"has no peaks in him." His literature was an admirable "by-product" of his almost limitless capacities; his actions and not his writings are the achievements of his life.

CHAPTER XII

CLEMENCEAU AND THE DREYFUS AFFAIR

IN December, 1894, Captain Dreyfus, a member of the General Staff, was found guilty of treason by a Court Martial. The court was unanimous. He was condemned to be sent to the Ile du Diable, there to expiate his offense by the prolonged torture of imprisonment and solitary confinement, in a tropical climate. It was a terrible punishment. But the offense of betraying France to Germany, committed by an officer entrusted with the military secrets of the Republic, was a terrible one too. It seemed so incredible, especially as Captain Dreyfus was a man of considerable means, that up to the last moment the gravest doubt as to the possibility of his having committed such a crime prevailed. When, however, the Court declared against him as one man, and without the slightest hesitation, there could no longer be any question of the correctness of the decision. For the trial had lasted four whole days, and Dreyfus had been defended by one of the ablest advocates at the Paris Bar. "What need have we of further witness?"

That was the universal feeling. Nearly a quarter of a century before, Marshal Bazaine had betrayed France to her mortal enemy, and had escaped the penalty which was his due. Common soldiers were frequently condemned to death and executed for impulsive actions against their superiors. High time an example should be made of a man of higher rank. Dreyfus was lucky not to be shot out of hand. That an Alsatian, a rich man, a soldier sworn to defend his country, an officer employed in a confidential post, should thus sell his nation to Germany was frightful. The thing was more than infamous. No punishment could be too bad for him. Permanent solitary confinement under a blazing sun is worse than immediate death. All the better. His fate will encourage the others.

And Captain Dreyfus was a Jew. That made the matter worse. Powerful as they are in politics and finance, Jews are not popular in France. By Catholics and sworn anti-Semites they are believed to be capable of anything. Even by men of open mind they are regarded with distrust as citizens of no country, a set of Asiatic marauders encamped for the time being in the West, whose God is a queer compound of Jahveh, Moloch and Mammon. There was thus the bitterest race and religious prejudice eager to confirm the judgment of the Court Martial. The case was decided. Dreyfus was sent off to the Island of the Devil.

Clemenceau shared the general opinion. He accepted the statement of the president of the Court Martial that "there are interests superior to all personal interests." And these were the interests which forbade that the Court Martial should be held in public, or that the secret evidence of treason should be disclosed. Given the honor, good faith, capacity and freedom from prejudice of the judges, this was a reasonable contention on the part of the chief officer of the Court. But there was that to come out, in this very Dreyfus case, which should throw grave doubt upon the advisability of any sittings behind closed doors of any court that deals with matters into which professional, personal or political considerations may be imported. Secrecy is invariably harmful to democracy and injurious to fair play.

Three years later Clemenceau began to understand what lay behind this veil of obscurity which he then allowed to be thrown over the whole of the Dreyfus proceedings. He took upon himself the full burden of his own mistake. When he had distinguished his fine career by the vigorous and sustained effort in favor of justice to the victim, he printed at full length his articles denouncing the man about whom he had been misled. "I cannot claim," he writes, "credit for having from the first instinctively felt the iniquity. I believed Dreyfus to be guilty, and I said so in scathing terms. It seemed to me impossible that officers should lightly inflict such a sentence on one of themselves. I imagined there had been some desperate imprudence. I considered the punishment terrible, but I excused it on the ground of devotion to patriotism." Nothing was farther from Clemenceau's thoughts, even at the close of 1897, than that Dreyfus should after all be not guilty. He laughed at Bernard Lazare when he said so. Meeting M. Ranc by accident, this politician and journalist confirmed the opinion of Lazare and declared that Dreyfus was innocent. Again Clemenceau smiled incredulously, and was recommended to go at once and see M. Scheurer-Kestner, Vice-President of the Senate, the famous Alsatian whose high qualities he many years afterwards proclaimed in a funeral oration.

The editor of *l'Aurore* called upon that courageous and indefatigable champion of Dreyfus; and comparison of the handwriting of Esterhazy, the chief witness against the captain, with that of the *bordereau* attributed to Dreyfus and decisive of his guilt, convinced Clemenceau, not that Dreyfus was innocent, but that the judgment had been quite irregular. Therefore he resolved to begin a campaign for a revision of the case. He did not share Scheurer-Kestner's view as to the enormous difficulty and danger of such an undertaking. Trouble and misrepresentation he anticipated. Bitter opposition from the members of the court and of the General Staff—Yes. Virulent misrepresentation due to priestly hatred—Yes. Unceasing malignity of anti-Semites—Yes. Strong political objection to any reopening of a *"chose jugée,"* on public grounds—Yes. But, in spite of all, the truth in modern France would easily and triumphantly prevail! "Events showed me how very far out I was in my calculations."

As on more than one occasion in his stormy life, therefore, Clemenceau underrated the strength of the enemy. He had to contend against a combination of some of the strongest interests and passions that can affect human life and sentiment. There had been from the very commencement a bitter feeling among some of the most powerful sections of French society against the Republic. As was shown in the rise of Boulanger, Clemenceau, by exposing the drawbacks of successive Republican Governments, had done much to strengthen this feeling among its opponents and to weaken the loyalty of its supporters. There was, in fact, nothing in the Republic itself to be enthusiastic about. It was essentially a bourgeois Republic, living on in a welter of bourgeois scandals, unbalanced by any great policy at home, any great military successes abroad, or any great personalities at the head of affairs. The glories of France were dimmed: the financiers of France—especially the Jew financiers—were more influential than ever. All this helped the party of reaction.

Religion, too, had come in to fortify finance and build up the anti-Semite group. The Catholics, to whom Jews and Free-Masons are the red flags of the political and social bull ring, had not very long before challenged the former to deadly combat in that Field of the Cloth of Gold on which, to use the phrase of one of their less enlightened competitors, they "do seem sort of inspired." It is possible that had the Catholic Union Générale listened to the advice of their ablest and coolest brain, who was, be it said, neither a Frenchman nor a Catholic, the great financial combination of the Church, with all its sanctified funds of the faithful behind it, might have won. Even as it was, it drove a Rothschild to commit suicide, which was regarded as a great feat at the time.

But M. Bontoux was too ambitious, he did not possess the real financial faculty, his first successes turned such head as he possessed. The Jews, therefore, were able to work their will upon the whole of his projects and groups, and the devout Catholic investors of Paris, Vienna and other places had the intolerable mortification of seeing their savings swept into the coffers of the infidel. This had happened some years before the Dreyfus case. But losers have long memories, and here was a sore monetary grievance superadded to the previous religious hatred of the Hebrew.

Dreyfus was a Jew. Nay, more, he came of financial Jews who had had their pickings out of the collapse of the Union Générale as well as out of the guano and other concessions malignantly obtained in the Catholic Republic of Peru. Monstrous that a man of that race and name should be an officer in the French Army at all!

THE DREYFUS AFFAIR

Still more outrageous that he should be placed by his ability and family influence in a position of military importance, and entrusted with serious military secrets! Something must be done.

Now the persons forming the most powerful coterie in the higher circles of the French Army at this time were not only men who had been educated at the famous military academy of St. Cyr and imbued with an *esprit de corps* cultivated from their school-days upwards, but they were officers who believed heartily, if not in the religion, at any rate in the beneficent secular persuasion of the Catholic Church. They were, as was clearly shown, greatly influenced by the Jesuits, who saw the enormous advantage of keeping in close touch with the chiefs of the army.

Then there were the monarchists and Buonapartists, male and female, of every light and shade, who were eagerly on the look-out for any stroke that might discredit the new studious but scientific and unbelieving class of officers, whom the exigencies of modern warfare were making more and more essential to military efficiency. Their interest was as far as possible to keep the main higher organization and patronage of the army and the General Staff a close borough and out of the hands of these new men.

All this formed a formidable phalanx of organized enmity against any officer who might not suit the prejudices or, at a critical moment, might be dangerous to the plans of people who, differ as they might in other matters, were at one in disliking capable soldiers who were not of their particular set. And here was Dreyfus, who embodied in his own person all their most cherished hatreds, who could be made the means of striking a blow at all similar intruders upon their preserve, in such wise as greatly to injure all their enemies at once. Unfortunately for him, Dreyfus was at the same time an able officer—so much the more dangerous, therefore—and personally not an agreeable man. Not even their best friends would deny to clever Jews the virtue of arrogance. Dreyfus was arrogant. He was not a grateful person to his superiors or to his equals. They all wanted to get rid of him on their own account, and their friends outside were ready enough to embitter them against him because he was a Jew.

This is not to say that there was an elaborate plot afoot among all who were brought in contact with Dreyfus, or that, when the charge against him was formulated, there was a deliberate intention, on the part of the members of the Court Martial, to find him guilty, no matter what happened. But it is now quite certain that, from the first, the idea that he was a spy was agreeable to his fellow-officers in the Ministry of War; and, being satisfied as to his responsibility for the crime that they wished to believe him guilty of, they did not stick at trifles, in the matter of procedure and testimony, which might relieve their consciences and justify their judgment. Knowing, then, the powerful combination which would oppose to the death any revision of Dreyfus's trial, Scheurer-Kestner, resolute and self-sacrificing as he was, might well take a less sanguine view than Clemenceau of the probabilities of certain victory as soon as the truth was made known.

But when once he began to doubt whether Dreyfus had had fair play, Clemenceau immediately showed those qualities of personal and political courage, persistence, disregard of popularity, and power of concentrating all his forces upon the immediate matter in hand, indifferent to the numbers and strength of his opponents, which had gained him so high a place in the estimation of all democrats and lovers of fair play long before. "If there are manifest probabilities of error, the case must be revised." That was his view. But the National Army and the National Religion, as bitter opponents of justice put it, were one and indivisible on this matter. Militarism and Jesuitism together, backed by the high society of reaction and a large section of the bourgeoisie, constituted a stalwart array in favor of the perpetuation of injustice. There was literally scarce a crime of which this combination was not capable rather than admit that by any possibility a Court Martial on a Jew captain could go wrong.

The Minister of War, General Billot, the Prime Ministers Méline and Brisson, generals of high standing such as Mercier, Boisdeffre, Gonse, Zurlinden and others, officers of lower rank and persons connected with them, were gradually mixed up with and defended such a series of attempted murders, ordered suicides, wholesale forgeries, defense and decoration of exposed spies, perjury, misrepresentation and false imprisonment that the marvel is how France survived such a tornado of turpitude. Clemenceau little knew what it would all lead to when, by no means claiming that Dreyfus was innocent, he and Scheurer-Kestner and Zola and Jaurès, and all honest Radicals and Socialists, demanded that, even if Dreyfus were guilty, he could not have been *legally* condemned on false evidence and forged documents: the latter never having been communicated to his counsel. It was on this ground that Clemenceau demanded a revision of the trial.

But quite early in the fray the defenders of the Court Martial became desperate in their determination that the matter should never be thoroughly investigated. The honor of the army was at stake. Colonel Picquart, a man of the highest credit and capacity, comes to the conclusion in the course of his official inspection of documents at headquarters that the incriminating paper on which Dreyfus was condemned, but which he was never allowed to see, was not in his handwriting at all, but in that of Major Esterhazy, an officer disliked and distrusted by all fellow-officers with whom he had served. Picquart, in fact, suspected that Esterhazy was a Prussian spy and that he forged the *Bordereau* which convinced the Court Martial of Dreyfus's guilt. But before this, in 1894, when the story leaked out that an officer having relations with the General Staff was suspected of treachery, it was not Dreyfus whose name was first mentioned. His old comrades said with one accord, "It must be Esterhazy: we thought so." Esterhazy, however, soon made himself necessary to the army chiefs and their Catholics. If his character was blasted publicly, down these gentry would come, and with them the whole of the proceedings against Dreyfus. They therefore suggested to Picquart that he should simply hold his tongue. *"You* are not at l'Ile du Diable," they said. But Picquart would persist, so they sent him off to Tunis. However, thanks to Scheurer-Kestner and others, the truth began to come out, and Picquart still refused to be silenced. So instead of dealing with Esterhazy, they arrested his accuser and gave the Major a certificate of the very highest character.

As it began, so it went on. Clemenceau's daily articles and attacks drove the militarists, the Catholics, the anti-Semites and the reactionaries generally, into a fury.

Colonel Henry, Colonel Paty du Clam, the Jesuit Father du Lac, the editors and contributors of the *Figaro,* the *Echo de Paris* (the special organ of the Staff), the *Gaulois* were in a permanent conspiracy with the generals named above, and the General Staff itself, to prevent the truth from being known. It was all of no use. Picquart under lock and key was more effective than Picquart at large. Slowly but surely men of open mind became convinced that, little as they wished to believe it, something was wrong. But these were always the minority. Few could grasp the fact that an innocent man was being put in chains on the Ile du Diable, virtually because there was an agitation in favor of his re-trial in Paris.

Then came Zola's terrible letter in the *Aurore,* which Clemenceau had suggested and gave up his daily article in order to give place to. He also supplied the title "*J'Accuse.*" Zola summed up the whole evidence relentlessly against the General Staff and its tools and forgers, Esterhazy, Henry, Paty du Clam and the rest of them.

Such an indictment formulated by a novelist who was universally recognized as one of the leading men of letters in Europe, quite outside of the political arena, would have attracted attention at any time. In the midst of a period when all feelings and minds were wrought up to the highest point of tension, it came as a direct and heavy blow at the whole of the military party. It is difficult to realize to-day the sensation produced. It had all the effect of a combined attack of horse, foot and artillery for which preparation had been made long before by a successful bombardment. There was no effective answer possible in words. This the military cliques and their friends at once saw and acted upon. They abandoned discussion and forced Zola and *l'Aurore* into court on a charge of treason and libel. The action stirred all Europe and riveted attention throughout the civilized world. This was due not merely to Zola's great reputation and popularity, to the political position held by Clemenceau, to the enthralling interest of the Dreyfus affair itself, to the excitement of the life-and-death struggle between freedom and reaction, but to the fact that behind all this lay the never-dying hostility of Germany to France.

All this was too much for the criminal champions of "the honor of the Army." *L'Aurore* and Zola must be prosecuted. They were. And Clemenceau conducted his own defense. It was a crucial case, and the famous advocate Labori had previously done his best for Zola, pointing out that the whole drama turned on the prisoner then suffering at the Ile du Diable: perhaps the most infamous criminal, perhaps a martyr, the victim of human fallibility. He had shown, however, that "all the powers for Justice are combined *against* Justice," and had called for the revision of a great case.

"After the jury have adjudicated, public opinion and France herself will judge you," said Clemenceau himself. "You have been told that a document was privately communicated to the Court. Do you understand what that means? It means that a man is tried, is condemned, is covered with ignominy, his own name, that of his wife, of his children, of his father, of all his connections eternally blasted on the faith of a document he had never been shown. Gentlemen, who among you would not revolt at the very idea of being condemned under such conditions? Who among you would not adjure us to demand justice for you if, brought before a tribunal, after a mockery of investigation, after a purely formal discussion, the judges, meeting out of your presence, decided on your honor and your life, condemning you, without appeal, on a document of whose very existence you were kept in ignorance? Who among you would quietly submit to such a decision? If this has been done, I tell you your one duty above all others is that such a case should be re-tried."

That was the main point, as Clemenceau saw even more clearly than M. Labori. No man, guilty or innocent, could be justly condemned and sentenced on the strength of a written document the purport and even the existence of which had been deliberately concealed from the prisoner and his counsel. It scarcely needed further argument, not even the direct proof which was forthcoming that Colonel Sandherr, the president of the Court Martial, had a bitter and unreasoning prejudice against Jews. If the validity of the document had been beyond all possibility of question; if witnesses whose good faith had been unquestionable had seen Dreyfus write it with their own eyes: even then the trial was legally vitiated by the fact that it had not been shown to the accused. But if the document was forged——? All the other points, serious as some of them were, counted little by the side of this.

That, therefore, Clemenceau dealt with most persistently. That, therefore, the General Staff, with its coterie of Jesuits, anti-Semites and spies, were determined to cover up. The generals who bore witness in the case against Zola and *l'Aurore* showed by their threats and their admissions they knew that it was they themselves and the members of the secret Court Martial who were really on their trial at the bar of public opinion.

It was in this sense that Clemenceau closed his memorable defense. He declared against the forger of the *bor-*

dereau, the Prussian spy, Esterhazy, who was sheltered and honored by the chiefs of the French Army. "Yes, it is we," he cried, amid derisive shouts and howls in court, "it is we who are the defenders of the army when we call upon you to drive Esterhazy out of it. The conscious or unconscious enemies of the army are those who propose to cashier Picquart and retain Esterhazy. Gentlemen of the jury, a general has come here to talk to you about your children. Tell me now which of them would like to find himself in Esterhazy's battalion? Tell me, would you hand over your sons to this officer to lead against the enemy? The very question is enough. Who does not know the answer before it is given?

"Gentlemen of the jury, I have done. We have passed through terrible experiences in this century. We have known glory and disaster in every form, we are even at this moment face to face with the unknown. Fears and hopes encompass us around. Grasp the opportunity as we ourselves have grasped it. Be masters of your own destinies. A people sitting in judgment on itself is a noble thing. A stirring scene also is a people deciding on its own future. Your task, gentlemen of the jury, is to pronounce a verdict less upon us than upon yourselves. We are appearing before you. You will appear before history."

CHAPTER XIII

THE DREYFUS AFFAIR (II)

THIS of Zola and *l'Aurore* was the greatest crisis in the long succession of crises which centered themselves round Dreyfus. The more serious the evidence against the conduct of the Court Martial and the honor of the army, the more truculent became the attitude of the militarists, Catholics, anti-Semites and their following. Passion swept away every vestige of judgment or reason. There was no pretense of fair play to the defendants. Inside the Court, which was packed to overflowing, inarticulate roars came from the audience when any telling argument or conclusive piece of testimony was put in on the side of truth and justice. Outside, an infuriated mob of reactionists demanded the lives of the accused. The smell of blood was in the air. The likelihood of organized massacre grew more obvious every day. Clemenceau told me himself—and he does not know what fear is—that if Zola had been acquitted, instead of being condemned, the Dreyfusards present would have been slaughtered in court.

How determined the whole unscrupulous and desperate clique were to carry their defense of injustice to the last ditch was displayed when M. Brisson, the President of the Republic, himself a man credited with austere probity and cool courage, was forced by them to authorize proceedings against Colonel Picquart, because he had offered the highest personage in France to help him to discover the truth. Picquart was therefore to be victimized still further: likewise for the honor of the army! He was duly incarcerated and degraded. France herself was being found guilty and cashiered by the persecution of this high-minded and courageous colonel. Esterhazy runs away when his treachery and forgeries are finally exposed. Clemenceau and the Dreyfusards are willing that he should have a safe-conduct back again, if his coming will help to manifest the truth. A very different attitude towards a culprit convicted, not by a secret Court Martial but by his own public actions and admissions. Yet General Gonse and the General Staff even were quite ready to aid and support Colonel Picquart in exposing Major Esterhazy as only a German spy in constant communication and collusion with Colonel Schwartzkopfen acting on behalf of the German Army and the German Government. Esterhazy was no direct agent of the French Staff! When, however, it was discovered that Colonel Picquart's investigations went far to clear Captain Dreyfus altogether, and proved that he had at any rate been condemned on a forged document, *then* Picquart himself was to be treated as a criminal, unless he suppressed the truth at once, and held his tongue for ever.

And so this extraordinary case was now being tried in the open street before the public of France and of the world—for every civilized nation followed the changes and chances of Dreyfus's martyrdom—and so day after day, week after week, month after month, year after year, Clemenceau, Scheurer-Kestner, Jaurès and the Socialists fought on for a re-trial. The highest Court of judicature in France, worthy of its history, accorded the right of appeal. A sense of doubt was beginning to creep through the community. Thereupon, the Generals, their Church, their Press, their Mob, *their* Army, began afresh a very devil dance of organized forgery, calumny, perjury, vituperation, attempted murder and concomitant infamies.

Looking back at that period of desperate antagonism, it seems strange that open conflict should have been averted. It was no fault of the General Staff and its myrmidons that it did not break out. That such a result of their campaign of injustice and provocation would have been welcomed by many of the chiefs of the French Army is beyond question. At more than one juncture the outlook was so threatening that two, if not three, pretenders to the throne of France were in the country at the same time. Things did not take the turn they expected, and they went off again. All this was known, of course, to Clemenceau, who was also well aware that a great deal more lay behind the Dreyfus affair than the guilt or innocence of Dreyfus. Nor did the fact by any means escape him that those semi-occult ecclesiastical influences which had been against him all his life, not for personal reasons, but because he was a Radical, a free-thinker and a champion of free speech, a free press, secular and gratuitous education, and separation of Church and State —that those hidden powers were at work behind the General Staff in the Dreyfus case in the hope of gaining ground on the side issue which they were losing steadily on the main field of battle.

This it was which made the collision between the two opposing forces so critical an event for France. This, too, accounted for the desperation of the losing party.

The Jesuits of the Dreyfus affair had none of the diabolical far-seeing coolness of the type represented by the Père Rodin in Eugène Sue's *Wandering Jew*. They were infuriated fanatics whose unreasoning anxiety to torture and burn their heretic opponents was reflected in the blundering mendacity and undisguised hatred of their tools of the military Staff. Hence, in the long run, they delivered themselves into the hands of the Frenchmen of the future—Zola, Jaurès, Picquart and Clemenceau. Clemenceau's daily articles, which constituted the most formidable barrage on behalf of Dreyfus, make up five closely printed volumes. They are full of life and fire; but they are full also of crushing argument enforced with irony and sarcasm and illustrated by telling references to recent history. Abuse and misrepresentation could not permanently hold their own in a discussion thus conducted. Forgery and perjury when brought home to the real criminals necessarily made their case worse. Nothing is more surprising than the lack of dexterity and acumen on the part of the reactionary forces. They forgot that a bludgeon is a poor weapon against a rapier in the hand of an expert.

Thus it came about that after a long contest, whose interest, even for outsiders, was maintained throughout by tragical incidents such as the suicide of Colonel Henry—the forger for *esprit de corps* as Esterhazy was the forger for money and power—the attempted poisoning of Picquart and the attack upon Labori, a re-trial was forced from the Government of the day. The names of the chief opponents are already forgotten, such minor actors and apologists of injustice, forgers and spies on the "right side" were scarcely remembered. Who now cares whether the *petit bleu* was written by Schwartzkopfen or not? Who can recall what Major Lauth did or bore witness to? The trail of the serpent is over them all. That is all the world bears in mind to-day. The

THE DREYFUS AFFAIR

broad features of the drama are recorded on the cinema film of history. The faces and characters of the villains of the piece are already blotted out. Only the heroes of the conflict remain. And of these heroes Clemenceau might fairly claim to be the chief. The re-trial at Rennes was, when all is said, mainly his work.

What a re-trial it was! The Court was still a Court Martial. The president of the Court, Colonel Jouaust, was still a violently prejudiced officer. The judges behind him were all inspired by that fatal *esprit de corps* which accepts and acts upon the Jesuit motto that the end justifies the means, where the interests of a particular set of men are concerned. In fact, the combination in favor of military injustice remained what it had been throughout: a body resolved that come what might the victim of the forged document and other criminal acts should not be formally acquitted, even if monstrous illegality at the first trial forced a revision.

Nearly five years had now elapsed from the date of Dreyfus's original condemnation, when, released from his imprisonment, he stood at the Bar after that long period of physical and moral torture. Clemenceau is not a man of sentiment: he had long doubted whether Dreyfus was really innocent: even the outrageous proceedings at the first Court Martial had failed to convince him that there might not be something behind the forged *bordereau,* concealed from the prisoner, which could in a degree justify his judges: not until the close of the case against Zola and *l'Aurore* was his mind made up that, "consciously or unconsciously," a terrible crime had been committed. But now, with Dreyfus himself present, with all the old witnesses contradicting, more directly than ever, one another's testimony, yet allowed incredible license of exposition and explanation by the court; with the evidence of General Gonse, General Mercier, Roget, Cinquet, Gribelin, Lauth and Junck cut to ribands by the questions of Dreyfus's advocates; with Colonel Picquart brought up short by Colonel Jouaust, who had allowed all sorts of long-winged and irreconcilable accounts to be given by his favorites subject to no interruption—with all this almost inconceivable unfairness going on all day and every day through the Rennes Court Martial, Clemenceau seems to have been really affected, not only by the injustice done, but by the personal sufferings which the prisoner on trial had undergone and was undergoing.

Colonel Jouaust's interruption of Colonel Picquart's closely knit but passionless statement by the exclamation *"Encore!"* was destined to become famous. It summed up in one word the whole tone of the prosecuting judges on the Bench. Yet as the case proceeded and the criticisms of Clemenceau and his coadjutors became still more scathing than they had been before, it was difficult to see how even a suborned court could avoid a verdict of acquittal. But this Court dared not be just. There was too much at stake. The whole of the chiefs of the army had taken sides against the prisoner. They were there to secure condemnation of Dreyfus again at all costs. The Court, headed by Colonel Jouaust, was forced to be the same. It was the "Honor of the Army" backed by Esterhazy, Henry and Sandherr against the character of one miserable Jew. There could be no hesitation under such conditions. Dreyfus was found "Guilty, with extenuating circumstances." Extenuating circumstances in the dealings of a spy and a traitor who, not being in any pressing pecuniary need whatever, had deliberately and infamously sold France to the enemy! Not one of the five judges who rendered this verdict could really have believed Dreyfus to be guilty. France was more dishonored by this decision than if the Court had definitely declared against the whole weight of the evidence that Dreyfus was a traitor.

Dreyfus was thereafter "pardoned" and released. That special plot of the anti-Republican clerico-military syndicate of Father du Lac, to use Clemenceau's phraseology, had after all miscarried. As the result of incredible efforts Dreyfus was at last a free man. The world could judge of the character of his accusers and of his champions. It did judge, and that verdict has never been revised. A gross injustice had been partly remedied but could never be fully obliterated. That Dreyfus was innocent the world at large had no doubt.

Yet, strange to say, there are still men, who certainly had no feelings against Dreyfus but quite the contrary, who were not convinced. I have heard this view expressed from several quarters, but the opinions of two personal friends of the most different character and career made a considerable impression upon me at the time. The first was my friend, the late George Henty, well known as a special correspondent and author of exceedingly successful books for boys. Henty was a thoroughgoing Tory, but he had no doubt that Dreyfus was a terribly ill-used man and the victim of a foul plot—until he went over to France to watch the re-trial by Court Martial at Rennes. He returned in quite a different frame of mind. He knew I was entirely favorable to Dreyfus, as he himself had been when he crossed the Channel. Meeting him by accident, I asked him his opinion: "All I can tell you, Hyndman, is that I watched the man carefully throughout and he made a very bad impression upon me indeed. The longer I looked at him the worse I felt about him. I don't deny for a moment that his first trial was abominably conducted and that he was entitled to fair play. I dare say I may be all wrong, the weight of the evidence might have overborne me as a juryman. But, as it was, I felt that if I myself had been one of the jury I should have given a verdict against him. The man looked and spoke like a spy, and if he isn't a spy," Henty went on in his impulsive way, "I'll be damned if he oughtn't to be one." That, of course, is simply the statement of an impressionable Englishman, who, however, understood what was going on.

The other anti-Dreyfusard was a very different personality. It was the famous German Social-Democrat Wilhelm Liebknecht. I *knew* him well. A man of a cooler temper or a more judicial mind I never met. As I have mentioned elsewhere, he and Jaurès, the great French Socialist leader and orator, were staying with me together in Queen Anne's Gate, just after the Rennes Court Martial. Jaurès had done immense service in the Dreyfus matter, second only to that of Clemenceau. He had studied the evidence thoroughly on both sides. Like Clemenceau, he had been forced to the conclusion that such methods of defense would never have been used unless they had been necessary to cover up the unjust condemnation of an innocent man, who was known to his judges to be innocent shortly after he had been shipped off to his place of punishment. Jaurès's articles in *La Petite République* had helped Dreyfus greatly in one way, though in another they told against him, as the Socialists themselves were unfairly charged with being anti-patriots and even in German pay. There seemed no possibility that he could be mistaken. Liebknecht was just as strong on the other side. He was confident that Dreyfus was a traitor. One of his main calculations rested on the statement that there existed an honorable understanding, never broken under any circumstances, between civilized Governments that, should a man be wrongfully accused of being a spy and be brought to trial for that offense, the foreign Government which he was supposed to be serving should notify the other Government concerned that it had got hold of the wrong man. Now the German Government had never done this in any way, at any period of the Dreyfus affair. Of this Liebknecht affirmed he was absolutely certain. Statements as to Dreyfus's innocence had been made by German military officers; but the German Government itself, which knew everything, had never moved. Therefore, urged Liebknecht, Dreyfus was a spy. But the German Socialist leader gave his own view too. "Have either of you," he asked Jaurès and myself, "read carefully through the verbatim report of the re-trial at Rennes?" I admitted I had not. Jaurès said he had. "Well," Liebknecht went on, "I was where I was in a position to read the whole of the pleading and the evidence day by day and word by word. For I was in prison the whole of the time, and the study of the verbatim report was my daily avocation. I am as certain as I can be of anything of the kind that Dreyfus had disclosed secrets to our Government. He may have done so in order to secure more important information in return. That is possible. But communicate French secrets to Germany, in my opinion, he unquestionably did." We debated the matter fully several times. Nothing Jaurès or I could say shook Liebknecht's conviction. Nor was it shaken to the day of his death. I have heard since, on good authority, that more than one of those who had risked much for Dreyfus never spoke to him again after the Rennes re-trial. That may easily have arisen from personal causes, for Dreyfus was not an agreeable man. But I have no ground for believing that Clemenceau ever saw reason to waver in his opinion in the slightest degree.

I recall this now, when the lapse of years has calmed down all excitement and many of the chief actors are dead, to show how, apart from the mass of sheer prejudice and unscrupulous rascality which had to be faced and overcome, there was also an element of honest intellectual doubt among the anti-Dreyfusards. The presence of this element in the background made Clemenceau's task more difficult than it would otherwise have been. Even at the present time there may be found capable observers who lived through the whole conflict, certainly not sympathetic to militarism, Catholicism or anti-Semitism, who are still ready to argue that Dreyfus may have been ill-used but that he deserved the fate to which he was originally condemned! This, however, may be said with perfect truth, that the victory of his opponents over Clemenceau, Jaurès, Zola and all they represented would have been a disaster to France, whatever view may be taken of Dreyfus himself.

In 1906 the first report of the Committee appointed to examine into the whole of the Dreyfus case was presented. It exonerated Dreyfus from all blame, declared him to have been the victim of a conspiracy based upon perjury and forgery. This report secured the complete annulment of the condemnation at Rennes and restored him to his position in the army, after years of martyrdom.

CHAPTER XIV

AS ADMINISTRATOR

AT this time Clemenceau, owing to his apparently resolute determination not to take office, no matter how many Ministries he might successfully bring to naught, had got into a backwater. He had become permanently Senator for the Department of the Var in 1902, a startling, almost incomprehensible move when his continued furious opposition to that body is remembered. However, having thus made unto himself friends of the mammon of unrighteousness, he found their "eternal habitations" a not unpleasing dwelling-place. His position as publicist and journalist was assured and nothing could shake it; his criticisms by speech and pen were as telling and vigorous as ever. But at sixty-five years of age he was still a free-lance, a force which all parties were obliged to consider but with which no Ministry could come to terms. It was a strange position. So his countrymen thought. Those who most admired his ability and his career saw no outlet for his marvelous energy that would be permanently beneficial to the country in a constructive sense. Perhaps no politician of any nation ever so persistently refused to "range himself" as did Clemenceau for thirty-five years of stormy public life. He reveled in opposition: he rejoiced in overthrow. He was on the side of the people, but he would not help them to realize their aspirations in practical life. He was a political philosopher compact of incompatibilities. As an individualist he was a stalwart champion of individual freedom: as a man of affairs he advocated the use of State power to limit the anarchic domination of personal power.

There was no understanding such a man. He would remain a brilliant Frenchman of whom all were proud until the end, when he would be buried with public honors as the champion Ishmaelite of his age. "When I saw he doubted about everything, I decided that I needed nobody to keep me ignorant," wrote Voltaire. Much the same idea prevailed about Clemenceau. He was the universal skeptic: the man whose sole intellectual enjoyment was to point out the limitless incapacity of others with epigrammatic zeal. I myself, who had watched him closely, was afraid that he would allow all opportunities for displaying his really great faculties in a ministerial capacity to slip by and leave to his friends only the mournful task of writing his epitaph: "Here lies Clemenceau the destroyer who could have been a creator."

But this was all nonsense. *"Ce jeune homme"*—Clemenceau will die young—*"d'un si beau passé"* had also before him *un bel avenir*. Nothing is certain with Clemenceau but the unforeseen. At the very time when people had made up their minds that he was a back number, he had a brand-new volume of his adventures ready for the press. After a few conversations with M. Rouvier and then with M. Sarrien, he became Minister of the Interior in the latter's Cabinet. He took office for the first time on March 12th, 1906, at a very stirring epoch.

It is difficult to exaggerate the impression produced by this step on the part of M. Clemenceau. His accession to M. Sarrien's Cabinet eclipsed in interest every other political event. Here was the great political leader and organizer of opposition, the Radical of Radicals, the man who had declined the challenge alike of friends and of enemies to take office, time after time, at last seated in a ministerial chair. All his past rose up around him. The destroyer of opportunism: the Guy Earl of Warwick of ministries: the universal critic; the immolator of Jules Ferry and many another statesman; the one Frenchman who had maintained the ideals of the French Revolution against all comers—this terrible champion of democracy *à outrance* now placed himself in the official hierarchy, whence he had so often ousted others. His victims of yesterday could be his critics of to-day. How would this terrible upsetter of Cabinets act as a Minister himself? That was what all the world waited with impatience to see. They had not days but only hours to wait.

That was the time when, M. Delcassé having been forced to resign from the Foreign Office, almost, it may be said, at the dictation of Germany, the Morocco affair was still in a very dangerous condition, threatening the peace of France and of Europe. But even the critical negotiations at Algeciras were for the moment overshadowed by a terrific colliery disaster in the Courrières-Lens district, causing the death of more miners than had ever been killed before by a similar catastrophe. This horrible incident occurred but a few days before Clemenceau became Minister, and it fell within the immediate sphere of his official duties.

The mines where the accident occurred had long been regarded as very dangerous, fire-damp being known to pervade them from time to time, and the miners throughout the coal regions had long held that the owners had never taken proper precautions to ensure the safety of the men. They went down the pits day after day, not only to work on very difficult and narrow seams, but at the hourly risk of their lives. Owing to the great social and political influence of the mine-owners it was practically impossible to get anything done, and the general treatment of the men employed was worse than is usual even in those districts in our own and other countries where coal magnates are masters. The pitmen under such conditions were less cared for and more harshly treated than animals, probably because they were less costly and could be more easily replaced.

Three days before the main explosion there had been an outburst of fire-damp at a small adjacent mine, whose workings were in direct communication with the larger pits. This alone ought to have been taken as a serious warning to the engineers in control. But markets were good, coal was in great demand, the "hands" were there to take risks. So this minor difficulty was dealt with in a cheap and convenient way, and the extraction of coal went on upon as large a scale from the imperiled shafts as it did before. Meanwhile the dangerous gases were all the time oozing in from the smaller pit to the larger ones. For three days this went steadily on, and nothing whatever was done, either in the way of taking further precautions where the original danger began, or of testing the character of the air in the bigger mines to which the other pit had access.

On Saturday, March 10th, no fewer than 1,800 men went down the shafts into the mines. A full account of what actually took place could never be given. All that was learned from the survivors was that the miners working with bare lights in these dangerous pits suddenly encountered an influx of fire-damp. Explosion after explosion took place. The unfortunate men below, threatened at once with suffocation or being burned alive, rushed in headlong disorder for the cages which would lift them to the surface. Horrible scenes inevitably took place. Those in front were pressed on by those behind, who, as one of them expressed it, were breathing burning air. For the majority there was and there could be no hope. Out of the 1,800 miners who went down in the morning, more than 1,150 were either stifled by the gas or burnt alive. The heroism displayed by the pitmen themselves, in their partially successful endeavors to rescue their entombed comrades, was the only bright feature in the whole of this frightful disaster. Some of these fine fellows went down to what seemed certain death, and others worked at excavation until almost dead themselves in their efforts to save a few from the general fate. No wonder that the feeling throughout the neighborhood was desperately bitter.

The war, sad to say, has much modified our general conception of the value of human life, even when unnecessarily thrown away. But sacrifices for a great cause on the battlefield or on the ocean, however serious, are made as a rule for high ideals. They differ widely from the loss of life deliberately occasioned by capitalist neglect or greed. Thus a mining accident on a large scale, or a conflagration in a peaceful city produces a stronger impression on the public mind than the loss of ten or twenty times the number of soldiers or sailors in a worldwide struggle. Among the widows and children and relations and comrades of the victims on the spot the exasperation against the employers was still greater. Class hatred and personal hatred were excited to a very high pitch.

This was the more natural for two reasons. First, the company on whose property the immolation of so many pitmen had occurred, and to whose mismanagement and cold-blooded indifference the avoidable explosions were due, had made enormous, almost incredible profits. From dividends of fifty per cent. in 1863 their returns had risen to profits of 1,000 per cent. in 1905. Yet they could not spare the comparatively small sum necessary to safeguard the lives of the men who obtained this wealth for the shareholders. Secondly, the Germans, who rendered assistance in the attempts to rescue the Frenchmen still in the workings below openly proclaimed that it was quite impossible—as indeed was the truth—that such an accident on such a scale should have occurred in Germany. That the Empire in Germany should be far more careful of the lives and limbs of the miners than the Republic in France, and that huge profits should have been made still higher by the refusal of the French coal-owners to adopt the ordinary precautions enforced by law on the other side of the frontier—these considerations, driven home by the results of the great catastrophe, rendered the situation exceedingly perilous from every point of view. A strike for increased wages seemed a very poor outcome of the horrors inflicted upon the actual producers of the coal under such conditions.

Clemenceau was perhaps the best man in the country to deal with the miners at such a juncture. A Socialist of mining experience would possibly have taken more decidedly the side of the men, but he would not have been able to carry with him to the same extent the support of the Chambers. And Clemenceau had gone very far already on collectivist lines. Not many years before, in an article on "The Right to Strike," he had put the case of the men very strongly indeed. In a vehement protest against the theory of supply and demand, as applied to the human beings compelled to sell labor power as a commodity, and the political economy of the profiteers based upon subsistence wages for the workers—all being for the best in the best of possible worlds—Clemenceau set forth how the system worked in practice:—

"The State *gives* to some sleek, well-set-up bourgeois immense coal-fields below ground. These fine fellows turn to men less well dressed than themselves, but who are men all the same, men with the same wants, the same feelings, the same capacity for enjoyment and suffering, and say: 'We will grant you subsistence; sink us some pits in the earth; go below and bring us up coal, which we will sell at a good price.'

"Agreed. The pits are sunk, the coal comes out of the earth.

"But, observe, those comfortable bourgeois for their outlay of *five hundred francs* ($100) have now a bit of paper which is worth *forty thousand francs* ($8,000).

"The miners, who watch what is going on, think this a good deal, and, as they have got nothing by way of profit, they protest and ask for a share.

" 'That, my friend, is impossible. The price of coal has fallen this year, the price of man must come down in proportion. All I could do for you is to reduce your wages. You object to that. All right; down the shaft you go: don't let us talk about it any more.'

"But the men won't go down.

" 'You don't make money this year. All right. But when you made huge profits, did you give us even the crumbs from your banquet?'

" 'I wasn't a shareholder then; it was my father.'

" '*My* father, like myself, was a miner. He died of consumption, his lungs choked with coal-dust. Now it is my turn to cough and spit black. And my wife, looking at her babes, asks herself whether I shall live long enough for them to be old enough, before my death, to go down into the mine which will kill them in turn. If I crock up too soon, misery, ruin, beggary, wholesale wretchedness for wife and children.'

"They don't come to terms. The strike begins.

"Economists argue, to begin with, that the State has no right to interfere in the relations between miners and mine-owners. The mine-owner is at home on his own property. Certain securities for life and limb may be demanded, nothing more. But no sooner does a strike begin than the State, which five minutes ago had no right to interfere, is called upon to bring in horse, foot and artillery on the side of the coal-owners. Then the miners have no rights left, and the judges decide against them on shameless pretexts and condemn them to prison, when they cannot bear false witness in support of the police and military."

Such were Clemenceau's views on the right to strike and the grievances of the men, before he accepted the post of Minister of the Interior and began to deal with the troublous state of things at Courrières-Lens, where the terrible accident had occurred and a strike been entered upon, and while the entire district was in a state of mind bordering upon anarchist revolt.

The first step he took was as bold and as remarkable an act as any in the whole of his adventurous life. He went down at once to Lens himself. Arrived there, he walked straight off, without any escort whatever, to meet and confer with the committee of the miners themselves.

AS ADMINISTRATOR

Courageous and honorable as this was, it failed at first to impress the strike committee. This was natural enough. They were lamenting the wholesale butchery of their comrades and were incensed against the employers who, with hundreds upon hundreds of dead pitmen below, would not deal fairly with the survivors. Clemenceau therefore met with a very cool reception. But he was nothing daunted, and began to address them. Gradually, he convinced the committee that he meant fairly by the men, and that he had not come down, alone and unarmed as he was, with any intention of suppressing the strike, but, so far as he could, to see that they had the fairest of fair play, according to their rights under the law.

Thereupon the committee agreed that Clemenceau should go with them to speak to a mass meeting of the miners. It was a doubtful venture, but Clemenceau went. In the course of his speech he reassured the men upon the attitude of the Government as represented by himself. He told them plainly: "You are entitled to strike. You will be protected by the law in doing all which the law permits. Your rights are equal to the rights of President or Ministers. But the rights of others must not be attacked. The mines must not be destroyed. For the first time you will see no soldiers in the street during the strike. True, soldiers have been placed in the mines, but solely to protect them, not in any way to injure you. On the other hand, you must not resort to violence yourselves. The strike can be carried on peacefully and without interference. Respect the mines upon which you depend for your livelihood."

This was plain enough, and Clemenceau adhered to his own program as he had formulated it. But the difficulty was apparent from the first, and it is a difficulty which must always recur when a great strike is organized. If the State claims the right to intervene, in order to protect the laws and liberties of those who wish to work for the employers, in spite of the strike and the decisions of the strikers, antagonism to such action is practically certain beforehand. For in this case, as the strikers say, the State is using the forces of the military and the police in order to protect "blacklegs" who, by offering their labor to the employers at such a time of acute class war, act in the interests of the coal-owners and against the mass of the workers. Socialists argue that the strikers are sound in their contention, and that by assuring to non-strikers the right to work the Government practically nullifies the right to strike. When, therefore, in this typical Courrières case, the strikers as a whole remained out, notwithstanding certain insufficient offers by the coal-owners, and a minority of non-strikers claimed the help of the law, with support of the State army, to weaken by their surrender the position of the majority of their fellow-workers in the same industry, then the ethics of the dispute between sections of the miners could not be so easily determined as M. Clemenceau from his individualist training assumed.

If the employers were in the wrong, as it appears they were, then to call out the military to protect those miners who showed themselves ready to make immediate terms with injustice was, however good the intention, to take sides against the main body of the men. So it seemed to these latter. When, therefore, the soldiers defended the non-strikers, the strikers assailed the military, who had not attacked them. Clemenceau accordingly decided that the strikers had broken the law, as undoubtedly they had, by stoning and injuring the servants of the State, who were upholding the law as it stood. The truth is that, so long as these antagonistic sections exist among the working class, and persist in fighting one another, it is practically impossible for the State not to intervene in order to keep the peace. There may be no sympathy with blacklegs, but the Minister of the Interior could scarcely be blamed for protecting them against an infuriated mob, which would probably have killed them, or for insisting upon the release of those whom the strikers had seized. That the temper of the crowd had become highly dangerous was apparent a little later, when the Socialist Mayor was knocked down as he was trying to calm them.

All this rendered M. Clemenceau's second and third visits to the scene of class warfare far more stormy than the first. Owing to the horror and hatred created by the avoidable holocaust in the Courrières mines, and the further discovery that engineers appointed by the State had played into the hands of the employers, the situation got worse from day to day. The strike itself was not only an effort to get more wages, but a declaration of hostility to the mine-owners, and those of the miners' own class who showed any tenderness towards them or were ready to take work under them. Their own leaders and representatives had no longer any influence with the men or control over them. M. Basly, the deputy who acted throughout for the miners, had as little power over the strikers as anybody else. The whole movement was taking an anarchist turn. Also agents were at work among them both from the reactionary and the revolutionary side whose main object, for very different reasons, was to foster disturbance and influence passion. Foreign emissaries likewise were said to be at work.

Clemenceau's task was therefore an exceedingly hard

one. He had ever in mind the old eighteenth-century watchword which, from his point of view, is the foundation of the French Republic—Liberty, Equality and Fraternity. And the greatest of these is liberty. He throughout forgot or overlooked that, even according to his own pronouncements, liberty in any real sense is impossible for the weaker—the majority who own no property—against the stronger—"Les Plus Forts," the minority who own all the property. This triune fetish Clemenceau, with all his keenness of criticism, might be said to worship: yet to worship in a more or less reasonable way. He could not shut his eyes to the truth that for men and women whose livelihood was at the mercy of capitalists there could be no real liberty, dominated as the workers were by their daily compulsion to obtain the wherewithal for the necessaries of life. The only way by which even partial justice could be secured under the system of payment of wages was combination among the wage-earners. Hence he recognizes the liberty to strike. But he was equally determined, as he puts it, to defend the liberty of those who would not strike. It was logical: it was in harmony with the law; but it was a virtual help to the employers none the less.

On the occasion of his second visit he enforced his view in his usual emphatic way. Three miners who would not join the strike were being paraded through the town by the strikers with an insulting placard hung around their necks: *"Nous sommes des poires cuites; des faux frères."* Clemenceau insisted that they should be released, and succeeded in freeing them. The very fact, however, that it was possible for the strikers to act in this way, without protest, showed how small was the minority and how strong the feeling against these claimants of the liberty of taking the other side. Clemenceau likewise acted with vigor against all who were guilty of any violence. But the strikes still spread.

Speaking at Lyons on May 3rd, he explained the difficulties of the situation:—"My position is between the political demagogues of the Church, the clericals and the reactionaries on one side, who tried hard to hound on the troops I was forced to call in to fire upon the strikers, who greatly provoked them. This the ecclesiastics and restorationists did with the hope of fomenting a revolt against the Republic—a revolt supported by certain military chiefs inspired by the clericals and their shameless lack of discipline." The Separation of Church and State was being decided while all this was going on. "Their object was to bring about a massacre in the interest of the Catholic Church and the monarchy. This plot was frustrated. Butchery was avoided.

"On the other side, I am accused by the revolutionary Socialists of indulging in brutal military oppression because I suppress anarchist rioting. This though no striker was killed or wounded. I acted for tranquillity, while the monarchists fostered disturbances. They wanted a Government of the Republic which should rely for support solely on the Right. The anarchists helped the monarchists, who had agents throughout the perturbed districts, by denouncing the Republic and excusing mob violence. Yet how stood the case? Was it I who organized a campaign of panic? Was it I who was responsible for the original explosion and strike? Was it I who brought about the state of things which resulted in general disturbance and might have tended towards another *coup d'état?* Nothing of the sort. I was suddenly called upon to deal with unexpected troubles. I acted for the maintenance of the Republic, and kept the peace under the law."

By taking office at the time when he did it was at once apparent that Clemenceau had brought himself into the full whirlpool of strike difficulties which then arose. He was called upon to solve in everyday life, as a man committed to a policy of justice to the workers, problems which, at critical moments, are almost insoluble under the capitalist system of wage-earning and production for profit. Has any section of the community the right to hold up the life of a nation or a great city in order to secure advantages for itself? At first sight the answer would undoubtedly be "No." But if the conditions of existence for those who act in this way are admittedly such as ought not to continue in any civilized country, it is not possible to reply so confidently in the negative. Neither can the "No" be repeated with certainty when employers, or the State itself, are guilty of a direct breach of faith towards the workers, unless, by ceasing to carry out their duties they actually imperil the welfare of the entire collectivity of which they form a part. In short, all depends upon the circumstances, which have to be considered most carefully in each case. It fell to Clemenceau's lot to decide in what might almost be taken as the test incident, the strike of the electrical engineers and workers of Paris.

There seems to be something in M. Clemenceau's horoscope which has decreed that his career shall be diversified and rendered interesting by a series of dramatic events. The strike of the electricians of Paris was certainly one of them.

Scene: Cabinet of the Minister of the Interior. The Minister, M. Clemenceau, at work at his desk and dictating to his secretary. Everything going on quite nicely. No sign of more than ordinary pressure. Electric light functioning as usual for the benefit of the Radical leader as well as for Parisians of every degree. Hey presto! Darkness falls upon the bureau of the Minister. Very provoking. What is the matter? Corridors and other bureaux suffering the like eclipse. Evidently something wrong at the main. Candles obtained, lamps got out from dusty cupboards, oil hunted up. Ancient forms of illumination applied. Darkness thus made visible. Telephones set going. All Paris obscured. A city of two or three millions of inhabitants suddenly deprived of light. What has happened? The entire electrical service disorganized until to-morrow by the sudden and unexpected strike of the whole of the skilled men in the electrical supply department. Lovers of darkness because their deeds are evil likely to have a good time. Business arrested, fathers and mothers of families perturbed. Dangers of every sort threatened. Apaches and other cutthroats preparing for action in the to them providential enactment of endless gloom.

Such is the baleful news borne over the telephone wires to the much troubled Minister of the Interior, with his wax tapers and old-world lamps glimmering around him. How preserve his Paris, his *ville lumière,* from the depredations of the miscreants engendered by the social system of the day, when light fails to disclose their approach? How protect the savings of the conscientious bourgeois and the diamonds of the high-placed *horizontale* from removal and conveyance under cover of the night? To surrender to the strikers is to admit their right as a few to blackmail the many. It is to sanctify the action of the despoiling minority above by giving way to the organized minority below. Immediate decision is essential. Night is upon us, when no man can work, save the man who communizes movable property to his own use. Light is a necessary of security for property, nay, even for life. The State must come in to fulfill the functions which the Creator neglected to provide for when He divided the night from the day. The sapper is the man to supplement the deficiencies of Providence and to mitigate the social revolution by electrical engineers. *Rien n'est sacré pour un sapeur!* No sooner thought of but acted upon. M. Clemenceau, as Minister of the Interior and trustee for the well-being of the citizens of Paris, calls upon the State engineers under military control to light up Paris afresh. The thing is done. Paris sees more clearly and breathes more freely. Society itself has the right to live.

But stay a moment: here is M. Jaurès. He has a word to say. What are you doing, M. Clemenceau? You are outraging all your own principles. You are interfering with that very right to strike which you yourself have declared to be sacred. You are using the military discipline of the comrades of the men out on strike against the electrical companies, to render their protest nugatory, by employing the sappers against them. You have, in fact, called out the powers of the State to crush the workers in a particular industry. If you were true to yourself, you would convert the electrical supply of Paris now in the hands of greedy monopolists into a public service, and give the strikers every satisfaction. That is the only real solution of social anarchy.

To him Clemenceau: "But this was not merely a strike or a limited liability class war against employers. It was a bitter fight between two irreconcilable antagonists against inoffensive passers-by. The people of Paris, for whom I am concerned, had nothing to do with the matter. I myself knew nothing about the decision to strike till my own work was rendered impossible by the sudden infliction of darkness upon me by these resuscitated Joshuas. Not only was the general security threatened, as I have declared, but the lives of your own clients, Jaurès, were threatened by immersion in a flood below ground. The inundation of the Metropolitan (the Underground Railway) had already begun. The workers of Paris who used that means of communication in order to return to their work would most certainly have been drowned owing to the suspension of electrical pumps and lifts, had not the sappers and the firemen, both of them sets of public functionaries, rushed at once to the rescue. Were the workmen of Paris engaged in other departments to be allowed to perish, with the State standing by, wringing its hands in hopeless ineptitude, while the electrical engineers got the better of their masters in a dispute about wages? This was a practical question which I had to decide at once. I decided in favor of the inoffensive people of Paris and against the electrical engineers on strike."

Taking a wide view of the whole question, I hold Jaurès's opinion to be the right one. But Clemenceau had to deal with an immediate practical difficulty of a very serious kind indeed. The lights went out at six o'clock. Night was coming on. No time could be lost in negotiating with the engineers. Still less was nightfall the period when a public service could be instituted in hot haste. The matter was settled in that form and for that occasion. But none the less the real point at issue was not thus easily disposed of. Clemenceau was right in preventing Paris from being left all night in darkness. Jaurès was right in claiming that the State should have a more definite and consistent policy than that of dealing with differences between wage-earners and employers by such hand-to-mouth methods.

It was just at this point that, notwithstanding all adverse criticisms in regard to the instability of Ministries, and the scenes of apparent disorder which sometimes arise, the French National Assembly displayed its immense superiority to the Parliaments of other countries when serious matters of principle were involved. The desire to get to the bottom of a really dangerous question, to hear the arguments on both sides taken, as far as possible, out of the narrow limits of personal or party politics, puts the French Assembly on a very high level. From the point of view of economic development France is far behind Great Britain, America and Germany. The great factory industry and the legislation growing out of it are not nearly so far advanced. But in the wish and endeavor to investigate the principles upon which the future regulation of society must proceed, France gives the lead.

This openness of mind and anxiety to let both views have fair play have grown under the Republic in a wonderful way. Where else in the world would men of all parties and all sections allow the two chief orators of the Left—Jaurès, the Socialist leader of the opposition, Clemenceau, the Individualist Minister—to debate out at length, in two long sittings, the issues between genuine Socialism and that nondescript reformist Collectivism which goes by the name of Socialistic Radicalism (the latter really meaning, to Socialists, capitalism palliated by State bureaucracy)?

AS ADMINISTRATOR

This was indeed a great oratorical duel, and those who contend that oratory has lost its significance and virtue in modern times would have to admit that they were wrong not only in this particular case but in regard to other speeches delivered by the two chief disputants afterwards. The debate itself was a contrast between styles just as it was a conflict of principles. Jaurès was an orator of great power and wonderful capacity for stirring the emotions. His voice, his face, his gestures, his method of argument and fusing of forcible contentions into one compact whole made so great an impression that he could capture a large audience with the same ease even on subjects remote from the immediate matter of his address—as once he held the Assembly entranced by a long digression on music in the course of a fine speech on the tendencies of the time.

If it might be urged that he occasionally used too many words to express his meaning, this was easily forgiven by his countrymen on account of his admirable turn of phrase and his understanding use of the modulations of the French language. However prejudiced his hearers might be against him (and his personal appearance was not such as to disarm an opponent), they had only to listen to Jaurès for ten minutes to feel interested in what he had to say. From this to admiration and excitement was no long step. Short, stout and somewhat cumbrous in figure, wearing trousers nearly halfway up his calves, with a broad, humorous, rather coarse face, his eyes full of expression and not wanting in fun, troubled with a curious twitching on the right cheek which affected his eye with a sort of wink, Jaurès was certainly not the personality any one would have fixed upon as the greatest master of idealist and economic Socialist oratory in

France, and perhaps in Europe. But his sincerity, his eloquence soon overcame these drawbacks on the platform and in the tribune, just as his bonhomie and good-fellowship did in private life. He had been a Professor of Literature in the University of Toulouse, and was a man of wide cultivation. But his learning never made him pedantic, nor did his great success turn his head. Gifted with extraordinary vitality, his powers of work were quite phenomenal. To say that he "toiled like a galley-slave" for the cause to which he devoted himself was no exaggeration. Yet he was always fresh, always in good spirits, always ready to contribute wit and vivacity to any company in which he found himself. Add to this much practical good sense in the conduct of his party and the affairs of the world, and all must admit that, in Jaurès, the Socialist party of France had a worthy chief and Clemenceau a worthy antagonist. The galleries, like the Assembly itself, were always crowded when either orator was expected to address the House.

Jaurès dealt with the development of society from the chaos of conflicting classes and mutual antagonisms to the coördination of common effort for the common good. This can and should be a peaceful social evolution. Property for all means a universal share, not only in politics, but in the production and the distribution of wealth. This could not be obtained under the conditions of to-day, where those who possessed no property but the labor in their bodies were at the mercy of the classes who possessed all else; where only by strikes in which the State took the side of the employers could the wage-earners obtain an infinitesimal portion of their rights. By collectivism leading up to Socialism, and general coöperation, every individual would have a direct interest in and be benefited by the general social increase of wealth due to the growing powers of man to produce what is useful and beneficial to all.

Socialism substitutes order for anarchy, joint action of every member of society for the mutual antagonism which is now the rule. Legal expropriation with compensation will gradually put the community in control of its own resources. Our task is to convince the small proprietor and the small bourgeoisie that they will benefit by the coming transformation. Incessant social reform on Socialist lines would lead to the realization of Socialist ideals in a practical shape. Such strikes as that at Courrières, followed by the military intervention of the State, at M. Clemenceau's direction, and repression of the strikers, displayed the injustice of the existing system and proclaimed the necessity for accepting the higher view of social duty by which all would benefit and none would suffer.

The speech thus briefly summarized was delivered at two sittings of the Chamber, and was listened to with profound attention by those present, the great majority of whom were directly opposed to Socialist views. No higher tribute could have been paid.

Clemenceau rose to reply to the Socialist leader a few days later. Twenty years had passed over his head since I last described his personal appearance, his vigorous individuality and his incisive, clear-cut, witty conversation and oratory. Time had affected him little. He was still the same energetic and determined but ordinarily cool political fighter that he had shown himself in the eighties of the last century. His head was now bald, and his mustache gray, but his eyes looked out from under the heavy white eyebrows with all the old fire, and the alertness of his frame was apparent in his every movement. Though many years older than his Socialist challenger, there was nothing to choose between them in regard to physical and mental vigor. Jaurès had been eloquent and persuasive; he brought in the ideals and the strategy of the future to illuminate the sad truths of the present. He relied upon the history of the past and the hopes of humanity ahead to constitute a policy of preparation for coming generations of Frenchmen, while applying the principles he advocated as far as possible to the events of the day. Clemenceau confined his answer, which also extended over two sittings of the Chamber, to the matters immediately in hand and the criticisms on his method of dealing with them. This sense of practicality, not devoid of sympathy with the disinherited classes of our day, gave the Minister of the Interior a great advantage and precisely suited his style. The interval between the two speeches also told in favor of Clemenceau. The ring of Jaurès's fine sentences had died down in the meantime. His glorious aspirations were discounted hour by hour by the continuance of the conflict, whose existence he himself could not but admit, which formed, in fact, part of his case, and in a way strengthened his indictment. Yet this had to be dealt with all the same.

Clemenceau began his oration with a glowing tribute to Jaurès's passion for social justice. But his magnificent eloquence has eliminated the whole of the bad side of life. He rises to the empyrean, whence he surveys creation through a roseate atmosphere which is raised far above plain facts. "For myself, I am compelled to remain in the valley where all the events which Jaurès leaves out of his picture are actually taking place. That accounts for the difference in our perspective. I am accused of attacking the workers and of doing worse than other Governments. I have never attacked the workers, I have never done them wrong. The duty of the Government is to maintain tranquillity. This I have done without injury to the toilers, though I had to face 85,000 strikers in the Pas de Calais and 115,000 in Paris—the largest number ever known on strike at the same time in France. I went down to Courrières to ensure liberty. We have all of us here to go through our education in Liberty. Education is not a matter of words, but of deeds. Those deeds formed part of the education. The working classes become worthy of taking over the responsibility of Government for themselves when their own deeds are in accordance with the law. If speeches alone could teach administration, the Sermon on the Mount would have dictated practical politics for centuries.

"In these disturbances my orders, issued through the highest police authorities, were precise. Maintain, I said, liberty to strike, liberty to work. Soldiers to be called in only in case of actual violence. But the miners themselves infringed the liberties of others. They indulged in the anarchical wrecking of houses belonging to men of their own class. I have here photographs of the destruction wrought. Were Monsieur Jaurès Minister of the Interior—misfortune comes so suddenly—he himself would send down troops to stop wholesale pillage. Yet, if he did, he would in turn be denounced by the anarchist heads of the General Confederation of Labor as the enemy of the class whose cause he now champions. I challenge M. Jaurès to say what he would do under such circumstances as I have had to face"—

the orator pauses and waits. There is dead silence. No answer. "By not replying, you have replied. There have, I repeat, been no dead or wounded among the working class. On May 1st, when general disorders were openly threatened, I took precautions against organized outbreak. No trouble arose."

The Republic, he continued, was a rule of freedom for the individual, so far as it could be secured under existing conditions. Those conditions and the law itself might work injustice, but it was then the duty of the State, and the Minister who had to translate its functions into action, to mitigate such harshness by protecting the weaker side. Soldiers had been sent down to Courrières not to attack the strikers—no attack had been made upon them—but to prevent the strikers themselves from destroying the mines and inflicting illegal punishments upon those of their class who did not agree with them. When this was done, the strikers molested the soldiers, who never fired a shot. The lieutenant in command was assailed, though his saber remained all the time in its sheath. The right of men to work on terms they themselves are willing to accept could not be contested as the law now stood. "But," says M. Jaurès, "by assuring non-strikers the right to work, I myself am violating the right to strike, which I have declared to be the inalienable privilege of the wage-earners. But then, I ask, what are the non-strikers to do? They also have wives and children who demand to be fed. What law justifies me in preventing them from working? Republicanism means the right of the individual to combine with others to resist oppression and obtain advantages. This freedom is admitted. It does not include the freedom to oppress others, still less to assault servants of the State who are acting in order to safeguard the law as it stands. When the Socialists of M. Jaurès's school begin to deal with facts, and not with ideals at present all in the air, what sort of program do they formulate?

"Here we have it. An eight-hours' working day for all trades. The right of State Employees to form Trade Unions and to strike. Proportional Representation. A progressive Income Tax, and so on. A nice little program, but a bourgeois program all the same. No idealism, no Socialism there! M. Jaurès, however, claims the immediate Nationalization and Socialization of all departments of industry, including the land. But such unification of society is in reality the Catholicization of Society. There is a definite program of Radical Reforms, nevertheless, constituting an advance towards a Socialist policy. They are formulated by the bourgeoisie, but Socialists threaten to vote against the Budget, which is necessary in order to carry out some of their own proposals. Take Old Age Pensions. These need money. The Socialists refuse the required funds. Yet Socialists are for the Republic. So far we cordially agree. So far I, of necessity, work with them. But if they at the same time denounce Republicans as the enemies of the workers and secure a majority of votes in that sense, then that is to vote for the defeat of the Republic. If Socialists would work with the Radicals in order to attain the ends they have in common, none would be more glad than I. But if such common action is impossible, then let each work on in their own way."

It was said at the time that at the close of the debate, when Clemenceau was leaving the Assembly, he remarked to Jaurès, "After all, Jaurès, you are not the good God."

To which Jaurès replied: "And you are not even the Devil."

I have dealt with this famous controversy at some length, without attempting to give the speeches in full, because although the discussion led to no decision at the moment, it certainly brought before the public of France and even the public opinion of Europe the direct theoretical and practical difference between Socialism and well-meaning Radicalism in an intelligible manner as nothing else would. The effect upon French politics within the next few months, in spite of further desperate outbreaks in 1907, was also remarkable. Jaurès's speech did much to consolidate the Socialist Party as a unified section of the Chamber; and Clemenceau himself was so far influenced by it and by the trend of events that, as will be seen, it affected his policy as Prime Minister in the formation of his own Cabinet shortly afterwards. Looking at the matter from the Socialist point of view, therefore, Jaurès was building better than his opponents in the Chamber knew, and Socialists had no reason to regret the apparent victory of his formidable antagonist at the time. In fact, as Bernard Shaw said in regard to a very different debate under widely different circumstances in London more than thirty years before: "The Socialist was playing at longer bowls than you know."

It is this power of detachment, this recognition that theory and sentiment play a great part in the molding of public character and public opinion, even in the practical affairs of everyday life, that renders France—independent, idealist, revolutionist, conservative and thrifty France—so essential a factor in the discussion of the world-problems of to-day. France alone among the nations rises above the smoke of class warfare, and though her own social and economic conditions are not themselves ready for the definite solution of social problems, she indicates the route which may be most safely followed by countries more economically advanced. Both Jaurès and Clemenceau, therefore, rendered good service to mankind when they used their utmost efforts to place before the peoples and the students of all nations the views of the Socialist with his outlook on the future, and the Radical with his policy of the present based on the traditions of the past. Jaurès, in the prime of his manhood and the fullness of his fame, was torn from the useful and noble work which lay well within his power and his intelligence by the murderous revolver of a reactionary assassin: a loss indeed to his party, his country, and the world at large! His antagonist, Clemenceau, still works on as nearly an octogenarian, with all the vigor and energy of his fiery youth, on behalf of that France, who, to-day, as for many a long year past, has been the mistress and the goddess of the materialist democrat and Radical champion of the people.

On October 23rd, after six months of service as Minister of the Interior, Clemenceau was called back from Carlsbad, whither he went every year before the war to conjure attacks of gout (which might at least, in all reason, have spared a lifelong teetotaler), in order to form a Cabinet of his own in place of M. Sarrien. That Cabinet was remarkable from many points of view. Comments upon its constitution and significance may be reserved for a wider survey. Suffice it to say here that Clemenceau himself, in addition to holding the Presidency of the Council as Prime Minister, remained Minister of the Interior, thus declaring his intention not to shirk any of the responsibility he had taken upon himself or the animosity he had incurred in his dealings with strikes and other social questions.

France was passing through a very difficult period. Whatever view a thoroughgoing Socialist may take as to the need for a wider general policy than that adopted by Clemenceau, it is not easy to see how, the French people being unprepared to accept a purely Labor or Socialist Government, the Republic could have been peacefully maintained but for the cool determination of the Radical Republican at the head of affairs. Scarcely a day passed without some fresh economic and social conflicts that called for prompt action. These, however, arose in provinces and cities and under conditions where the antagonism between wage-earners and employers, between capital and labor, in the ordinary way offered no exceptional features for the statesman. But in the spring and summer of 1907 a more complicated and dangerous uprising, which developed into little short of an attempt at an Anarchist-communist, anti-Republican revolution, broke out in the South of France among the wine-growers.

The peasants of the districts round Narbonne and Montpellier, together with many of the inhabitants of those towns who were themselves dependent upon the wine industry, made, in fact, a desperate local attack upon the existing Government of France. Disaffection had been growing for a long time and was due to a series of economic and agricultural troubles among the wine-growers, which successive Ministries had not understood, far less attempted to cope with. It had its direct origin in a natural cause. This cause was the appearance in the Bordeaux country of the deadly enemy of all *vignerons,* large and small—the much-dreaded phylloxera. The vineyards of the Gironde were devastated and the famous clarets shipped from Bordeaux ceased to be the product of Bordeaux grapes. Thereupon the inferior vintages of the Midi came into abnormal demand. But the wine-producers of the West were not wholly defeated, even while the phylloxera continued his ravages and no method of checking the mischief had been discovered. There are ways and means of meeting even such a calamity.

"Would your lordship like madeira served with that course?" said a butler to a well-known bishop who was giving a dinner, in days long before the war, to a number of his clergy. "Madeira!" was the reply, in great surprise. "Why, I have not a single bottle in my cellar." "Oh, yes, my lord, you have. *Monseigneur oublie peut-être que je suis de Cette.*" Madeira, so the story goes, was duly served. But Cette is not the only town in France where the art of blending and refining wine for foreign and even home palates has been brought to a high pitch. At any rate, during the phylloxera period, Australian, Algerian, Spanish and other wines which previously had been regarded contemptuously by foreign and French consumers of claret were, it was alleged, imported at Bordeaux in great quantity and came out again with the old familiar Bordeaux labels and duly impressed corks.

Thus adulteration, which John Bright declared was a legitimate form of competition, made its appearance in a widely different industry from his own, to the detriment, even thus early in the struggle, of the legitimate growers of more acid but more genuine beverages in the South. Adulteration became a war-cry among the peasants, who felt themselves defrauded. Republicans of great commercial reputation and high standing in finance were accused, rightly or wrongly, of being deeply and profitably concerned in this nefarious traffic. That was all bad enough. But at last, a remedy for the vineyard plague was discovered and widely used, with the aid of the Government, partly by chemical applications to the vines, partly by bringing in new stocks from without. Then followed exceptionally good vintages in the Bordeaux country, while the adulteration, falsification, manipulation of other wines with sugar and the like continued. Hence an abnormal glut of wine of every degree, with a corresponding fall in price.

The peasants, whose views of the admirable law of supply and demand were very crude, only discovered that the more wine they produced the less money could they get for it. To produce for the consumer, at a loss to themselves, at once struck them as an unfair dispensation in the order of the market since it affected the sales of their wines. Obviously, they said, the Government was to blame. How could they pay taxes when wine was fetching a derisory price? Why should they borrow to pay taxes when wine was fetching a derisory price? Let Government take short order with the adulterators and big producers out there in the West, who were preventing the hard-working toilers on the soil in the South from disposing of their sole saleable product at a profit. A Republic which couldn't protect the backbone of the nation, the Southern wine-growers, to wit, was of no use to them. And the people of the South, as M. Clemenceau knows very well, for he is Senator for the Var, are a vivacious and an excitable folk. But their vivacity and excitement had already been worked up to a high pitch by gradual exasperation before M. Clemenceau himself took office. It was his hard fate to meet the full fury of the storm as Premier of France.

No trifling storm it was. The whole countryside, in the late spring and summer, was aflame. Commune after commune, district after district, took part in the agitation. Peasants and *prolétaires* made common cause against the authorities. Taxes should not be paid. Tax-gatherers should appear at their peril. The Government was an unjust Government, and should be defied. And it was so. Meetings were held in every town and village. Capable representatives and leaders, of whom a M. Albert was the chief, were chosen by the men themselves. Attempts to confer with the people as a whole resulted in failure. The old story was told again. The reactionaries of the Right took the side of the people, and shouted against "adulteration," because they were victims of a chaotic economic system, because also they objected to the use of troops who belonged to and were paid by the whole people in order to maintain that system in full vigor. What was to be done? Things got worse and worse. The Minister of the Interior felt obliged to call out the troops in order to prevent downright ruin being wrought in Narbonne, Montpellier and St. Béziers. There were killed and wounded on both sides. Hence a serious ministerial crisis was threatened which, as matters stood, could scarcely fail to tell in favor of reaction and against the only Republic then possible.

The facts were beyond dispute. In consequence of the causes and results summarized, the temper of the people became unmanageable. There were terrible riots of a wholly anarchist character. The doors of public buildings were soaked with kerosene and then set on fire. At Narbonne, Montpellier and St. Béziers attacks were made on peaceful citizens at dead of night by uncontrolled mobs of armed men recruited from the worst members of the population. Soldiers on the spot refused to fire in reply to revolver shots aimed at them. The provocations to the troops, who were brought in solely to maintain order, were almost intolerable, but they were borne with heroic calm. At first they fired in the air. Then they fired in earnest, and there were killed and wounded on both sides. Hence there was the greatest excitement in the Chamber and unrest throughout Paris, where the wildest rumors were spread.

Everything pointed to a serious political upset when Clemenceau rose to give an account of the circumstances and to defend the action of the Government. This is, in brief, what he said: "I did my best to avoid sending troops, and directed that they should not be used except in case of absolute necessity. But can a Government allow a wine-growers' committee to forbid the villagers to pay taxes? Can it quietly permit tax-collectors to be molested when they arrive in the communes? Can it look on with indifference while 300 mayors of communes declare a general strike and hold up the entire business of the community? Everywhere the committees of the wine-growers took upon themselves to give their orders in place of the constituted authority, and were obeyed. Soldiers who mutinied against their officers were applauded and a large sum was raised for their compensation. No Government could stand that. Citizens were bound to pay their taxes. No Minister can deny that. I could have resigned. I do not want office. But I felt it my duty to remain when the troops were attacked."

After this speech the ministerial crisis ended. The difficulties on the spot slowly calmed down, owing largely to the good sense and loyalty to the Republic of M. Albert and other leaders of the men. But the Socialists have never forgiven M. Clemenceau for calling in the military at Courrières and Narbonne, and particularly for the bloodshed at the latter town. This has been a great misfortune for both sides, the rather that both could plead justification for the course they took. The Socialists contended that the troubles arose in the North and in the South from causes whose development the Government ought to have watched and whose results it should have foreseen. The State ought to have made ready, and introduced adequate legislation to encounter and overcome these troubles by peaceful methods which all governments have, or ought to have, at their command. Clemenceau could and did answer that he was in no wise to be held responsible personally for outbreaks which had arisen from circumstances over which he had no control, and that all he had to do was to prevent any mistakes that had been made from leading to violent action that must harm innocent persons and injure the Republic. The split between Radicals and Socialists remains unbridged to this day.

Yet in the Senate on more than one occasion in 1906 Clemenceau, interrupting a speaker, declared: "I claim to be a Socialist!" And again, "When I accepted the offer to form a Government I conceived the idea of governing in a Socialist sense. Years ago I offered to coöperate with M. Jules Guesde to carry Socialist measures on which we mutually agreed." This has never been denied. It ought to have been possible to come to terms on palliative measures at least.

For the strike difficulties did not end in 1906 and 1907, nor did Clemenceau change his policy in dealing with them. Non-strikers were always to be protected against strikers: anything in the shape of violence on the part of strikers, no matter how great the provocation, was to be repressed by the forces of the State. Also civil servants, being the servants of the State, were not to be allowed to combine in trade unions against the State as employer. Still less could Clemenceau allow them the right to strike against the State. They then became, as he expressed it, "rebellious bureaucrats," allied with those who would like to destroy *"la Patrie."* To them the amnesty granted to the rebellious wine-growers and rural anarchists of the South must be denied. Civil servants in revolt and the bigots of anti-militarism—Hervé was at this time an ardent peace-at-any-price man and fanatical anti-militarist—were guilty of a crime against their country; and with such criminals the Government was engaged in battle.

Once more an actual strike close to Paris gave point to all these declarations, and put Clemenceau and his Government again at variance with the Socialists by the acute difference of principle which was then accentuated in practice. This was at Vigneux, when there was a strike of the workers in the sandpits. Clemenceau, who was still Minister of the Interior as well as Prime Minister, used the gendarmes to protect the non-strikers or blacklegs still working in the pits. As a result, there was open conflict between the two sides. Two of the men on strike were killed, and several of the gendarmes were injured. This aroused great indignation against the Government among the organized workers. They felt that the right to strike became illusory if at any moment the Ministry could turn the scale against the strikers, no matter how great their grievances or how just their claims might be, by bringing in the State to uphold the minority of the men in standing by the masters.

In practice, as has often been found in England, such intervention on behalf of the blacklegs means that the strike may be broken in the interest of the capitalists. The deputies of the places where the strikes took place interviewed Clemenceau on the matter. It is clear that the antagonism went very deep. In answer to a bitter attack Clemenceau again defended his action in the Chamber. The question was one not of mere opinion, but of justice. "When the workers are in the wrong they must be told the truth about it. The Government will never approve of anarchy." ("You are anarchy enthroned yourself," cried Jaurès.) "My program is Social Reform under the law against grievances, and Social Order under the law against the revolutionists." Finally the National Assembly passed a vote of confidence in Clemenceau as against the Socialists. That, of course, was to be expected.

have given a fairly detailed account of these affrays—they were no less—between Clemenceau and the Socialists because they are of great importance, not only as explaining the vehement hostility which has since existed between them, but because the points at issue affect every civilized country to a greater or less degree. Capital and labor, capitalists and wage-earners, are at variance everywhere. Their antagonism can no more be averted or bridged over than could the class struggle between land and slave-owners and their chattel slaves, or the nobles and their serfs. Only the slow process of social evolution leading up to revolution can solve the problem. Meanwhile combination on the one side is met by combination on the other. Outside political action, which is ineffective until the workers themselves understand how to use it, there is no weapon for the wage-earners or wage-slaves but the strike. They suffer, even when they win, far more than the capitalists or employers, who are only deprived of the right to make profits out of their hands while those same hands are undergoing the pangs of hunger and every sort of privation, not only for themselves but for their wives and children.

Arbitration, when the social conditions have reached the stage where this is feasible, may postpone the crucial battle and smooth over the matter temporarily; but it can do no more than that. A step towards this arbitration was made under M. Millerand's measure declaring strikes illegal unless decreed by a majority of the employees upon a referendum and the enactment of an arbitration clause. But when strikes actually take place and the men's blood is up, then comes the real tug-of-war.

Should the State—obviously the capitalist State to-day—interfere to keep order and maintain the right to work for non-strikers, or should it refrain from interference altogether? When Jaurès and the Socialists were challenged to say what they would do under the circumstances, they failed to answer, as already recorded. This put them in a weak position. An opposition must have a policy which it would be prepared to act upon if it took office. Socialism, however desirable, could not be realized all at once. But, it was open to Clemenceau as to any other Minister entrusted with full powers by the State, *to bring at least as much pressure to bear upon the capitalists and employers as upon the strikers* and to insist that they should yield to the demands of the men and continue to work the mines, out of which, by the purchase of the labor-power of the pitmen, they had derived such huge profits. This course was not adopted by the Minister of the Interior, nor does it seem to have been demanded by Jaurès. The troubles in the wine districts arose from different economic causes, and had to be dealt with in a different way. But the truth is that, in periods of transition, no Government can go right. It was Clemenceau's lot to have to govern at such a period of transition.

CHAPTER XV

STRENGTH AND WEAKNESS OF CLEMENCEAU

STRIKES and anarchist troubles, however, formidable as they were in the North and in the South, were by no means the only serious difficulties which Clemenceau had to cope with, first as Minister of the Interior and then as Premier. The danger from Germany, as he well knew, was ever present. Anxious as France was to avoid misunderstandings which might easily lead to war, eager as the Radical leader might be to enlarge upon the folly and wickedness of strife between two contiguous civilized peoples, who could do so much for one another, it was always possible for the German Government to put the Republic in such a position that the alternative of humiliation or hostilities must be faced. Less than a year before Clemenceau accepted office, the German Kaiser himself had taken a most provocative step in Morocco, the object of which can now be clearly seen. Germany had no real interests in Morocco worthy of the name. Several years later the German Minister of Foreign Affairs pooh-poohed the idea that Germany, distant from Morocco as she was, with only 200 Germans in the country, and not more than $1,000,000 worth of yearly commerce, all told, with the inhabitants, could be concerned about political matters in that Mohammedan kingdom.

With France the case was very different. Algeria was adjacent to the territories of the Sultan of Morocco, and if the wild tribes on the frontier were stirred up against the infidel, the most important French colony was threatened with serious disturbance. It was all-important for France, therefore, that there should be a government at Fez strong enough and enlightened enough to keep peace on the border. Clemenceau, who had always been so stern an opponent of colonial adventures and had overthrown several Cabinets which he considered were prone to encourage harmful exploits, had himself spoken out very plainly about Morocco. Long before capitalist interests were involved on any large scale the French ownership of Algeria necessitated a definite Moroccan policy. This again brought with it the obligation of constant pressure upon the Sultan to induce him to consider French interests. These interests could be harmonized with those of Spain and Great Britain, and were so settled by special agreements in April, 1904, just a year before the German Emperor's *coup de théâtre* startled the world. France's special interests in Morocco were thus recognized all round, and Germany, far from raising any objection, expressly disclaimed any desire to interfere, so long as "the open door" was left for German goods. But the general antagonism between France and Germany was a matter of common knowledge.

It was natural, therefore, that the Sultan of Morocco, alarmed lest French attempts to introduce "order" and "good government" into his realm might end, as it had always done elsewhere, by destroying his independence, should appeal to the Kaiser, who had proclaimed his sympathy for the Moslem, to help him against the less sympathetic infidel. For a long time these appeals fell upon deaf ears. Even when the Kaiser visited Gibraltar, after an interview with the King of Spain, he refused pressing invitations to cross the Straits and meet envoys of the Moroccan potentate at Tangier. This was in March, 1904. But in March, 1905, when everything looked peaceful, the Kaiser went to Tangier in the *Hohenzollern,* landed with an imposing suite, met the uncle of the Sultan, who came as a special envoy to the German Emperor, and addressed him in the following terms:—

"I am to-day paying my visit to the Sultan in his quality of independent sovereign. I hope that under the sovereignty of the Sultan a free Morocco will remain open to the peaceful competition of all nations, without monopoly and without annexation, on the footing of absolute equality. The object of my visit to Tangier is to make known that I have decided to do all in my power to effectually safeguard the interests of Germany in Morocco. Since I consider the Sultan an absolutely free sovereign, it is with him that I desire to come to an understanding on suitable measures for safeguarding these interests. As to the reforms that the Sultan intends to make, it seems to me that he must proceed with much caution, having regard to the religious feelings of the population, so that public order may not be disturbed."

Such was the declaration of the German Emperor. What gave special point to his address was the fact that at that very moment a French delegation was at the capital, Fez, in order to obtain necessary reforms from the Sultan, and was meeting week after week the most obstinate resistance from him and his Government. It was obviously open support of the Sultan in his refusal to accept French representations, and a declaration of hostility to France on the part of the Kaiser. Nothing more arrogant or offensive can well be imagined. France, from the Socialist point of view, was wrong in her attempt to instruct the Sultan how to deal with a state of things which undoubtedly threatened the peace of Algeria, but the Kaiser's intervention after such a fashion was wholly unwarrantable, and threatened the peace of the world.

What was the meaning of this extraordinary display of Imperial diplomacy and Prussian direct action? There were statesmen—Sir Charles Dilke was one—who believed that the German Emperor was really devoted to peace, and that no war could take place in Europe so long as he lived. There was a general feeling in England to the same effect, largely engineered by Lord Haldane and others of like nature, whose spiritual or political home was in Germany. But all can see now that this was an illusion. The only difference between the Kaiser and the most aggressive and bloodthirsty Junker or pan-German was as to the time and season when the tremendous Central European and partially Mohammedan combination that he had formed should commence the attack. William II wished to wait until the road had been so completely prepared for the aggressive advance that victory on every side would be practically certain. The Junker party, with which the Crown Prince identified himself, were in a hurry, and the Emperor could only keep them in good humor by these periodical outbursts which enabled him to pose as the dictator of Europe.

All through, the Kaiser's real ambition was that which he occasionally disclosed in a well-known drawing-room in Berlin. He would not die happy unless he had ridden at the head of the Teutonic armies as the Charlemagne of modern Europe. But this megalomania was only indulged in with his intimates. Elsewhere he stood forth as the rival of his uncle as the Prince of Peace. According to him, therefore, it was M. Delcassé who forced him to act in this peremptory way at Tangier, and efforts were made to convince all the Governments in Europe that the French Minister of Foreign Affairs had tried to boycott Germany out of Morocco. France, rather than take up the challenge, got rid of M. Delcassé. Thus the Emperor displayed his power for the appeasement of his Junkers, established a permanent source of difficulty on the flank of France, and gave the Mohammedan world to understand once more that Germany, not England, was the champion of Islam.

Meanwhile, German political, financial and commercial influence of every kind was making astounding advances, not only in France itself, but also in every country that might at the critical moment be able to help either France or Russia; while German armaments, military and naval, and German alliances for war were being worked up to the point which, if carried on for ten, or perhaps even for five years more, would have rendered the German power almost, if not quite, irresistible by any combination that could have been made in time against it. The Kaiser, in short, was playing a successful game of world-peace in order to make sure of playing at the right moment a successful game of world-war. Desperate as the conflict has been, it may have been fortunate for mankind that the Junkers, his son and the General Staff forced the Emperor's hand.

When, consequently, Clemenceau took the lead in French affairs, he soon found that the sacrifice of M. Delcassé, the friend of Edward VII, to the pretended German injury had been made in vain. There was no intention whatever, either then or later, of coming to a really permanent settlement of outstanding grievances against France, although the position in Morocco was eventually used to gain great advantages in other parts of Africa. Germany was, in fact, a permanent menace to the peace of Europe and the world; but those who said so, and adduced plain facts to justify their contentions, were unfortunately denounced both by capitalists and Socialists in every country as fomenters of war. This insidious propaganda, which tended to the advantage of Germany in every respect, was already going on in 1906, when M. Clemenceau joined M. Sarrien's Cabinet, and when he formed a Cabinet of his own. This was publicly recognized.

This is what M. Clemenceau said at Hyères, after some furious attacks had been made upon France in the German official newspapers; no German newspapers being allowed to print comments on foreign affairs without the consent of the Foreign Office: "No peace is possible without force. When I took office I myself was persuaded that all European nations were of one mind in wishing for peace. But almost immediately, without any provocation whatever from us, a storm of calumny and misrepresentation broke out upon us, and we were compelled to ask ourselves, 'Are we prepared?'"

On October 23rd of the same year, M. Sarrien resigned, and M. Clemenceau formed his Cabinet. It comprised, among others, Messrs. Pichon (Foreign Affairs), Caillaux (Finance), Colonel Picquart (War), Briand (Justice and Education), Viviani (Labor), and Doumergue (Commerce). A more peaceful Cabinet could hardly be. M. Pichon, who took the place from which M. Delcassé had been forced to resign because he too strongly opposed German influence in Morocco and refused a European Conference on the subject as wholly unnecessary, was an old friend and co-worker with Clemenceau on *La Justice,* and had gone into diplomacy at Clemenceau's suggestion. He had since held positions in the East and in Tunis, and he and Clemenceau were believed to be entirely at one in abjuring all adventurous colonial policy. M. Caillaux, at the head of the Department of Finance—people are apt to forget that M. Caillaux, now in jail under serious accusation, was thus trusted by Clemenceau—was certainly not opposed to Germany, but even at that time was favorable to a close understanding with that power. Colonel Picquart, who now received his reward for having, though personally an anti-Semite, destroyed all his own professional prospects in his zeal to obtain justice for the Jew Dreyfus, was certainly as pacific a War Minister as could have been appointed. But what was more significant still, M. Briand, himself a Socialist, and the hero of the great inquiry into the separation of Church and State which had now become inevitable, was placed in a position to carry that important measure to its final vote and settlement; and M. Viviani, likewise a Socialist, became head of the new department, the Ministry of Labor. When I saw these two men, Briand, whom I remembered well as a vehement anarchist, and Viviani, who was a vigorous Socialist speaker and writer, in the Cabinet of which Clemenceau was the chief, I could not but recall the conversation I had with the French Premier sixteen years before.

Seated comfortably in his delightful library, surrounded by splendid Japanese works of art, of which at that time he was an ardent collector, M. Clemenceau had spoken very freely indeed. Of course he knew quite well that I was no mere interviewer for Press purposes, and, indeed, I have always made it a rule to keep such conversations, except perhaps for permitted indiscretions here and there, entirely to myself. There is no need for me to enlarge upon his quick and almost abrupt delivery, his apt remarks and illustrations, his bright, clever, vigorous face and gestures. I put it to him that Socialism was the basis of the coming political party in France and that, vehement individualist as he might be himself, it was impossible for him to resist permanently the current of the time, or to remain merely a supremely powerful critic and organizer of overthrow. Sooner or later he must succumb to the inevitable and take his seat as President of Council, and to do this with any hope of success or usefulness he would have to rely in an increasing degree upon Socialist and semi-Socialist support.

To this Clemenceau answered that he was quite contented with his existing position; that he had no wish to enter upon office with its responsibilities and corrupting influence; while, as to Socialism, that could never make way in France in his day.

"Looking only at the towns," he said, "you may think otherwise, though even there I consider the progress of Socialism is overrated. But the towns do not govern France. The overwhelming majority of French voters are country voters. France means rural France, and the peasantry of France will never be Socialists. Nobody can know them better than my family and I know them. Landed proprietors ourselves—my father's passion for buying land to pay him three per cent. with borrowed money for which he had to pay four per cent. would have finally ruined him, but that our wholesome French law permits gentle interference in such a case—we have ever lived with and among the peasantry. We have been doctors from generation to generation, and have doctored them gratuitously, as I did myself both in country and in town. I have seen them very close, in birth and in death, in sickness and in health, in betrothal and in marriage, in poverty and in well-being, and all the time their one idea is property; to possess, to own, to provide a good portion for the daughter, to secure a good and well *dot*-ed wife for the son. Always *property,* ownership, possession, work, thrift, acquisition, individual gain. Socialism can never take root in such a soil as this. North or south, it is just the same. Preach nationalization of the land in a French village, and you would barely escape with your life, if the peasants understood what you meant. Come with me for a few weeks' trip through rural France, and you will soon understand the hopelessness of Socialism here. It will encounter a personal fanaticism stronger than its own. Your Socialists are men of the town; they do not understand the men and women of the country."

Now the same M. Clemenceau, after a long struggle side by side with the Socialist Party, first in the Dreyfus case and then in the anti-Clericalist and Separation of Church and State movement, finds that events have moved so fast, in a comparatively short space of time, that he is practically compelled to take two active Socialists into his own Cabinet. This, too, in spite of the fact that his action in calling in the troops at Courrières and insisting upon liberty for non-strikers or blacklegs had turned the Socialist Party, as a party, definitely against him. No more significant proof of the advance of Socialist influence could well have been given. That it was entirely on the side of peace and a good understanding with Germany cannot be disputed.

But this did not make the Morocco affair itself any less complicated or threatening. Notwithstanding the Conference which Germany succeeded in having convoked at Algeciras, and the settlement arrived at in April, 1906, after a sitting of more than three months, the condition of Morocco itself had not improved. The fact that the Conference gave France the preference in the scheme of reforms proposed and in the political management of Morocco, against the efforts of Germany and Austria, suited neither the Sultan nor the Kaiser. Troubles arose of a serious character. The French considered themselves forced to intervene. The old antagonism broke out afresh. So much so that the French Premier spoke with more than his usual frankness in an interview with a German newspaper in November:—

"The Germans have one great fault. They show us extreme courtesy to-day and marked rudeness the day after. Before this Morocco affair, feeling in France had much improved. Many of us thought an understanding with Germany very desirable, and I freely admit your Emperor did a good deal to engender this feeling. Then, although we had dismissed Delcassé, the German press attacked us. It went so far as to declare that you were to extort from us the milliards of francs necessary to finance an Anglo-German war. . . . I do not want to have any war, and if we desire no war we necessarily wish to be on good terms with our neighbors. If, also, our relations are unsatisfactory, we are anxious to improve them. Such is my frame of mind. Moreover, if I have a chance of doing so, I shall be glad to act on these lines. Of course it is imperatively necessary for us to be always strong and ready for all eventualities. That, however, does not mean that we want war: quite the contrary.

To wish for war would mean that we were mad. We could not possibly carry on a war policy. If we did, Parliament would soon turn us out, as it did Delcassé."

Nothing could be clearer than that. And what made the pronouncement more important even than the strong but sober language used was the fact that, after as before the Conference of Algeciras, there was really a great disposition among certain sections in France to come to terms with Germany rather than to strengthen the understanding with England. The expression of this opinion could be frequently heard among the people. It was fostered even in the face of the German press campaign against the Clemenceau Administration, by powerful financial interests and by Clerical reactionary elements which were at this time less hostile to Germany than to England.

Throughout, however, Clemenceau stood for the *Entente* with the latter power as the only sound policy for his country. In this respect he was at one with the old statement of Gambetta that a breach of the alliance with England would be fatal to France. For Clemenceau, therefore, who had more than once in his career suffered so severely for his friendship for England, to state that an understanding with Germany had been seriously contemplated was a striking testimony to the immediate tendency of the time at that juncture. Whether the whole of this fitful friendliness on the side of Germany was simulated in order to foster that remarkable policy of steady infiltration of German interests, German management, and German goods into France, with far other than peaceful aims, is a question which can be much more confidently answered now than at the period when this peaceful offensive was going on. Enough to say that the

Clemenceau Ministry was not, at first, at all averse from a permanent arrangement for peace with Germany, so long as English animosity was not aroused.

It must be admitted, nevertheless, that French policy in Morocco was, in the long run, quite contrary to the views on colonial affairs which Clemenceau had so strongly expressed and acted upon hitherto. Whatever excuse may be made on account of the proximity of Morocco to Algeria and the necessity for France to protect her own countrymen and secure peace on the border, the truth remains that the French Republic was allowed by her statesmen to drift into what was virtually a national and capitalist domination of that independent country, backed up by a powerful French army. Clemenceau in his defense of these aggressions recites those familiar apologies for that sort of patriotism which consists in love of another people's country and the determination to seize it, which we Englishmen have become so accustomed to in our own case. If we didn't take it, somebody else would. If we leave matters as they are, endless disturbances will occur and will spread to our own territory. A protectorate must be established.

But a protectorate must have a powerful armed force behind it, or there can be no real protection. National capital is being invested under our peaceful penetration for the benefit of the protected people. The rights of investors must be safeguarded. Our countrymen—in this instance Frenchmen—have been molested and even murdered by the barbarous folk whom we have been called upon to civilize. Such outrages cannot be permitted to go unpunished. Towns bombarded. Villages burnt. Peace reëstablished. More troops. "Security of life and property" ensured by a much larger army and the foundation of civilized Courts. Protection develops insensibly into possession. The familiar progression of grab is, in short, complete.

That is pretty much what went on with Morocco, whose entire independence as a sovereign State had only just been internationally acknowledged. What is more, it went on under M. Clemenceau's own Government, consisting of the same peaceful politicians enumerated above. No doubt the action of Germany against France and French interests, on the one side, and the support by England of France and French interests, on the other, hastened the acceptance of the "white man's burden" which her capitalists and financiers were so eager to undertake; if only to upset the schemes of the Brothers Mannesmann in the troublous Mohammedan Sultanate. But it is strange to find Clemenceau in this galley. For, unjustifiable as were the proceedings of Germany at the beginning and all through, it is now obvious that France, by her own policy, put arguments into the mouth of the peace-at-any-price and pro-German advocates; that also she played the game of the Kaiser and his unscrupulous agent Dr. Rosen. This worthy had been in the employment of Prince Radolin, who thus described him: "He is a Levantine Jew whose sole capacity is intriguing to increase his own importance." It was disgraceful of Germany to make use of such a man to stir up Morocco against France. But it was certainly most unwise, as well as contrary to international comity, for France to put herself in the wrong by an aggressive policy in that State. Especially was this the case when such a terrible menace still overhung her Eastern frontier and, as events proved, not a man could be spared for adventures in Morocco or elsewhere.

The war between rival Sultans and the attack upon the French settlers at Casablanca could not justify such a complete change of front. Jaurès, in fact, was in the right when he denounced the advance of General Amadé with a strong French army as a filibustering expedition, dangerous in itself and provocative towards Germany. But Clemenceau supported his Foreign Minister, Pichon, in the occupation of Casablanca, which had been heavily bombarded beforehand, and, on February 25th, declared that France did not intend to evacuate Morocco, neither did she mean to conquer that country. He had, he averred, no secrets, and, as in the matter of the anarchist rising in the South, said he was ready to resign. This was evidence of impatience, which was harmful at such a critical period in French home and foreign affairs. It looked as if Clemenceau had been so accustomed to turn out French Governments that he could not discriminate even in favor of his own! But the Chamber gave him a strong vote of confidence, and he remained at his post.

There were two important developments in foreign affairs going on during this year, 1908, of which the difficulties in Morocco, serious as they were, constituted only a side issue. The one was open and above-board: the other was known only to those who kept very closely in touch with German politics.

The first was the rapid improvement in the relations between France and Great Britain, for which Clemenceau himself and King Edward VII were chiefly responsible. We are now so accustomed to regard the *Entente* as part and parcel of English foreign policy that it is not easy to understand how bitter the feeling was against Great Britain which led important Frenchmen to take the view of an agreement with Germany spoken of above.

English domination in Egypt to the practical exclusion of French influence and control even over the Suez Canal; English conventions with Japan, checking, as was thought, that legitimate French expansion in Asia by which M. Jules Ferry had hoped to counterbalance the defeats of 1870-71; English settlement of the irritating Newfoundland Fisheries question; English truculence and unfairness in the infamous Boer War; English antagonism to Russia, France's trusted ally and heavy debtor—all these things stood in the way of any cordial understanding. It may well be that only Clemenceau's strong personal influence, supported by his nominee President Fallières, prevented steps being taken which would have been fatal to the revival of genuine good feeling between the Western Powers. The following passage in the *Encyclopædia Britannica* does no more than justice to Clemenceau's services in this direction:

"M. Clemenceau, who only late in life came into office and attained it when a better understanding with England was progressing, had been throughout his long career, of all public men in all political groups, the most consistent friend of England. His presence at the head of affairs was a guarantee of amicable Anglo-French relations, so far as they could be protected by statesmanship." This tribute in a permanent work of reference is thoroughly well deserved.

Happily, too, his efforts had been earnestly supported long before, and even quietly during, the Boer War by Edward VII, as Prince of Wales and as King. But this very connection between the French Radical statesman and the English monarch was the subject of most virulent attacks. It was, in fact, made the groundwork of an elaborate accusation of treachery against Clemenceau, who was represented as the mere tool of Edward VII in promoting the permanent effacement of France. The King was an English Machiavelli, constantly plotting to recover for the British Empire, at the expense of France, that world-wide prestige which the miserable Boer War and the rise of German power on land and sea, in trade and in finance, had seriously jeopardized. A book by the well-known M. Flourens, written at this time to uphold that thesis, went through no fewer than five editions. Here is the pleasing picture of the late King presented for the contemplation of the Parisian populace by this virulent penman: *

"*Edouard VII montait sur le trône à l'age où, si l'on consulte les statistiques, 75% des rois sont déjà descendus dans la tombe. Il sortait d'une longue oisiveté pour entrer dans la vie active a l'époque où, dans toutes les carrières et fonctions publiques, les hommes font valoir leurs droits à la retraite.*

"*S'il y avait un conseil de revision pour les rois, comme il y en a un pour les conscrits, il eût été déclaré impropre au service.*

"*L'obésité déformait son corps, alourdissait sa marche, semblait, sous le développement des tissus adipeux, paralyser toute activité physique, toute force intellectuelle. Sa figure, contractée par la douleur, trahissait,*

---

* "*Edward VII ascended the throne at the age at which, as we may learn from statistics, 75 per cent. of all kings have already descended into the tomb. He came out of a prolonged period of idleness, in order to enter active life at the time of life when men in all public careers and functions claim the right to retire.*
"*If there were an Exemption Board for kings, as there is for conscripts, he would have been reported unfit for service.*
"*Obesity deformed his body, hampered his movements, and beneath the accumulation of adipose tissues, seemed to paralyze all physical activity, as well as all intellectual force. His features, contracted by pain, betrayed momentarily the sufferings which a will of iron strove*

par moment, les souffrances qu'une volonté de fer s'efforcait de maîtriser, pour dissimuler aux yeux de ses sujets la maladie qui, à cet instant même, menaçait sa vie.

"A voir sa corpulence maladive, on ne pouvait s'empêcher de se rappeler les paroles que Shakespeare met dans la bouche d'un de ses ancêtres à l'adresse du fameux Falstaff, le compagnon dissolu des égarements de sa jeunesse: 'Songe à travailler, à diminuer ton ventre et à grossir ton mérite—quitte ta vie dissolue! Regarde la tombe, elle ouvre, pour toi, une bouche trois fois plus large que pour les autres hommes!'

"De tous côtés, les lanceurs de prédictions, depuis le fameux archange Gabriel jusqu'à la non moins fameuse Mme. de Thèbes, s'accordaient pour entourer son avènement des plus sinistres prévisions, pour annoncer sa fin prochaine et l'imminence d'une nouvelle vacance du trône d'Angleterre.

"Symptôme plus grave! Les oracles de la science n'étaient pas moins menaçants que les prophéties des devins. Deux fois, les pompes de son couronnement durent être décommandées, deux fois les fêtes ajournées

to master, in order to hide from his subjects the malady which even then was menacing his life.

"Beholding his unhealthy corpulence, one could not help recalling the words which Shakespeare puts into the mouth of one of the king's fore-runners regarding the famous Falstaff, the dissolute companion of his youthful errors:

> 'Make less thy body hence, and more thy grace;
> Leave gormandizing; know the grave doth gape
> For thee thrice wider than for other men.'

"On all sides, the makers of prophecies, from the famous archangel Gabriel to the not less famous Mme. de Thèbes, agreed in surrounding his future with the most sinister predictions, including his early demise and the imminent prospect of a new vacancy to the throne of England.

"Grave symptom still! The oracles of science were no less menacing than the prophecies of the inspired. Twice the preparations for his coronation had to be countermanded, twice the festivities were postponed and the illuminations extinguished. The princely guests, gath-

et les lampions éteints. Les hôtes princiers, convoqués a grands frais de tous les points du globe, pour participer à ces réjouissances, attendirent, dans l'angoisse, l'annonce d'une cérémonie plus lugubre.

"*La volonté d'Edouard VII triumpha de toutes ces résistances. Il déclara avec une indomptable énergie que, coûte que coûte, il était décidé à ne pas descendre dans la tombe avant d'avoir posé sur sa tête, avec tout l'éclat, avec toute la solennité traditionnels, aux yeux des représentants émerveillés de tout son vaste empire, aux yeux de l'Univers jaloux, la couronne de ses Pères, sa double couronne de Roi et d'Empereur, que les mains avides de la mort semblaient vouloir lui disputer.*"

His account of Edward VII reads curiously to-day, the more so when we recall the fact that M. Emile Flourens was at one time French Minister of Foreign Affairs, and that, at the moment when the book first appeared, the King was frequently in Paris, and on good terms with Republicans of all sections.

After pointing out how scrupulously he had as Prince of Wales suppressed his political opinions, during his mother's lifetime, even when his power, had he exerted it, might have been advantageous to his country, the French critic gives him full credit for having made the best of his life in many ways. He had traveled all over the world, had studied humanity and society in all shapes, had "warmed both hands before the fire of life" in every

---

ered together at great expense from all corners of the globe, to participate in these rejoicings, awaited anxiously the announcement of a more lugubrious ceremonial.

"But the will power of Edward VII triumphed over all these hindrances. He declared with unconquerable energy that, cost what it might, he had decided not to descend to the tomb until he had had placed upon his head, with all the traditional magnificence and solemnity, the crown of his Fathers, the double crown of King and Emperor, which the covetous hands of Death seemed eager to wrest from him."

quarter of the globe. But, though his features as a private personage were familiar to everybody, he remained a sphinx, mysterious and unfathomable, even to his friends, in public affairs. He was well known to Parisians everywhere, and was as popular in working-class centers as in the most aristocratic *salons*. Paris was, in fact, the only city where he was at his ease and at home, where, in fact, he was himself. By far the most sympathetic Briton to Parisians who ever was in Paris, he exercised a real influence over all classes. They were kept carefully informed as to his tastes, his manner, his intimates, his vices and his debts, and were the more friendly to him on account of them. The warmest partisans of his accession, however, were his creditors, who were mortally afraid that his habits would not give him the opportunity for discharging his liabilities out of his mother's accumulations.

The description of the position of the British Empire at the close of the Boer War was less flattering even than the personal sketch of its King and Emperor. "At this moment the astounded peoples had felt the Britannic colossus totter on its foundation, this colossus with feet of clay which weighs down too credulous nations by its bluff, by its arrogance, by rapine, by insatiable rapacity, which already grips the entire globe like a gigantic cuttle-fish and sucks its marrow through the numberless tentacles of its commerce, until the day when it shall subjugate the whole planet to its domination—always provided that it does not encounter on its way another still more powerful octopus of destruction which will attack and destroy it."

Needless to say that this challenger of the British supremacy was the rising power of Germany. As an Englishman I admit the infamy of the Boer War, and recognize that our rule in India and Ireland has been anything but what it ought to have been. M. Clemenceau knew all that as well as we British anti-Imperialists do. But even in 1907-8 much had happened since 1900. Democracy was slowly making way in Great Britain likewise, and freedom for others would surely follow emancipation for herself. It was not to be expected that all Frenchmen should see or understand this. A nation which has under its flag a fourth of the population and more than a seventh of the habitable surface of the world can scarcely expect that another colonial country, whose colonies the British have largely appropriated, in the East and in the West, will admit the "manifest destiny" of the Union Jack to wave of undisputed right over still more territory. There was a good deal to be said, and a good deal was said, about British greed and British unscrupulousness: nor could the truth of many of the imputations be honestly denied.

It called, therefore, for all Edward VII's extraordinary knowledge of Paris, his bonhomie, shrewd common sense, and uncanny power of "creating an atmosphere" to overcome the prejudice thus created against himself as a master of intrigue and Clemenceau as his willing tool. Matters went so far that at one moment the King's reception in his favorite capital seemed likely to be hostile, and might have been so, but for the admirable conduct of the high-minded conservative patriot, M. Déroulède. But, luckily for France, Great Britain and the world at large, these difficulties had been overcome; and almost the only good feature in the trouble with Morocco was the vigorous diplomatic help France received from England—a good feature because it helped to wipe away the bitter memories of the past from the minds of the French people. The extremely cordial reception of President Fallières and M. Clemenceau in London, and the King's own exceptional courtesy at all times to M. Delcassé, whom the French public regarded as the victim of German dictatorial demands, tended in the same direction. All the world could see that Clemenceau's Administration had so far strengthened the Anglo-French *Entente* as to have brought it almost to the point of an alliance: nor thereafter was the Triple Entente with Russia, as opposed to the Triple Alliance, very far off.

At this same time, however, matters were going so fast in Germany towards an open breach that the only wonder is that the truth of the situation was not disclosed, and that Germany, quite ready, and determined to be more ready, for war at any moment, was allowed to continue her policy of pretended peace.

England and, to a large extent, France still believed in the pacific intentions of the Fatherland. Yet a meeting was held in Berlin of the heads of all the departments directly or indirectly connected with war, at which the Kaiser delivered a speech which could only mean one thing: that Germany and her Allies would enter upon war so soon as the opportunity presented itself, and the preparations, including the completion of the Kiel Canal (or perhaps before that great work had been accomplished), gave promise of a short and decisive campaign. Rumors of this address reached those who were kept informed as to what was being contemplated by the Kaiser, his Militarist Junker *entourage* and the Federal Council. Unfortunately, when the statement was challenged, a strong denial was issued, and the pacifists and pro-Germans, honest and dishonest, laughed at the whole story as a baseless scare.

How far it was baseless could be learned from deeds that spoke much louder than words. Even thus early great accumulations of munitions of war were being made at Cologne, and the military sidings and railway equipments, which could only serve for warlike and not commercial purposes, were being completed. Six years before the war all the work necessary for an aggressive descent on the West and for the passage through Belgium had been done.

Europe was comfortably seated over a powder magazine. M. Clemenceau might well discuss in London, when he came over to Sir Henry Campbell-Bannerman's funeral, as Premier of France, how many hundred thousand men, fully equipped for war, England could land within a fortnight in North-Eastern France, should a sudden and unprovoked attack be made. But he got no satisfactory answer.

It is evident, therefore, that what with strikes, anarchist outbreaks, the troubles in Morocco, the menacing attitude of Germany—who, as Clemenceau put it, said, "Choose between England and us"—and the attempts to form an enduring compact with England, Clemenceau as President of Council, with all his energy, determination and versatility, had enough on his hands to occupy all his thoughts. But this did not exhaust the catalogue of his labors during his term of Premiership.

CHAPTER XVI

END OF CLEMENCEAU'S MINISTRY

IT it easy to be tolerant of the Catholic Church and Catholics in a Protestant country; though even in Great Britain, and of course only too sadly in the North of Ireland, there are times when the bitterness inherited from the past makes itself felt, on slight provocation, in the present. At such times of sectarian outburst we get some idea ourselves of what religious hatred really means, and can form a conception of the truly fraternal eagerness to immolate the erring brethren, nominally of the same Christian creed, which animated the true believers of different shades of faith, whether Orthodox or Arian, Catholic or Huguenot, in days gone by. Those who chance to remember what Catholicism was in Italy, the Papal States, or Naples two generations ago, the Church then claiming for itself rights of jurisdiction and sanctuary, outside the common law—those who understand what has gone on in Spain quite recently, can also appreciate the feeling of Frenchmen who, within the memory of their fellow-citizens still living, and even themselves in some degree under the Empire, had suffered from Clerical interference and repression, when the chance of getting rid of State ecclesiasticism was presented to them at the beginning of the twentieth century. The Church had entirely lost touch with the temper of the time. Though it may have been impossible for the Vatican to accept the brilliant suggestion that the great men of science should all be canonized and the discoverers of our day should receive the red hat, as secular Cardinals, there was no apparent reason why a form of supernaturalism which had lived into and out of two forms of human slavery, and was passing through a third, should have been unable to adapt itself in some degree to modern thought. A creed which, in its most successful period, had conveniently absorbed ancestor-worship as part of its theological propaganda in China need not, one would have thought, have found it indispensably necessary to the salvation of its votaries to cleave to all the old heresies inculcated in days when criticism of the incomprehensible and unbelievable involved the unpleasant possibility of being tortured to death, or burnt alive.

Nor certainly could its worst enemy have predicted that the infallibility of the Pope would be invented and thrust upon the faithful, as a doctrine whose acceptance was essential to their spiritual welfare, in a period when it was being proved every day and in all departments of human knowledge that what was universally believed to be a certainty yesterday is discounted as a fallacy tomorrow. Nothing in all the long controversy about the Separation of Church and State in France produced a greater or more permanent effect upon intelligent Frenchmen than this preposterous claim of Papal infallibility. Explain it away, whittle down its significance by any amount of Jesuitical sophistry, and still this declaration that a mere man could never be mistaken, because he was the Vicegerent of God, shook the whole framework of Catholic domination, so far as any participation of the State in the matter was concerned. And the career and character of many of the Pope's predecessors rendered the dogma more utterly preposterous to all who had even a smattering of the history of the Vatican than might otherwise have been the case. That John XXIII should have been infallible threw a strange light upon Catholic morality in its highest grades. Yet if Pius infallible, why not John?

What, however, had more practical effect in turning the scale of public opinion against the Papacy, its nominees and believers as servants and paid employees of the State, was the fact that in all the practical affairs of French life the Catholic Church, as represented by its ecclesiastical hierarchy, had taken the wrong side. Theoretical or theological difficulties would never have upset the regard of the French people for the National Church. But, time after time, the Clerical party ranged itself with the reactionists, throwing over all its wisest counselors, whose devotion to the Church had never been questioned, when they advised standing by the cause of the people, and relied solely upon the judgment of bigoted Jesuits. Zola, whom these creatures hated, showed in his "Germinal," thoroughgoing materialist as he was, what a noble part a priest of the Church could play, when the young ecclesiastic stands between the strikers who form part of his flock and the soldiers who are about to fire upon them. Individuals might thus rise up to and above the level of their creed, but the Church in France, as a whole, was represented by men of God who were a good deal worse than men of Belial. Nor was this all. They pursued a policy of relentless obscurantism. Their object was not to develop education but to stunt its growth; not to teach the truth but to foster lies. So manifest was the determination to take no high view of their duties that such a man as the venerable Dr. Leplay, a Catholic of Catholics whose religious convictions did not prevent him from becoming a master of the theories of Marx, lamented that his Church was proving itself wholly incompetent to cope with or to stem what, as a Christian, he recognized was the rising tide of infidelity.

Of this infidelity, the freethinker and champion of secularism, Clemenceau, was a type and a prominent example. He saw the Church as a pernicious influence. His feeling towards it was even more vehement than that of Voltaire or Gambetta. *"Ecrasez l'infâme!"* *"Le cléricalisme voilà l'ennemi!"* If thought was to be free, if Frenchmen were to be emancipated from superstition and intolerance, the power of the Catholic Church must be weakened and, if possible, destroyed. For him in this matter compromise was impossible. His begettings, his surroundings, his education, his profession, his political life all made him relentless on this point. Behind the Duc de Broglie, behind the persecutor of Dreyfus, behind the pretender Boulanger, behind reaction in all its forms hid the sinister figure of the unscrupulous power, working *perinde ac cadaver* against all that was noblest in France, against all that was highest in the ideals of the Republic. And if Clemenceau knew well that under all circumstances and at every turn of events the Catholic Church was the enemy of France and of himself, the Church had no doubt that Clemenceau was its most formidable foe in French political life.

Long before, and after his defeat in the Var, in 1893, the Catholics never hesitated to join with their enemies, if only this combination would help them to overthrow Clemenceau. Whatever differences the French Premier might have with the Socialists on strikes and social affairs generally, on the matter of the separation of Church and State they were heartily at one. In fact, Clemenceau was even more uncompromising than they. The whole texture of his thought revolted against showing any consideration for a Church which, from his point of view, had been for centuries the chief and most formidable enemy of progress in France and the most capable organizer of attacks upon all democratic and Republican ideals.

The greatest names in French history are the names of those whom the Catholic Church has persecuted or martyred. Its leaders would resort to the same tactics now, and have only failed to do so because the power has slipped from their hands as the truths of science and the wider conceptions of human destiny have permeated the minds of the masses. There was no likelihood that as Prime Minister Clemenceau, the free-thinker and materialist, would be inclined to modify his opinions in favor of what might be regarded as statesmanlike concessions to the Right on ecclesiastical matters. The danger lay in the other direction. It was one of the remarkable incidents, in connection with his first tenure of the Presidency of the Council, that the final settlement of this important question of the relations of Church and State should come when he himself was at the head of the French Government.

When M. Briand's measure for the complete laicization of the Church so far as the State was concerned was introduced into the Chamber, he pointed out in his report that the proposal for complete separation was not dictated by hatred or political prejudice, nor did it involve anything at all approaching to the change in the relations of property when, at the time of the French Revolution, the Church owned one-third of the total wealth of France. This Act was the assertion of definite principles which were necessary in order to secure for the State full mastery in its own country. Freedom of worship for all. No State payment to ministers of any creed. Equitable management of Church property taken over by the towns and Communes.

The Bill, after considerable debate in the National Assembly, was passed by a large majority. In the Senate M. Clemenceau denounced the settlement as too favorable to the clergy. His criticism was as mordant as usual. But he neither proposed an amendment nor voted against the Bill, which passed the Senate without even the alteration of a word, by a greater proportional majority than it did in the Lower House.

This, it might have been thought, would have been the end of the matter for Clemenceau. He had done his full share towards putting the Catholic Church out of action, and might have been contented, as Premier, with any further settlement that M. Briand, the member of his own Cabinet responsible for this important measure, and M. Jaurès, the powerful leader of the Socialist Party, might come to in regard to the properties of the Church, about which there had been much bitter feeling. But Clemenceau has the defects of his qualities. The Pope had refused to permit his clergy to avail themselves of the excellent terms French Republicans, Radicals and Socialists had been ready to accord to them. He had issued two Encyclicals which could certainly be read as intended to stir up trouble in the Republic,—which, in fact, had brought about some disorder. When, therefore, everything seemed arranged on this prickly question of valuations and appropriations, Clemenceau could not resist the temptation to show the unsatisfactory nature of the entire business to him. It was one of those moments of impulse when "the Tiger" could not refrain from giving free play to his propensities at the expense of his own kith and kin, failing the presence of his enemies to maul. It was thought that the Ministry must come down; for both M. Briand and M. Jaurès took this outburst amiss. But a conversation in the lobby brought the great irreconcilable very sensibly to a compromise, and Clemenceau failed to give the Catholics the malicious enjoyment they anticipated. It was a strange ebullition which exhibited the perennial youth of this statesman of the unexpected.

In other directions than social affairs and Morocco, where he unfortunately relied upon the Right more than upon the Left in the Assembly for the support of his Administration, Clemenceau proved that his claim to act as the advocate of reform as well as the upholder of order was no pretense.

Whatever may have been its alleged deficiencies in some respects, Clemenceau's first Ministry was by far the most Radical Government that had held office under the Republic. And the boldness and decision which he and his Cabinet displayed in dealing with what they regarded as Anarchist action—it is fair, perhaps, to recall that Briand himself had first achieved fame as an Anarchist—on the part of the workers, they also put in force when high-placed officers, with a powerful political backing, tried to impose their will upon the State. Thus the navy, as has too often happened in French annals, had been allowed to drift into a condition which was actually dangerous, in view of what was going on in the German dockyards, and the probable combination of the Austrian and Italian fleets, with German help, in the Mediterranean. At the same time admirals were in the habit of acting pretty much as they saw fit in regard to the fleets and vessels under their control. Consequently, important men-of-war had been wrecked time after time, and more than one serious accident had occurred. In almost every case also, so powerful was the *esprit de corps,* in the wrong sense, that the officers in command at the time were exonerated from blame. There was, therefore, a strong public opinion in favor of something being done to improve both the fleet itself and the spirit which animated its commanders. Admiral Germinat, a popular officer with, as appears, a genuine loyalty to his profession and a desire to remedy its defects, thought proper to write a very strong letter to a local service newspaper, making a fierce attack upon the general management of the navy, without having given any notice of his views either to the Minister of Marine or the Prime Minister.

Thereupon, M. Clemenceau at once put him on the retired list. Immediately a great hubbub arose. The very same people who had approved of Clemenceau's policy in regard to those whom they called anarchist workmen were now in full cry after the President of Council, for daring to deal thus drastically with a man who, however good his intentions may have been and however distinguished his career, was beyond all question an anarchist admiral. The matter became a question of the day. It was brought up in the Senate amid all sorts of threats to the stability of the Government. M. Clemenceau, as usual, took up the challenge boldly himself. His speech was so crushing that the whole indictment against the Ministry collapsed. The evidence of indiscipline on the Admiral's part, not only on this occasion but on several others, and the declaration that Admiral Germinat would not be excluded from the navy, when he had purged his offense and when his services would be advantageous to the country, settled the matter and strengthened the Ministry.

By acquiring the Chemin de Fer de l'Ouest and combining it with other Government railways, the Ministry made the first important step towards nationalization of railways. Clemenceau defended this measure on grounds that would be, and were, accepted by Socialists, but events have shown in this particular case that a good deal more is needed than the establishment of another department of State bureaucracy to render the railways a national property really beneficial to the community. As carried out in practice, the acquisition of the Chemin de Fer de l'Ouest has rather set back than advanced the general policy of railway nationalization in France.

A more important measure was that introduced by M. Caillaux and, amazing to say, passed through the Assembly, for a graduated income-tax. How this majority was obtained has always been one of the puzzles of that period. There is no country in the world where a tax upon incomes is more unpopular than in France, and from that day to this, in spite of the desperate need for funds which has arisen, this tax has never yet become law. But it was a genuine financial reform and creditable to the Government. The Socialists supported it, though in itself it is only a palliative measure of justice in purely bourgeois finance. From this period dates the close alliance between the Socialists as revolutionaries and M. Caillaux as the adventurous financier and director of the Société Générale, which later produced such strange results in French politics, and intensified Socialist hatred for M. Clemenceau. But at this time M. Caillaux, with the full concurrence and support of the Prime Minister, was attacking all the bourgeois interests in their tenderest place. The wonder is that such a policy did not involve the immediate fall of the Ministry. Quite possibly, had Clemenceau remained in office, it might have become a permanent feature in French finance. Boldness and boldness and boldness again is sometimes as successful in politics as it is in oratory. Although, therefore, to attack pecuniary "interests" of a large section of the nation is a far more hazardous enterprise than to denounce eminent persons or to overthrow Ministries, this move might then have been successful if well followed up.

On March 8th, in this year 1909, Clemenceau unveiled a statue to the Radical Minister Floquet, with whom he had worked for many years. The revolutionary Socialists announced their intention of demonstrating against him on this occasion. They objected to him and his administration on account of the expedition to Morocco—in which Clemenceau had certainly run counter to all his previous policy on colonial affairs—on account of cosmopolitan finance, Russian loans and the shooting down of workmen on strike. It was the last that occasioned the bitterest feeling against him, and this was really not surprising.

Clemenceau had made the workers' liberty to strike in combination secure, but he did not use the power of the State against the employers, who, in the mines especially, could on his own showing be considered only as profiteering trustees under the State. Also he refused to all Government servants the right to combine or to strike. This disinclination to take the capitalists by the throat, while using the official power to restrain the workers, had a great deal more to do with the menacing attitude of the Socialists than Morocco or finance. However, there was no disturbance. Clemenceau took advantage of the occasion to deliver a speech which was in effect a powerful defense of the idealist Republicanism of the eighteenth century against the revolutionary Socialism of the twentieth.

The French Revolution is deified by nearly all advanced Frenchmen. Its glorification is as much the theme of Jaurès and Vaillant as of Gambetta and Clemenceau. Bourgeois revolution as it turned out to be, owing to economic causes which neither individualists nor collectivists could control, orators of the Revolution overlook facts and cleave to ideals. Thus Clemenceau told his audience that the French Revolution was a prodigious tragedy which seemed to have been the work of demigods, of huge Titans who had risen up from far below to wreak Promethean vengeance on the Olympians of every grade. The French Revolution was the inevitable culmination of the deadly struggle between the growing forces of liberty and the worn-out forces of autocracy without an autocrat. Yet, said he, the Revolution itself was made by men and women inspired with the noblest ideals, but educated, in their own despite, by the Church to methods of domination, condemned also by the desperate resistance of immeasurable powers to prompt and pitiless action followed by corresponding deeds of brutal reaction. The people who had just shed torrents of blood for the freedom of the world passed, without audible protest, from Robespierre to Napoleon. Yet the Revolution is all of a piece. The Republic moves steadily on as one indissoluble, vivifying force. Compare the France of the panic of 1875 with the France of to-day. Her position is the result of understandings and alliances and friendships based on the authority of her armed force. France has resumed her position in Europe, in

END OF CLEMENCEAU'S MINISTRY

spite of a few weak and mean-spirited Frenchmen whose opposition only strengthened the patriotic enthusiasm of the nation at large. The history of the Republican Party had been one long consecration of the watchwords of the French Revolution. Liberty of the Press. Liberty of public meeting. Liberty of association. Liberty of trade unions. Liberty of minds by public schools. Liberty of thought and religion. Liberty of secular instruction. Liberty of State and worship. Laws had been passed for relief of the sick. A day of rest had been prescribed for all. Workmen's compensation for injury had been made imperative. The Income Tax had been passed by the Assembly. "The Revolution is in effect one and indivisible and, with unbroken persistence, the work of the Republic goes on." "A fine record." So argued Clemenceau.

Notwithstanding all the mistakes which Socialists so bitterly resented, this was a great victory for the Republicans and for the Administration of which Clemenceau was the head. Not the least important claim to national recognition of good service done was the establishment of the Ministry of Labor, over which Viviani, the well-known Socialist, presided. The pressure of events, as well as the pressure of the Socialists themselves, might well have pushed the Radical-Socialist Premier farther along the Socialist path.

Unfortunately for the Prime Minister and, from more than one point of view, for the nation, M. Clemenceau had another of those strange fits of impatience and irascibility which he had exhibited more than once before. The political antagonism between M. Clemenceau and M. Delcassé was of long standing, and was intensified by personal bitterness. During his tenure of the office of Minister for Foreign Affairs, a position which he had held for seven years, in successive Administrations of widely different character, M. Delcassé had been subjected to vehement attacks by the leader of the Radical Left. His policy in relation to Morocco had been specially obnoxious to M. Clemenceau. That policy M. Clemenceau had most severely criticized at the time when M. Delcassé was stoutly resisting that extension of German influence in Morocco that led to the Foreign Minister's downfall and the Conference of Algeciras, which M. Delcassé had refused to accept. The relations between the two statesmen could scarcely have been worse, but hitherto the Radical leader had carried all before him.

Now came a dramatic climax to the long struggle. A debate arose in the French Assembly on the condition of the navy. It was admittedly not what it ought to have been. M. Picard, the Minister of Marine, made a conciliatory reply to interpellations on the subject of promised immediate reforms and even complete reconstitution. But this was not enough for M. Delcassé. The Assembly was not hostile to M. Clemenceau, and certainly had no desire to oust his Administration. Yet M. Delcassé's direct attack upon the Premier brought the whole debate down to the level of a personal question. Nevertheless, what he said was quite legitimate criticism. M. Clemenceau had been a member of the Commission of Inquiry on the Navy, and could not get rid of his responsibility for the present state of things. The great critic of everybody and everything was open to exposure himself. He who had enjoyed twenty-five years of running amuck at the whole political world was now being called to account in person as an administrator. So far M. Delcassé. Clemenceau retorted that M. Delcassé had himself been on the Naval Commission of 1904. He was full of great policies here, there and everywhere. What had they resulted in? The humiliation of France and the Conference of Algeciras. Clemenceau was evidently much incensed. The fact that he had been obliged, as he thought, by Germany's action to follow M. Delcassé's Moroccan tactics rendered the position exceptionally awkward. It raised the whole question of M. Delcassé's foreign policy. This gave him a great advantage when it came to direct political warfare. For M. Delcassé was considered, even by those who opposed him, as the victim of German hatred, since he had refused to surrender to German threats and was sacrificed simply because France dared not face a war. So when he recounted his agreement with Spain, his agreement with Italy, his agreement—"too long delayed"—with England, his mediation in the Spanish-American War and his Treaties of Arbitration, the Assembly went with him. Then, too, his assaults upon Clemenceau raised the fighting spirit on Delcassé's side. The feeling was: "This time Clemenceau is getting as good as he brings." The Prime Minister has not done his duty either as President of the Inquiry or as President of Council. "I say to him as he said to Jules Ferry: 'Get out. We won't discuss with you the great interests of this nation.'"

Very good sword-play. But had Clemenceau kept cool, as he certainly would have done on the duel ground, there might have been no harm done. However, he burst out into furious denunciation, exasperated by the ringing cheers which greeted his opponent's conclusion. It was M. Delcassé's fault that France had to go to Algeciras. M. Delcassé would have carried things with a high hand. "But the army was not ready, the navy was not ready. I have not humiliated France: M. Delcassé has humiliated her." A purely personal note, disclosing facts that were the more bitter to the Assembly inasmuch that they were true. It was indecent—that was the sensation that ran round the House—for a Premier thus to expose the weakness of his country on a personal issue, no matter what provocation he may have received. The hostile vote, therefore, was given against Clemenceau himself, not against his Government, and he promptly resigned.

Had he desired to bring about his own overthrow he would have acted precisely as he did; and some thought that this was his intention. It was an unworthy conclusion to a Premiership which, whatever its shortcomings, had done extremely good work for the Republic, and to a Government which had lasted longer than any French Administration since the downfall of the Empire. The character and leadership of the Ministry under M. Briand, which succeeded Clemenceau's Cabinet, proved that only by his own fault had he ensured his official downfall.

As usual, he turned round at once to other work, and accepted an engagement to speak throughout South America, publishing a pleasant record of his experiences in an agreeably written book. The Prime Minister of yesterday was the genial lecturer the day after.

CHAPTER XVII

CLEMENCEAU AND GERMANY

CLEMENCEAU flung himself out of office in an unreasonable fit of temper. A man of his time of life, at sixty-eight years of age, with his record behind him, had no right to have any personal temper at all, when the destinies of his country had been placed in his hands. Probably he would admit this himself to-day. But, during his exceptionally strenuous period of office, he had, as we have seen, more than once shown an impulsiveness and even an irritability that were not consonant with his general disposition. Throughout there appeared to be an inclination on his part to take opposition and criticism too much to heart. As if, in fact, the great Radical overthrower of opportunism was annoyed at being compelled, as all administrations must be, to adopt to some extent a policy of opportunism himself. His outburst against all compromise with the Church was one instance of this. His uncalled-for resignation on account of M. Delcassé's attack was another. This might well have been the end of his official experiences. Certainly no one would have ventured to predict that eight years later would come the crowning achievement of his remarkable career. His own remark on leaving office was not calculated to encourage his personal adherents or to give his country confidence in his leadership. "I came in with an umbrella, I go out with a stick," was all very well as the epigram of a journalist: it was too flippant a remark for a serious statesman such as Clemenceau had shown himself to be. But the time was not far off when all his main policy, as man of affairs, politician, and publicist, would be overwhelmingly justified. As we have seen, Clemenceau was all his life strongly opposed to colonial expansion. His action with regard to Morocco, apparently so contrary to this, arose from an even stronger motive,—his desire to build up French defense against Germany on every side.

But his general distrust of colonization by conquest in Egypt, China, Madagascar, and elsewhere had been based upon France's need for using all her strength and all her resources to build up the power of the French Republic within the limits of France. This is true of all nations at a period when the power of man over nature is increasing so rapidly in every department: perhaps, properly understood, in agriculture most of all, when science is capably applied to production of the land. That is to say, that even in countries such as England, where the cry of over-population is so frequently raised, and where the cult of colonization and emigration has been exalted to the position of a fetish, it would be far better to devote attention to the creation of wealth at home than to the development of waste lands, however fertile, abroad. Concentration of population, given adequate regulation of employment in the interests of the whole people, and attention to the requirements of space, air and health, is not only devoid of danger but is an element in national prosperity—"nothing being more plain than that men in proper labor and employment are capable of earning more than a living," as John Bellers wrote more than two hundred years ago; and "a nation wherein are eight millions of people is more than twice as rich as the same scope of land wherein are but four," as Petty wisely stated, about the same date.

If this was so obviously true at the end of the seventeenth century, it is tenfold, not to say a hundredfold, more certain in the twentieth, having regard to the marvelous discoveries and inventions since made and still but partially applied in every direction. But France is the land where such considerations are most decisive in dealing with the basis of national polity. France has enormous advantages in regard to soil, climate, the industrious habits and skill of her people, and the consequent monopoly on the world market of whole branches of commerce, where taste and luxury have to be gratified. Moreover, she possesses a source of income unparalleled in Europe and scarcely worth noting elsewhere, except in the case of Italy. I calculate that France receives, one year with another, from visitors who come thither, merely to see and to spend, an amount, by way of profit, of not less than $350,000,000. This large sum alone, if used for enhancing the productiveness of the French soil and French industry generally, would immensely benefit the people in every respect. French thrift, again, had piled up out of the products of industry immense pecuniary accumulations. There could have been no better investment of these funds possible than the improvement of the defenses of France against invasion, the completion of her railway and canal system, the development of her mines, so greatly coveted by her aggressive neighbor, the concentration of her military and naval forces at home, instead of scattering any portion of them abroad, the expenditure upon thorough education and scientific agricultural and industrial experiments. All this even Imperialist Frenchmen can see now.

So with regard to Russia. The alliance of the French Republic with the Empire of Russia gave France, apparently, a better position in Europe, the pusillanimous and short-sighted English statesmen having rejected an alliance which was afterwards forced upon Great Britain when wholly unprepared for war. Here also Clemenceau's views were justified by the event. The close connection between a democratic Republic and an autocratic Empire put France in an unenviable moral position before the world. More materially serious than this ill-fated combination, ethically, was the necessity imposed upon the French of lending continually to Russia, until the total amount of the Russian loans held in France amounted to many hundreds of millions sterling.

Such huge sums, again, would have been far more advantageously spent at home than in building strategical and other railways and financing gold and other mines in the vast Muscovite Empire. Financiers gained largely by these loans. But the peasants and small bourgeoisie of France were unknowingly dependent for their interest upon a poverty-stricken agricultural population, which could not possibly continue to pay the large sum due yearly on this amount to their Western creditors without utter ruin. Thus unsound finance followed hard on the heels of more than doubtful policy, and France was the weaker and the poorer for both.

This was all the more fatal to real French interests, inasmuch that, at the same time, the home population of the Republic was slowly decreasing, while the population of her threatening rival, Germany, was steadily growing, and the wealth of the German Empire, both agricultural and mineral, was likewise rapidly expanding with every decade. Consequently, the position of France was becoming more and more precarious, and the relative strength on the two sides of the frontier less and less favorable to the Republic. It must be admitted, under such circumstances, that those who favored a Russian alliance, in spite of all its manifest drawbacks, had a great deal to say for themselves. But that Great Britain should have failed to see that the declension of French power was a peril to herself, long before the *Entente* was brought about by Edward VII, and that a pacific understanding alone was not sufficient to ensure the maintenance of peace, is a truly marvelous instance of the blindness of British statesmanship! Only the phenomenal good luck that has so far attended the United Kingdom hindered our governing classes from landing this country, as well as the French, in overwhelming disaster. How narrow the escape was is not yet fully understood.

Clemenceau was at all times in favor of an Anglo-French offensive and defensive alliance, and he clung to this policy in the face of the most serious discouragement from abroad and, as has been seen, at the cost of vitriolic misrepresentation and hatred at home. It was in vain, however, that for many years he preached this political doctrine. Even when the relations between the two countries were greatly improved, the very proper Liberal and Radical and Labor dislike in England of the entanglement with Czarist Russia rendered the close combination which seemed so essential to all who, like Clemenceau himself, knew what was really going on in Germany, exceedingly difficult to bring about.

The terrific war has thrown into high relief facts

always discernible except by those who were determined not to see. Here Clemenceau's own bitter experience of the war of 1870-71, and his yearly visits to Austria, enabled him to form a clearer conception of the real policy of Germany and the ruthless brutality which underlies modern Teutonic culture than any of his contemporaries. It is no longer doubted that the Franco-German war was welcomed by Prince Bismarck and made inevitable by him in order to crush France and ensure German military supremacy in Europe. Bismarck himself made no secret of the manner in which he had deceived Benedetti at Ems by a forged telegram; and the refusal of the Germans to make a reasonable peace with France immediately after Sedan was conclusive evidence of what was really intended. During the campaign also the Germans resorted to the same hideous methods of warfare on land, on a smaller scale, which have horrified the entire civilized world, on land and on sea, during the great war which commenced forty-four years later.

All this Clemenceau himself saw. While, therefore, in his speeches and writings he never shut out the possibility that the people of Germany, rising superior to their militarist rulers, might come to terms for permanent peace with the people of France, he at the same time cherished no illusions whatever as to the policy of those military rulers and the small probability that German Social-Democracy would be able to thwart the designs of the German aggressionists. Unfortunately, in France, as in Great Britain, a considerable section of all classes, but especially of the working class, represented by Labor Unions and Socialists, would not believe that at the end of the nineteenth and beginning of the twentieth century any great civilized power could be harboring such designs as those attributed to Germany. Vaillant, for example, who, like Clemenceau, had seen the horrors inflicted upon France in the war of 1870, was vehement on that side. So enamored was he of peace that he never lost a chance of assuring Germany that under no circumstances would the French Republic go to war. He advocated a general strike, in all countries affected, should a rupture of peace be threatened, entirely regardless of the fact that the Social-Democrats themselves had declared that such a strike was absolutely impossible in Germany itself.

The same with Jaurès. Not only did this great Socialist believe that peace might be maintained by concessions to Germany; but, although in favor of "the Armed Nation" for France herself, for the purpose of defending her against a German invasion, he actually came over to London and addressed a great meeting called by anarchist-pacifists who were all strongly in favor of the reduction of the British fleet. That fleet which, as Bebel himself put it, was the only counterbalance in Europe for Germany herself against Prussian militarism and Junkerdom, Jaurès spoke of with regret as a provocation to war. Germany could, in fact, always rely in all countries upon a large number of perfectly honest pro-Germans, and a lesser proportion who had purely financial considerations in view, to oppose any policy which was directed against the spread of German domination. This was the mania of anarchist-pacifism and anti-patriotism which Clemenceau, both in and out of office, did his utmost to expose and resist. Honesty of purpose could be no excuse whatever for fatuity of action.

Clemenceau, therefore, from the moment when he

gave up the Premiership, lost no chance of inculcating the need for vigorous preparation. France must be ready to meet a German assault by land and by sea. When the time came she was not ready on either element, and without the help in finance, in munitions, in clothing, and by arms, on land and on the ocean, at once given by England—whom Clemenceau always upheld as the friend of the Republic—France would have been overrun and crushed before she could possibly have obtained aid from elsewhere. In spite of the Franco-German agreement of 1909, the danger of such an attack in 1911 was very great: so much so that war was then commonly expected, and was only averted because Germany thought she would be in a more commanding position to carry out her predetermined policy three or four years later. The Franco-German Convention relating to Morocco, of November 4th, 1911, after the Agadir difficulty, was no better than a pretense. It was not intended, in good faith, to ensure a permanent peace, so far as Germany was concerned. This Clemenceau felt sure of, though the treaty was by no means unfavorable to France. He was ready to make all sacrifices, however mortifying, provided only a genuine treaty of peace and understanding between the two peoples could be secured. But this must not be done blindly. It must be an integral part of a serious policy.

Therefore, speaking in the Senate on the 12th February, 1912, in opposition to the treaty with Germany about Morocco, he went on: "We shall make every effort to give fresh proofs of our goodwill—we have given enough and to spare already during the past forty years—in order that the consequences of this treaty may fructify under conditions worthy of the dignity of the two peoples; but we must know what the other party to the treaty is about, what are his intentions, what he thinks, says, proposes to do, and what signs of goodwill *he* likewise has vouchsafed. That is the question we must have the courage to ask ourselves. This question I deal with at my own risk and peril, without being concerned as to what I have to say, because I have at heart no bad feeling, no hatred, to use the right word, towards the German people. I want no provocation; firmly resolved as I am to do nothing to sacrifice a vestige, however trifling, of our capacity to win if attacked, I am equally convinced that peace is not only desirable but necessary for the development of French ideas in the domain of civilization. . . . The German people won two great victories which changed the equilibrium of Europe, in 1866 and in 1870. . . . *We then knew, we had the actual proof in our hands, that if the enemy had occupied Paris the capital of France would have been reduced to ashes.* Prince Bismarck, in reply to the expostulations of Jules Favre, declared that the German troops must enter at one of the gates, 'because I do not wish, when I get home, that a man who has lost a leg or an arm should be able to say to his comrades, pointing to me: That fellow you see there is the man who prevented me from entering Paris.' When Jules Favre said that the German Army had glory enough without that, M. Bismarck retorted, 'Glory! we don't use that word.' The German, so far as I can judge of him, is above all the worshiper of force, and rarely misses an opportunity of saying so; but where he differs from the Latin is that his first thought is to make use of this force. As the vast economic development of the Empire is a perpetual temptation in this respect, he wants the French to understand that behind every German trader there stands an army of five millions of men. That is at the bottom of the whole thing." Moreover, he continued, having pocketed a fine indemnity last time, Germany is greedy for a much bigger one now. "Even quite lately the German Press has never wearied of proclaiming that France shall pay out of her milliards the cost of building the new German fleet. That frame of mind of Germany, that is the truth which clearly appears in your treaty: Germany thinks first and foremost of using to advantage her glory and her force.

"But this is not all. She has conquered her unity by force, by iron, by blood; she has so fervently yearned for this unity—nothing more natural—that now she wants to apply it; she wishes to spread her surplus population over the world. She finds herself compelled, therefore, by a fatality from which she cannot escape, to exercise pressure upon her neighbors which will compel them to give her the economic outlets she needs. . . . There is always land for an owner who wishes to round off his estate. There are always nations to be attacked by a warrior nation which would conquer other peoples. I am not here for the purpose of criticizing the German people, I am trying to describe their state of mind towards us. . . .

"And now what of us, the French people? The people of France are a people of idealism, of criticism, of indiscipline, of wars, of revolutions. Our character is ill adapted for continuous action; doubtless the French people have magnificent impulses, but, as the poet says, their height has ever been measured by the depth of their fall."

After a survey of "the terrible year" and its results,

the orator recounts what difficult work it was that Frenchmen had to carry out after the collapse. It was not only that they had to change their Government, but this Government must be taught how to govern itself.

"That has created a hard situation for us. We are absorbed in this great task. We hope to bring it to a successful conclusion. The intervention of public opinion to-day in its own affairs, calmly, soberly, without a word of braggadocio, that is one of the best signs that France has yet given.

"The work we have done must be judged not by what we see but by the ideas, the spirit that we have breathed into the heart of all French citizens."

After giving conclusive proof that in 1875, in the Schnäbele affair, as well as at Tangier, Morocco and Casablanca, Germany's policy had been to wound, weaken and irritate France, Clemenceau wound up as follows:

"In all good faith we desire peace, we are eager for peace because we need it in order to build up our country. But if war is forced upon us we shall be there! The difficulty between Germany and ourselves is this: Germany believes the logical consequence of her victory is domination. We do not believe that the logical consequence of our defeat is vassalage. We are peaceful but we are not subjugated. We do not countersign the decree of abdication and downfall issued by our neighbors. We come of a great history and we mean to continue to be worthy of it. The dead have created the living: the living will remain faithful to the dead."

This great speech was prophetic. Clemenceau knew what were the real intentions of Germany. It was this fact that made him so bitter against all who, honest, patriotic and self-sacrificing as they might be, were in favor of weakening France in the hour of her greatest danger. His warning against the financiers who were so solicitous that foreign policy should be guided by manipulators of loans, interest and discounts was also specially appropriate at a time when German influence was becoming dominant in many of the banks and pecuniary coteries of Paris. Such warnings were also timely in view of the strange hallucinations—or worse—which then dominated English politicians.

For it was in this same year that Lord Haldane, having reduced the English artillery, full of sublime confidence in the rulers of Germany, returned from Berlin to tell us through Mr. Asquith and Viscount Grey that never were the relations between Germany and England better! It was in this same year, too, that Mr. Lloyd George and the whole Radical Party were convinced that Great Britain might safely reduce her armaments on land and on sea, and the Unionists themselves scarcely dared to take up the challenge. It was in this same year, again, that nearly all the leaders of the Labor Party convinced themselves that the Germans had the best of good feeling towards France and England. Having been most artistically and hospitably "put through" in the Fatherland, they returned to England brimful of zeal against all who, knowing Germany and Germans well for some fifty years, could not take the asseverations of the Kaiser, or of his trusted friend Lord Haldane, at their face value: a value which this legal nobleman admitted a few years later he knew at the time to be wholly illusory and not at all in accordance with what he then declared to be the truth.

Clemenceau did not condescend to such shameless falsification. Whatever mistakes he made, from the Socialist and anti-Imperialist point of view, in matters of domestic importance or concerning Morocco, where the danger of France from the other side of the frontier had to be considered, whether in office or out of it, he treated his countrymen with the utmost frankness.

So time passed on. The preparations of Germany were getting more and more complete. The influence of the pan-German Junkers and their flamboyant young Crown Prince was becoming so powerful that the Kaiser felt his hand being forced before success in "the great design" appeared quite so certain as he would like it to be. The German army was largely increased, powerful war-vessels were being added to the navy. A policy was being pursued which roused fears of aggression. All through 1913 and the first months of 1914 Clemenceau in his new paper, *L'Homme Libre,* continued day after day his warnings and his injunctions to all Frenchmen. He had no mercy for those who unceasingly preached fraternity and disarmament for France when Germany, more powerful and increasingly more populous, was arming to the teeth.

"Such fraternity," he said, at the unveiling of Scheurer-Kestner's statue, "is of the Cain and Abel kind. Against the armed peace and armed fraternity with which Germany is threatening us nothing short of the most perfect military education and military organization can be of any avail. All Europe knows, and Germany herself has no doubt whatever, that we are solely on the defensive. Her fury for the leadership of Europe decrees for her a policy of extermination against France. Therefore prepare, prepare, prepare. Here you see 870,000 men in the active army of Germany on a peace footing, better trained, better equipped, better organized than ours, as opposed to 480,000 Frenchmen on our side. Doesn't that convince you? And Alsace-Lorraine at the mercy of such creatures as Schadt and Förstner? Observe, Germany has great projects in all parts of the world. It would be childish for us to complain. What is intolerable is her pretension to keep Europe in perpetual terror of a general war, instead of general international discussion of her claims. Every Frenchman must remember that, if Germany's increasing armaments do impel her to war, the loss of the conflict would mean for us the subjugation of our race, nay, even the termination of our history. Meanwhile, with Alsace-Lorraine before me and the statue of Scheurer-Kestner now unveiled, I claim for us the right never to forget. To be or not to be, that is for us the question of the hour. Gambetta, after Sedan, called upon all Frenchmen in their day of deepest depression to rise to the level of their duty. He consecrated once again Republicans as the party of patriotic pride. France must live. Live we will!"

Unfortunately, one of the chief reasons why France was unready to meet the onrush of the modern Huns was that the Socialists were all bemused with their own fatuous notion that the German Social-Democracy could stop the war. Instead, therefore, of investigating the truth of Clemenceau's statements, they merely denounced him as a chauvinist and an enemy of the people, and twaddled on about a general strike on both sides of the Rhine. As an old Socialist myself, who, as a member of the International Socialist Bureau, had discussed the whole question at length with Liebknecht, Bebel, Singer, Kautsky and others, I knew that, as they themselves explained to me, there was little or no hope of anything

CLEMENCEAU AND GERMANY 275

of the sort being done when war was once declared. I viewed this whole propaganda, therefore, with grave alarm, and Bebel himself warned the French that the Social-Democrats would march with the rest. If an opportunity came something might be done, but—— Since then the old leaders had died and the new chiefs, as we all see now, were Imperialists to a man. Thus Clemenceau's prognostications and warnings were only too completely justified. Prince Lichnowsky's revelations conclusively prove this, and the German Social-Democrats have been at pains to confirm it. On March 11th, 1914, Clemenceau stated precisely what they would do.

How anxious, how eager, the French were at the critical moment to avoid even the slightest cause of offense is shown by the fact that all their troops were withdrawn fully eight miles back along the German frontier, a portion of French territory which the Germans made haste to seize. Even before this, every effort was made to provoke the French troops by petty raids across the frontier, and at last the Germans declared that the French had sent aeroplanes to drop bombs on Nuremberg—a statement which the Germans themselves now admit to have been a pure fabrication. But the facts of the invasion of Belgium and France are too well known to call for recital here.

Clemenceau did what might have been expected of him. He appealed to all Frenchmen of every shade of opinion to sink all minor differences in one solid combination for the defense of the country. Day after day this powerful journalist and orator labored to encourage his countrymen and to denounce unceasingly all who, honestly or dishonestly, stood in the way of the vigorous and successful prosecution of the war which should free France for ever from yet other attempts by Germany to destroy her as an independent nation. The memory of the dark days of 1870 was obliterated by the horrors of 1914 onwards. In good and bad fortune the Radical leader kept the same resolute attitude and used the like stirring language. *L'Homme Libre,* defaced and then suppressed by the Censor, was succeeded by *L'Homme Enchaîné.* Ever the same policy of relentless warfare against the enemy at the front and the traitors at the rear was steadily pursued. Ministry might come, Ministry might go, but still Clemenceau was at his post, save when illness compelled him to quit his work for a short time.

Nor did he waver in his views as to the general strategy to be pursued. Without making any pretense to military knowledge, but well advised by experts on military affairs, and firmly convinced that whatever success Germany might achieve elsewhere she would never be satisfied unless France was crushed, he persistently opposed diversion of strength from the Western front. *There* this terrific struggle for world-domination would eventually be decided. The civilization of the West must be subdued to German culture, France and England must be brought under German control, before the great program of Eastern expansion for the Teutonic Empire could be entered upon with the certainty of success. These were the opinions he held as to Germany's real objects.

Therefore, in opposition to the views of important personages in Great Britain and in Allied countries, Clemenceau withstood any frittering away of force on tempting adventures, away from the main field of warfare. This not because he confined himself to the narrow program of freeing France from the invaders, but because the waste of troops on wild-cat enterprises weakened the general strength of the Allies at the crucial point of the whole struggle. In that decision his judgment was at one with the ablest British strategists, and the event has shown that he did not underrate the importance of the warfare on the Western front. There alone, especially after the collapse of Russia, was it possible to deliver a crushing blow at the German power. There alone could all the forces of the Allies of the West be effectively concentrated for the final blow.

CHAPTER XVIII

THE GREAT WAR

THE events of the great war, from 1914 onwards, are too recent and too deeply graven on all our minds to call for lengthy recital or criticism. What many if not most people believed to be outside the limits of calculation occurred. The German armies commenced their campaign by outraging the neutrality of Belgium, which, in 1870, even Bismarck had respected. In a few days they crashed down the great Belgian fortresses, which capable experts had calculated would check the Teutonic advance for at least a month, with howitzers specially constructed and tested for that purpose; soon they exhausted the resources of barbarism in torturing, butchering and shooting down unarmed men, women and children whose country they had solemnly sworn to safeguard; and they devastated and destroyed homes, beautiful buildings, and great libraries, which even a Turcoman horde might have spared, and extorted tremendous ransom and blood-money from the defenseless inhabitants.

That accomplished, this torrent of ruffianism and infamy poured in upon France with almost irresistible fury. The horrors of 1870-71 were far outdone. The defeats of Mons, Charleroi and Metz, the impossibility that their opponents should resist such overwhelming odds, made the Germans believe that for the second time in half a century they would force Paris to surrender. Then they were prepared to wreak upon the great city, the social capital of Europe, full vengeance of destruction.

It is not easy, even for those who remember what occurred in the terrible year of the downfall of the Second Empire and the prostration of the French Republic before the German invaders, to imagine what were the feelings of all Frenchmen who went through that period of martyrdom for their country when they saw a still worse storm of brutality and hatred breaking out upon them—when, too, more rapidly than before, Amiens was in danger and Paris seriously threatened. Clemenceau, with his devotion to France and almost worship of the city where he had spent his whole manhood, was more hardly hit than perhaps any of his countrymen. He had experienced the horrors of the former invasion; and though, when France was at its lowest, he never despaired of the Republic, no ordinary man of seventy-three could possess the resource and resilience of a man of thirty.

Yet Clemenceau showed no loss of vigor compared with his former self. No Englishman has ever undergone what he underwent at that period. Undoubtedly, when the news came to us of the great retreat of August, 1914, our heartfelt sympathy went out to our own men. We were all likewise full of admiration for our French comrades who still held the Franco-British line unbroken. But at least our hearths and homes were kept in safety for us—the raids of aircraft excepted—by the magnificent courage of our sailors in the North Sea and our soldiers who freely gave their lives to protect us from the enemy. If we would fully appreciate what was happening to France and Belgium, in spite of all their efforts, we must imagine the county of Durham completely occupied by the German hordes, Yorkshire overrun and the chance of saving London from the enemy dependent upon the result of a battle to be fought in the neighborhood of Cambridge. It would be well if we could display at such a crisis in England the same cool courage that the Parisians did; if we had generals at our disposal such as Joffre and Foch and Gallieni; and statesmen in reserve such as Clemenceau. That was how things looked prior to the first battle of the Marne, which checked the early flood of German invasion and removed for the time being the necessity for retiring from Amiens and Epernay and moving the seat of government from Paris.

During the whole of this trying period Clemenceau never lost heart for a moment, nor his head either; and day after day in his journal he surveyed the whole situation without fear, devoid of illusion, yet confident always that France and her Allies could not be beaten to their knees. When things looked worst and Paris was being drained of her population by order, in preparation for a siege, and when the Government was about to be removed to Bordeaux, this is how Clemenceau wrote, recalling the past to cheer his countrymen in the present:

"The seat of government at Bordeaux is a new phase of the war which must follow its course: a renewal of the war in the Provinces as in the days of the Gambettas, of the Freycinets. The same struggle against the same German invasion, with the capital of France reduced to the simple condition of a fortress, with France herself—provincial France, as we say—taking in hand her own defense outside the traditional lines of political and administrative concentration in which she has lived.

"How men and times have changed! . . . And now after full four-and-forty years I find myself again at Bordeaux, before the theater I had not seen since 1871, looking for men who had undergone the misery of survival and failing to find them. Who now remembers that Jules Simon on his arrival had in his pocket an order for the arrest of Gambetta? In the Provinces, as in Paris, foreign war and civil war were being carried on. I only recall these terrible memories of past dissensions to enhance the value of the magnificent consolation that uplifts our hearts at the spectacle of the truly fraternal union of all the Frenchmen of to-day. Gambetta maintained the war against invasion in the midst of the most cruel attacks of a merciless opposition. Compare this with the present attitude of all parties in the presence of a Government from which all only demand that every means should be used with the maximum of efficiency." Nor does the writer hesitate even at this moment of trial to criticize the shortcomings of his countrymen. As opposed to the persistent preparations of Germany, Frenchmen, he says, have been too careless, too light-hearted, too apt to rely upon the inspiration and enthusiasm of the moment to repair their neglect, "while an implacable enemy was sharpening his sword against us with unwearying zeal." And this had been proved to be the truth years before; while so lately as November 22nd, 1913, the French Ambassador in Berlin, M. Jules Cambon, had solemnly warned M. Pichon, then as now French Minister for Foreign Affairs, "For some time past hostility against us is more marked, and the Emperor has ceased to be a partisan of peace."

The man who used his pen to tell Frenchmen disagreeable truths in this wise and followed them up by giving chapter and verse from the French Yellow Book, with the text of the threatening conversations of the Emperor and General von Moltke with the King of the Belgians, may be granted the credit of entirely disregarding his own political interests, at least.

So also when the Anglo-French forces had won the great seven days' battle on the Marne, Clemenceau at once uttered a note of warning against undue confidence and excessive elation. "Let us be very careful not to believe that we can reckon upon an uninterrupted series of successes up to the final destruction of the aggressor. The curtain falls on the horrible scenes of foreign invasion in Belgium and France. A mortal blow has been inflicted upon the invincible Kaiser who had never fought a battle. . . . But it would be sheer madness to imagine that we have nearly finished with an enemy who will shortly obtain fresh forces, vast forces even, from his uninvaded territory. A great part of his military resources are still untouched. Automatic discipline will soon reassert itself. The struggle will last very long yet and be full of unforeseen dangers. The stake is too heavy for the German Empire to decide suddenly to give up the game. Remember your mistakes of the past, rejoice soberly in your victory of the present, make ready now for still heavier trials in the future." Such was the counsel of Clemenceau to Frenchmen on September 15th, 1914. Above all, "Leave nothing you can help to chance. Our military leaders have just victoriously undergone racking anxieties. It is for us to show our confidence in them by giving them credit for the patience and firmness which they will desperately need."

That is the tone throughout. But here and there in *L'Homme Enchaîné* we find Clemenceau the controversialist in a lighter but not less telling style. I give an extract from his scathing attack on the Danish littérateur, M. Brandès, in the original:—

"Oui, retenez-le, lecteur, la crainte de M. Brandès dans les circonstances actuelles est que l'Allemagne puisse être humiliée! Le Danemark a été humilié par le *peuple de seigneurs* qu'est la race allemande. La France aussi, je crois, et la Belgique même; peut-être Brandès le reconnaitra-t-il. Il n'a pas protesté. Il refuse même de s'expliquer a cet égard, alléguant que son silence (assez prolixe) est d'or—d'un or qui ne résisterait pas à la pierre de touche. Mais sa crainte suprême est que les machinateurs du plus grand attentat contre la civilisation, contre l'indépendance des peuples, contre la dignité de l'espèce humaine, les auteurs des épouvantables forfaits dont saignent encore la Belgique et la France n'éprouvent une *humiliation*." * Brandès among the neutrals is of the same type as Romain Rolland and Bertrand Russell among the belligerents. All their sympathies are reserved for the criminals. And there are others, who are actually eager to embrace the murderers as their "German friends"!

But during the whole of the struggle, even when the

* "Yes, bear in mind, reader, Monsieur Brandès's fear under existing conditions is that Germany may be humiliated. Denmark has been humiliated by the people of Supermen who constitute the German race. France, also, I take it, and even Belgium: perhaps Brandès himself will admit that. He has not protested. He even refuses to explain himself on this point, declaring that his silence (prolix enough) is golden— that sort of gold which won't stand the touchstone. But his overmastering dread is that the organizers of the greatest crime against civilization, against the independence of the peoples, against the dignity of the human species, the authors of the appalling atrocities from which Belgium and France are still bleeding, may not themselves undergo *humiliation*."

military situation looked most desperate for the future of his country, Clemenceau never lost confidence. His faith in France and her steadfast ally Great Britain never wavered. That was a great service he then rendered to France and civilization. But he did more. At a time when on the other side of the Channel, as in Great Britain, in Italy, and in Russia, the national spirit was clouded by deep suspicion of enemy influence, bribery and corruption in high places, and almost criminal weakness, when strength and determination were essential to success, Clemenceau did not hesitate to denounce treachery where he believed it to exist. Nothing like his courage in this respect has, unfortunately, been shown by statesmen in any other of the Allied countries. The fact that fomenters of reaction were, for their own ends, engaged on the like task of exposing the men who were unworthy of the Republic did not deter him, bitterly opposed as he was to the Royalist clique of which M. Léon Daudet was the chief spokesman, from demanding thorough investigation and the punishment of traitors, if traitors there were, in their midst. The time has not yet come to estimate the full value of the work he thus did, or the dangers from which by his frankness he saved the Republic.

But already we can form a judgment of the perils which surrounded France in 1917. The feeling of depression and distrust was growing. The organization of the forces of the Allies was inferior to that of the enemy. The effect of the collapse of Russia was becoming more serious each day. Great Britain, which had rendered France quite invaluable aid in all departments, had accepted Mr. Lloyd George's personal strategy, which consisted in breaking through to the Rhine frontier by way of Jerusalem and Jericho, owing to the apparent hopelessness of a favorable decision on the West front. The French Government itself, alarmed at the enormous sacrifices France was making in every way, discouraged at the progress of the defeatist movement which weakened the position of Socialists in the Cabinet, and alarmed at the manner in which German agents and German spies, whom they were afraid to arrest, pervaded almost every department—the French Government, itself shaken daily by attacks from the Right and from the Left, felt incapable of dealing with the situation as a whole. There was for a moment a sensation in Paris not far removed from despair.

At this juncture a cry arose for Clemenceau. For many years he had predicted the German attack. For more than a full generation he had adjured his fellow-Frenchmen to prepare vigorously for the defense of *la Patrie*. That he feared nobody all were well aware. Of his patriotism there was no doubt. To-day, as more than forty years before, he never despaired of the Republic. Old as he was, whatever his defects of temper, whatever his shortcomings in other respects, the one man for such a crisis was Georges Clemenceau. Office was thus forced upon him, and, as he stated, he accepted power strongly against his will. At seventy-six, and approaching seventy-seven, not the most ambitious politician would be eager to take upon himself the responsibility of coping with such difficulties as Clemenceau was called upon to face. It was hard enough to undertake as Minister of War the work of that exhausting department.

But still more trying was the necessity imposed upon him of dealing with the traitors of various degree who had been trading upon the lives and sacrifices of the men at the front. Probably no other French statesman would have dared to enter upon this dangerous and difficult task. The suspected men were highly placed, both politically and financially. They were surrounded by influential cliques and coteries, in Parliament and in the Press, to whom it was almost a matter of life and death to prevent disclosures which would inevitably be made, if the various cases were brought into court. It was even doubtful whether he would get the support of the Assembly, the Senate, or the Presidents of Council who preceded him, if he decided to push things to extremity, as, in view of his own criticisms and denunciations, he was bound to do. Should such misfortune occur or should the malefactors be indicted and acquitted, all that Clemenceau had been saying against them would turn to the advantage of the domestic enemy. It was a great risk to run.

There was also another obstacle in the way of Clemenceau's acceptance of the Premiership. The relations between himself and M. Poincaré, the President of the Republic, had been anything but good. M. Clemenceau had energetically championed the claim of M. Pams for the Presidency. M. Pams had been, in fact, M. Clemenceau's candidate, as MM. Sadi-Carnot, Loubet and Fallières had been before him. This time he did not win. The fight was fierce, the personal animosity between the parties very keen, and M. Poincaré's victory was asserted to have been achieved by intrigue of a doubtful character. The war had called a truce to individual rancor and the *union sacrée* was supposed to inspire all hearts. Still it was by no means certain that trouble would not come from that quarter. A President of Council with a hostile President of the Republic over against him must find the difficulty of the post at such a time immensely increased.

Then there were the Socialists to consider. True, they had taken office in the Cabinet of M. Briand, whose policy towards strikers of anarchist methods had been even more stern than that of M. Clemenceau. But they regarded Clemenceau as an unforgivable enemy. The calling in of the military at Courrières, at Narbonne, Montpellier and St. Béziers had never been forgotten. Clemenceau for them was the Tiger crossed with the Kalmuck. It was far more important, the French Socialists apparently thought, to hamper Clemenceau, and prevent him from forming an administration, than it was to beat the German armies and clear France of the Boches. Such, at any rate, was the opinion of a minority which afterwards became the majority of the party. Therefore, even Socialists who thoroughly sympathized with Clemenceau in his policy towards Germany, and had previously taken part in a Cabinet pledged to carry on the war *"jusqu'au bout,"* would have nothing to do with a Clemenceau Administration. The upshot of these fatuous, anti-patriotic and anti-Socialist tactics on their part will be seen later. But the knowledge that the Socialists as a whole would give him at best a lukewarm support, and at worst would vigorously oppose him, was not an encouraging factor in the general calculation of what might occur.

Neither could high finance be relied upon. The great bankers, great brokers, and great money institutions as a whole were heartily sick of the war. They wanted peace with Germany on almost any terms, if only they could get back to business and begin to recoup their losses during more than three years of war. Nor, apart from downright treachery of which he held positive proof, could the proposed new Premier close his eyes to the fact that German influence had so subtly and thoroughly pervaded the French money market that many Frenchmen were still looking at the economic problems of France through spectacles made and tinted in Germany.

There was consequently a combination possible which might drive Clemenceau headlong out of office at any moment, if he entered upon his second attempt to control French affairs at such a desperately critical stage of the war.

But the formidable old Radical leader did not hesitate. Skeptic as he might be in all else, one entity he did believe in: the unshakable greatness of France: one Frenchman he could rely upon—himself.

CHAPTER XIX

THE ENEMY WITHIN

DURING the whole of the war, as for many years before the Germans began their great campaign of aggression, every country with which the Fatherland might in any way be concerned was permeated with German agents and German spies. Great Britain was one of the nations specially favored in this respect. The ramifications of their systematic interpenetration of the social, political, financial, commercial and even journalistic departments of our public life have never yet been fully exposed; nor, certainly, have the very important personages who conducted this sinister propaganda been dealt with. Even when the Defense of the Realm Act is ended and the Censorship is abrogated, it is doubtful if the full truth will ever be generally known, so powerful are the influences directly interested in its suppression.

In the United States of America, where similar work was done upon an enormous scale and at vast expense, under circumstances still more favorable to success than in this island, the American Government acted with a decision and a vigor that are not yet understood. Even so, the amount of mischief done was very great, and, for the first two years of the war at least, the German efforts were largely successful. That a duly accredited Ambassador to a friendly power should have been at the head of this vast conspiracy in America, as Count Bernstorff unquestionably was, introduces a new and most dangerous precedent into the comity of international relations. Italy, in like manner, suffered very seriously from German intrigues. The history of the carefully organized disaster upon the Isonzo has yet to be written. That it was the result of well-arranged collaboration between clerical organizers of treachery, inspired by Austria, German agents, with unlimited financial backing, who had sympathizers in high place, and honest and dishonest fanatics of the pacifist persuasion, does not admit of question. Certain it is that in this one case alone German underground machinations were responsible for the crushing defeat of an army of 500,000 men, holding a position where 50,000 good troops could have held a million at bay.*

But if Great Britain, the United States, and Italy were thus honeycombed with secret service agents from Germany, the nation which the Kaiser, his Chief of Staff and the Junkers were most anxious to crush down beyond the possibility of recovery was still more imperiled by astute German infiltration. Up to the crisis of Agadir in 1911, French finance was, to an ever increasing extent, manipulated by German Jews, who made it their special business to become more Parisian than the Parisians themselves. They were consequently regarded with favor by people whose patriotism was beyond question. Scarcely a great French finance institution but had close relations in some form with Germans, whose continuous attention to business and excellent general information rendered them valuable coadjutors for the French, who, as a rule, are not very exactly informed on foreign matters. Very few saw any danger in this. It seemed, indeed, a natural

* I happen to know the configuration of this district well, having walked all over it in 1866, after I went up into the Tyrol with Garibaldi.

result of the great growth of German trade, as well as of the position which Germans had acquired as capable managers of the growing French factory industry in the North-Eastern provinces.

This latter point is of importance. So long as any industry remains in the old form, where individual skill, meticulous attention to detail, and close observance of quality are the rule, the French are second to none in their methods. But when the next stage is reached, and machine production reigns on a very large scale, with its concomitant standardization of output, then the French seem to fail for lack of the thorough organizing faculty of the German or the American. Hence in many directions the highly educated, methodical, progressive foreigner from across the frontier had begun to take the place of the more conservative Frenchman. This process could be observed in the department of motor-cars, where the French, who were undoubtedly the pioneers, had begun to fall behind upon the world market in the time just anterior to the war. Not only the Americans, but the Germans, and even Italy, showed more capacity to gauge the necessities of the coming period than France in their output of cars.

But, in addition to this, Frenchmen, the most thrifty people in the world, are disinclined to use their savings in the development of their own country. In literature, in science, in art, they display great faculties of initiative. In the matter of investment they prefer to rely upon others. Even the underground railways of their metropolis were started by a foreigner: the French investors only coming in to buy the debentures of companies which they might just as well have started themselves. They complained that the Germans were making vast profits out of "their own" iron mines of Lorraine which had been taken from France in an undeveloped state in 1871; yet they failed to exploit the still richer deposits in Briey, of which the Germans were so envious that the desire to possess them was one of the minor causes of the war. Similar instances of neglected opportunities could be pointed out in many districts.

This indifference of the thrifty French investors to the possibility of enriching their own country by the use at home of the money capital obtained from their own savings, and the profits derived from visitors, astonished lookers-on. Clemenceau denounced the folly of financial wars of conquest in semi-civilized countries when France needed her own resources for the improvement of her own soil and what underlay it, as well as to make adequate preparation for war. But the loans to foreign nations and foreign banks were economically as prejudicial to her real interests as the injurious colonial policy. That was proved only too clearly, even in the field of military preparation when, in August and September, 1914, tens of thousands of men, unsupplied with clothing and equipment, were to be seen in and around Paris. England had to provide them with what they required.

In such a state of affairs, where neglect of consideration as to the purposes of loans was the rule, so long as the interest seemed quite secure, German banks could and did act with great advantage. They borrowed French savings at a low rate and employed them for profitable objects, or for their own more complete war preparations on economical terms. After the shock of Agadir, when war at one period seemed certain, the French called in most of their loans and thenceforward were rather more cautious. But, in the meantime, and even afterwards,

France's savings had been used to strengthen her bitterest enemy. And this was the end the Germans kept constantly in view when they borrowed. France, in fact, built up German credit against herself, at the same time that Germany was able to estimate exactly the economic power of her destined victim, and to investigate, without appearing to do so, the weak points in French preparation for defense. The German banks and their French friends played together the same game, in a different way as the Deutsche Bank and the Dresdner Bank in London and the Banca Commerciale in Italy. The whole formed part of the vast economic octopus scheme, in finance and in industry, which went hand in hand with the co-ordination of military effort destined for attack.

It is easy to discern how all this peaceful financial manipulation played into the hands of the German Government and fostered German influence in Paris and in France. There was nothing which could be reasonably objected to, under the conditions of to-day, if Holland, or Belgium, had been the nation concerned. But with Germany it was quite different.

Not only was French money being used on German account, but, under cover of quite legitimate finance and apparently genuine newspaper enterprise, most nefarious schemes were hatched in peace whose full utility to the enemy would only be disclosed in war. Taking no account even of the actual operations of bribery, which we now know were carried on upon a very large scale, everybody who was directly or indirectly interested in the various forms of parasitical Franco-German finance had personally excellent reasons for pooh-poohing distrust of the friendly nation on the other side of the frontier. Thus the most pressing warnings addressed to the French Government might be rendered almost useless—as, in fact, they were—by influence brought to bear from quarters that were pecuniarily above suspicion. An atmosphere favorable to German propaganda was created which covered up and favored the sinister plans of men and women who were actually in German pay. This went on long before the war, and was continued in still more dangerous shape after the war had begun.

Then there were the honest pacifists, who regarded all war, even defensive war, as disastrous to the workers. Whether Germany won or France won in any conflict, the capitalists and the capitalists alone were the real enemy. Two such different men as Edouard Vaillant and Gustave Hervé held this opinion; and both at great international Socialist congresses declared that every effort should be made to prevent France from coming to an actual struggle with Germany, no matter what the provocation might be. When, however, they saw what the policy of the Kaiser and his Junker militarists really meant they changed their minds. So, in the early days of the war, did the majority of French Socialists; and several of their principal men, including Jules Guesde, the leader of the Marxists, and Albert Thomas, joined M. Briand's Cabinet.

But there was always an active section left which in all good faith stood to their views that under the capitalist system nothing could justify the workers of one country in killing the workers of another. They had no interest in their own nation which was worth defending in the field. The past of France was for them a record of class oppression, the present of France the continuance of chattel slavery in disguise, the future of France no better than the permanence of penal servitude for life as wage-slaves to the bourgeoisie. German domination could be no worse for them than the economic tyranny of their own capitalist countrymen.

This form of social fanaticism now exists in every European nation. It is as bitter and, given the opportunity, as unscrupulous and cruel as any form of religious intolerance that ever exercised control. Economic theory entirely obscures history and facts with such men. Not even the awful horrors of the German invasion, horrors quite unprecedented in modern warfare and systematically practiced in order to engender terror, and destroy the means of creating wealth, could convert Socialists of this school. As a Socialist I understand their fanaticism, though I despise their judgment. Capitalism under the control of home employers and financiers is bad, but it can be controlled by educated workers. Capitalism in victorious alliance with foreign Junkerdom would have made France uninhabitable for Frenchmen, and would have thrown back democratic Socialism for at least two generations throughout Europe.

Nevertheless, this furious minority, in conjunction with Socialists of political intrigue, among whom Jean Longuet (son of Charles Longuet the member of the Commune and grandson of Karl Marx) was the leader, became eventually the majority, owing to the weakness of the heads of the patriotic section. This success laid the French Socialist Party open to the charge of being not only anti-patriotic but definitely pro-German. It led to the retirement of forty-one Deputies from the "unified" combination. The violent animosity of the main body to Clemenceau at the time when he was forced into office, and the refusal of Socialists to accept portfolios in his Cabinet, when the cause of the Allies was at its lowest point, from November, 1917, to July, 1918, looked to outsiders a miserable policy for the party, not to be explained by the devotion of its members to MM. Malvy and Caillaux.* Personal malevolence and political pusillanimity together were the imputations made against those who thus declined to serve France in her utmost need. Happily for Europe, their strength was not equal to their ill-will, and Clemenceau, after his first month of power, was able to treat them as a negligible quantity. So they remain to-day. A very great opportunity of serving the workers of their country has been missed: that the bitterest enemy of France and of freedom has not been greatly helped in her war for universal domination is no fault of theirs.

During the first three years and more of the war, however, a conspiracy was being conducted which, aided unfortunately by much of apathy and ineptitude on the part of successive French Governments, and supported unintentionally or intentionally by one of the leading statesmen of France, went near to wrecking the fortunes of the Republic. That this fateful plot failed to achieve the full success which the Germans anticipated from it is due

* Since the extreme pacifist and anti-nationalist section of Socialists captured the French Socialist Party a body of the French Socialist Deputies have constituted a group of their own in the Assembly. They number in all forty-one and they have a well-edited and well-written daily journal, *La France Libre,* which represents their views. Among their leading members are the Citizens Varenne De la Porte, Compère Morel, Albert Thomas and others. They are thoroughly sound Socialists in all domestic affairs, but they cannot accept the views of those who are now led by Jean Longuet and Marcel Cachin on questions affecting the independence and welfare of France as a nation. Their opinions are, in fact, much the same as those which have been so vigorously and successfully championed by the National Socialist Party in Great Britain. It seems a pity that none of their party have seen their way to accept the positions in the Cabinet offered by M. Clemenceau. The results of the General Election in Great Britain may give them encouragement to do so.

to Clemenceau. Sordid monetary sympathy with the enemy is difficult to forgive: Socialist fanaticism and Socialist intrigues which must tell to the disadvantage of the nation are hard to reconcile with common honesty; but downright infamous treachery, bribery, corruption, and wholesale attempts to organize defeat put all who are guilty of them outside the law. Yet matters had come to such a pass that all these various forms of treason to France, to the Allies, and to soldiers at the front could be carried on with impunity.

Though the guilty persons were well known and their German plots were scarcely concealed, none of the Ministers responsible for the public safety dared arrest them. Journals that were obviously published in the interest of the enemy were allowed to spread false information as they pleased, and to attack with vitriolic misrepresentation all statesmen and politicians who were honestly trying to serve France. Day after day this went on. Day after day, as the situation without grew more precarious, the chiefs of this criminal endeavor to bring France to ruin grew bolder in their well-paid treachery. The people of Paris and the soldiery in the trenches, whose minds also German agents strove to debauch with plausible lies, were becoming hopeless of justice being done. Ministry succeeded Ministry and still the traitors were treated with consideration by the Minister of the Interior, M. Malvy, and other men in high place.

Beyond question the man officially responsible for all this shameful laxity, at one of the most trying crises of the whole war, was M. Malvy, who enjoyed the whole-souled support of the Socialist Party, on account of creditable behavior towards the workers, altogether outside of questions arising from the war. But his conduct in regard to traitors and pro-Germans had become so weak as to be capable of the worst interpretation.

On July 24th, 1917, Clemenceau declared that he utterly distrusted M. Malvy. It was known even thus early that this Minister had shown deplorable incapacity in his dealings with men who are known to have been actual traitors. He had, in fact, decided not to arrest persons enumerated in what was called "List B," that is to say, men and women more than suspected of criminal intrigue against France. Had not Almereyda himself assured M. Malvy, as Minister of the Interior, that he and all other Anarchists and anti-patriotic agitators would really desist from their sinister proceedings? This was enough. Without taking any steps against them, or even obtaining any security for the fulfillment of this promise in the air, M. Malvy left these miscreants alone to do what they pleased. So things went on as before; though, as has since been proved, several of these active agitators for peace, disaffection and surrender were paid agents of the German Government.

When, therefore, a resolution of confidence in M. Ribot's Administration was proposed in the Senate, Clemenceau voted for the resolution, but made special exception in the case of M. Malvy, in whom he declared he had no confidence whatever. Later, Clemenceau boldly accused M. Ribot and his whole Administration of being themselves all responsible for the existence of the treacherous German *Bonnet Rouge* and Bolo conspiracy. Most unfortunately, notwithstanding the universal distrust thus awakened and spreading from Paris throughout France, Republican Ministers, who ought to have been the first to move to safeguard the interests of France and her Republic, against the dangerous plots of men known to be immersed in abominable dealings with the enemy, failed altogether in their duty. They left it to avowed Royalists and reactionaries to lead the attack upon persons guilty of these crimes. What, consequently, ought to have been done at once, legally and thoroughly, by men who had received political power by vote of the French people, and were trustees for the defense of the country, against the foreign enemy from without and the domestic enemy within, was left largely to be accomplished by M. Léon Daudet and M. Barrès.

These men made no secret of the fact that they were actuated by motives entirely antagonistic to the democratic policy of the Allies and hostile to the only form of government possible in France. This did not render their indictment less crushing when the facts were fully disclosed, but it certainly weakened the force of the attack. What is more, it gave a large and, later, apparently the largest section of the Socialist Party the excuse, which they were eager to grasp, for supporting M. Malvy, and more particularly their friend M. Joseph Caillaux, against what they were pleased to denounce as abominable detraction.

Newspapers to-day are credited, perhaps, with more political influence than they really possess. But it is clear that if nearly the whole of the important press of a country can be captured by a particular faction, and only such news is allowed to be published as suits the convenience of the Government in power, the people at large have no means of correcting the false impressions of events thus thrust upon them. That is an extreme case, which has, so far, been realized, in practice, in only one country. But the German agents who were so active in Paris were fully alive to the advantages of such a policy of purchase and manipulation of the press for their own ends. They made efforts to secure a control of the majority of the shares in some of the most influential journals of Paris. How far this process was surreptitiously carried will never be known: not far enough, certainly, to affect the tone of the organs they were anxious to manipulate.

But enough was done to show the great danger which would have resulted to the community, had a newspaper trust been successfully created on the scale contemplated, but fortunately never carried out, by the infamous Bolo Pasha and his associates. Their own journal, *Le Bonnet Rouge,* even when increased during the war from a weekly to a daily issue, was not by any means sufficient for their needs, although that traitorous sheet alone was able to do a great deal of mischief. But their control was extended to the *Journal,* a paper, prior to the war, of considerable circulation and influence. Their attempts to expand further were in full swing when, thanks to the work of MM. Léon Daudet and Barrès in the *Action Française,* and still more to that of their bitter opponent Clemenceau in *l'Homme Enchaîné* and in the Senate, the French Government was forced to arrest the proprietors of the *Bonnet Rouge* and put them on their trial as traitors. It was known that M. Caillaux and M. Paix-Séailles—the latter connected with M. Painlevé's Cabinet and the repository of anti-French confidences—had contributed considerable sums to the support of the incriminated paper.

When M. Almereyda, one of the most important persons connected with the *Bonnet Rouge* (to whose columns a leading Socialist was a contributor), died suddenly in prison, the editor of that journal telegraphed to M. Caillaux concerning the lamentable departure of "our friend." As these facts were accompanied by other revelations still more compromising, public opinion became greatly excited. There could be no doubt that the conspiracy was more than a mere anti-patriotic newspaper intrigue of financial origin, or an attempt of discredited politicians to float themselves back into office on the wave of discouragement and defeatism: it was an endeavor, supported throughout by German funds, to destroy French confidence in order to ensure French destruction. A complete exposure of the whole plot, in which M. Caillaux and Bolo Pasha were alleged to be the leading figures, was threatened in the course of the *Bonnet Rouge* trial. Eleven members of the Army Committee of the Senate were appointed to consider M. Caillaux's connection with M. Almereyda and the *Bonnet Rouge*.

M. Caillaux has been by far the most formidable advocate of a German peace from the first. That an ex-Premier of France should take up such a position would seem almost incredible, but that Signor Giolitti in Italy and Lord Lansdowne in England have pursued the same course in a less objectionable way. The political relations between Clemenceau and M. Caillaux in the years prior to the war had not been unfriendly. M. Caillaux had been Finance Minister in Clemenceau's Cabinet in 1907, and they had both worked together for M. Pams against M. Poincaré in the contest for the Presidency. But two more different personalities it would be difficult to find.

M. Caillaux is a financier of financiers. His whole career has been associated with the dexterous manipulation and acquisition of money in all its forms. Clemenceau never had anything to do with finance in his life, and wealth is the last thing anybody could accuse him of possessing. Clemenceau, though no sentimentalist, makes an exception in his view of life where Frenchmen, France and Paris are concerned. With Caillaux audacious cynicism in everything is the key-note of his character all through. Moreover, the one is very simple in his habits, and the other is devoted to ostentation and display. Caillaux's cynicism is as remarkable as that of Henry Labouchere, though more malignant. When he carried the Income Tax through the Assembly and was upbraided for having made himself the champion of such a measure, he claimed that, though he had obtained for his measure a majority in the Assembly, he had used such arguments as would destroy it in the country.

Whatever may be the truth of that story, it is certain that the result has been as predicted. So in the course of the Agadir affair. M. Caillaux, as Prime Minister during the whole of the proceedings, was reluctant, and perhaps rightly so, to assert the claims of France with vigor. He was, in fact, quite lukewarm on behalf of his country, the representatives of other nations doing more for France, it is said, than she, or her Premier, did for herself. No sooner, however, was the business settled than M. Caillaux, the judicious but unavowed anti-expansionist, claimed that he had secured Morocco for France! However this may be, M. Caillaux has always favored a close political and financial understanding with Germany, as by far the more advantageous policy for France, in opposition to a similar *entente* with England: a view which, of course, he was quite entitled to take and act upon, though its success in practice must have reduced France to the position of a mere satellite of the Fatherland. Before the war it was possibly a justifiable, though scarcely a far-seeing, policy.

The war itself rather strengthened than weakened his tendency in this direction. Having comfortably recovered from the unpleasing effect of the murder of M. Calmette of the *Figaro,* for which crime his wife was acquitted, he used all his influence, in and out of France, to bring about a peace with Germany, which could with difficulty be distinguished from complete surrender, as soon as possible. This while the German armies were in actual occupation of more than a fifth of his devastated country, that fifth being the richest part of France. His interviews with Signor Giolitti, a vehement partisan of Germany, and certain strange intrigues in Rome and elsewhere, could only be regarded as the more suspicious from the fact that he traveled with a passport made out in a fictitious name. Altogether M. Caillaux's proceedings at home and abroad, in Europe and in South America, gave the impression that he was pursuing a policy of his own which was diametrically opposed to the welfare of his countrymen.

Some who have watched closely M. Caillaux's career from his youth up are of opinion that the man is mad. But there is certainly method in his madness. Whatever the defects to which the high priests of international financial brotherhood may plead guilty, they never admit lunatics into their Teutono-Hebraic Holy of Holies. Access to the interior of that sanctuary is reserved for the very elect of the artists in pecuniary conveyance. But it is precisely within this innermost circle of glorified Mammon that M. Joseph Caillaux is most at home and most influential. And these people, so ensconced in their golden temple, were the ones most anxious to bring the war to an end, no matter what became of France. This, as has been well said, was a civil war for Jews; but for the Jews of the great international of Mammon it was civil war and hari-kari at one and the same time. So there was weeping and wail in Frankfurt-am-Main, there was wringing of hands in Berlin on the Spree, and the Parisian devotees of the golden calf were not less profuse in their lamentations.

As a matter of fact, international finance was, and is, the most pacifist of all the Internationals, and M. Joseph Caillaux as director of the *Société Générale,* a portion of the great *Banque de Paris et Pays Bas,* represented its view perfectly. But that he is not devoid of political as well as financial astuteness is apparent from the extraordinary success he has achieved in securing close intimacy and friendship with the French Socialists. This has assured him the support not only of Jean Lonquet and his friends, with whom he was specially bound up, but also of *L'Humanité,* with Renaudel, Sembat, Thomas and others connected with that useful journal. It has, indeed, been very difficult to understand the bitter hatred which the Socialists of France have manifested towards the thorough-going patriot Clemenceau, and their persistent championship of pro-Germans such as Caillaux and Malvy. But the dry-rot of pro-Germanic pacifism has infected a large proportion of the younger school of international Socialists in every country. With Socialism, as with commerce and finance, the German policy of unscrupulous penetration has been pursued with great success. Honest fanatics as well as self-seeking intriguers have fallen victims to their wiles. Caillaux was equally fortunate in capturing both sections. Even the rougher type of German agents, such as Bolo and Duval, were not without their friends in the Socialist camp.

The investigation of his conduct before the Army Committee of the Senate was, in effect, an informal trial of M. Caillaux, M. Malvy's case having already been remitted by the same body for definite adjudication by the High Court. Naturally, M. Caillaux and his friends strained every nerve, first to prevent Clemenceau from being forced into office by public opinion; and then, when his assumption of the Premiership became inevitable, to upset his Ministry while its members were scarcely warm in their seats. The French Socialist Party, unfortunately, aided M. Caillaux and his friends in their attacks, after having declined the Premier's offer of seats in his Cabinet. Shortly afterwards Clemenceau himself was summoned to appear as a witness before the Committee of the Senate on this serious indictment. It is difficult for us to imagine the sensation which this produced. Here was M. Caillaux, who had been Prime Minister of France only a few short years before, who had previously been Clemenceau's intimate colleague, openly charged with the despicable crime of trading France away to the enemy.

No wonder a great many thoroughly patriotic Frenchmen could not believe, even in the face of the evidence, that a statesman of M. Caillaux's ability, with a great future before him after the war, could be guilty of such actions as those which were imputed to him. But his old colleague who had just taken office was in possession of documents which threw an ugly shadow upon all M. Caillaux's recent proceedings. As usual Clemenceau went straight to the point. The Government had not furnished the members of the Committee with mere surmises or doubts cast upon the general conduct of the incriminated person. There were printed statements already at their disposal of the gravest character. With three notorious persons M. Caillaux had intimate connections. One of them, when arrested, had died suspiciously in prison; the two others were still under arrest upon most serious charges. If this were the case of a common citizen he would have been brought at once before a magistrate. The whole country was crying out for the truth in this Caillaux case as well as in the Malvy affair.

This happened soon after Clemenceau had accepted office. A month later, M. Caillaux being in the meantime protected against arrest by his position as deputy, Clemenceau repeated that if all the probabilities accumulated against Caillaux had been formulated against any private person his fate would have been practically decided already. "The Government has undertaken responsibilities. The Chamber must likewise shoulder responsibilities. If the Chamber refuses to sanction the prosecution of M. Caillaux, the Government will not remain in office."

M. Caillaux's admitted conferences with well-known defeatists in Italy were of such a nature that Baron Sonnino, the Italian Minister for Foreign Affairs, had himself informed the French Government that he was inclined to expel Caillaux forthwith. No doubt he would have done so, but for the fact that M. Caillaux had been, and might possibly still be again, an important personage in French and European affairs. Throughout, Clemenceau promised that the public should have the full truth. He kept his word. The delays in bringing M. Caillaux to a definite judgment have not been due to him. M. Caillaux's immunity as deputy was suspended. He was arrested and imprisoned on January 15th, 1918. Four days later came the partial disclosure of the documents found in his private safe in Florence.

That such papers should ever have been left by a man of M. Caillaux's intelligence where they might quite conceivably be attached, and that he should have carefully put in writing the names of men whom he hoped to use for the purpose of furthering a *coup d'état,* do unquestionably support the theory that he is subject to intermittent fits of madness. His extraordinary proceedings at Buenos Aires, where, according to the United States representative in the Argentine capital, he entered into a series of most compromising negotiations with the German von Luxburg, were no good evidence of the permanent sanity of this successful and experienced man of affairs. But "madness in great ones must not unwatched go." His object was avowed in that remote city: to make peace with Germany at any price, for the purpose of reviving international finance. All these statements coming in succession, and accompanied by the formulation of the cases against M. Malvy, Bolo Pasha, with Duval and others of the *Bonnet Rouge* clique, at length roused furious public indignation, which the actions of M. Humbert, the senator and owner of the *Journal,* the paper that Bolo had in effect bought, further inflamed. Who could be regarded as entirely free from treacherous designs, when such a crushing indictment as that officially formulated against Caillaux could be accepted as correct?—when a Minister of the Interior could be publicly charged with criminal weakness towards persons more than suspected of high treason of the most sordid type?—and when a man of Bolo Pasha's career and associations evidently exercised great influence, not to say authority?

The revelations at the trials of the accused persons,

and the ugly evidence submitted not only made matters look worse for M. Caillaux, but roused general amazement that such deadly intrigues should have been allowed to go so far under the very eyes of the authorities. The career of Bolo Pasha, the direct agent-in-chief of the main conspiracy, was well known. The men with whom he was on terms of close intimacy were suspected persons, long before any action was taken. The secret service department was well aware that he had huge sums of money at his disposal that were very, very far in excess of any that he could command from his private resources. The origin of his title of dishonor from the Khedive could not have escaped notice. Yet he, a born Frenchman, all whose begettings and belongings were a matter of record, pursued his shameless policy in the interest of Germany with apparent certainty of immunity from interference.

It was this very same certainty of immunity that made all but a few afraid to speak out. Bolo, in fact, was a privileged person, until there was a statesman at the head of affairs who not only did not fear to take the heavy responsibility of the arrest and imprisonment of M. Caillaux, but was also determined that the proceedings in the other cases already commenced should be pushed to their inevitable conclusion. "The unseen hand" in France, therefore, was no longer unseen. Yet so wide was the reach of the octopus tentacles, directed by underground agency, that even to this day not a few innocent, as well as guilty, people are in mortal fear lest disclosures may be made which will in some or other way implicate them. For the trial of M. Caillaux has yet to come.

The two really dramatic episodes in all this gradual exposure of infamy were the arrest and imprisonment of

M. Caillaux, upon the suspension of his privileges as deputy, and the public trial of Bolo Pasha. After what had happened since August, 1914, it seemed almost impossible that any Minister, however powerful he might be, would venture to go to the full extent of what was indispensably necessary with M. Caillaux. A man who had been Prime Minister of France, who in that capacity had gathered round him groups of politicians whose members looked to him to ensure their personal success in the future, was formidably entrenched both in the Senate and in the Assembly. To incur the personal enmity of such a capable statesman and such a master of intrigue as Joseph Caillaux was more than any of the previous Ministries had dared to risk. There were too many political reasons against it. Even the most honest of the Socialist Ministers themselves seem to have felt that. All the time, likewise, an influential portion of the Press vigorously supported the ex-Premier. They carried the war into the enemy's camp by denouncing his critics either as unscrupulous and lying reactionaries, who were endeavoring to ruin a really progressive statesman, as men imbued with such lust for slaughter and eagerness for revenge that they had lost all grip of the actual situation, or as malignant intriguers behind the scenes whose one object was to blacken the character of an opponent who stood in the way of their schemes for personal aggrandizement.

Furthermore, M. Caillaux, holding the eminent position already referred to in the world of finance, had the wholesouled and entire-pocket backing of the French and German-Jew international money-lords. These magnates of plutocracy, marvelous to relate, found themselves on this issue hand in glove with the most active international

French Socialists. Nobody who was in the least afraid of political cliques, of journalistic coteries, of financial syndicates, or of Socialist rancor, could put Caillaux under lock and key. And the military outlook lent itself to the encouragement of the leading advocate of surrender and his acolytes. The word was assiduously passed round that, now Russia was out of the fray, a drawn battle was the very best that the Entente could hope for.

France was bled white, Great Britain was war-weary and her workers were discontented, Italy—think of Caporetto—while, as to the United States, America was a long way off, President Wilson was still "too proud to fight" in earnest, American troops could never be transported in sufficient numbers across the Atlantic, and, to say nothing of dangers from submarines, there was not enough shipping afloat to do it. All pointed, therefore, to prompt "peace by negotiation," and what better man could there be to negotiate such a peace than M. Joseph Caillaux? It was because he was the one political personage in France who could secure fair terms for his distressful country, at this terrible crisis, that he was so persistently attacked by the Chauvinists as a pro-German and accused of the most sordid treachery by men who envied him his power at the international Council Table!

Such was the situation. So long as M. Caillaux was at large and able to direct the whole of the forces of defeatism, no genuinely patriotic Ministry could be successfully formed, or, if formed by some fortuitous concurrence of circumstances, could last for three months. Treachery breeds treachery as loyalty engenders loyalty. When Clemenceau took office, therefore, everything depended upon what he did with Caillaux. Paris and all France held their breath as they awaited the event.

Patriots were doubtful: defeatists were hopeful: soldiers were on the look-out for a man.

On January 15th, then, M. Caillaux was arrested and put in prison by Clemenceau and his Ministry. All the predictions of upheaval and disaster, indulged in by M. Caillaux's friends, were falsified. The country breathed more freely. Thenceforward, France knew whom to back. But, supposing that M. Caillaux had still been within the precints of Parliament and carrying on his political plots when the terrible news came of the disasters of Cambrai and St. Quentin, and when the German armies were within cannon-shot of Paris—how then? Those who knew best how things stood believe themselves that counsels of despair and pusillanimity might have prevailed, to the ruin of the country.

No such fateful issue as that involved in Caillaux's arrest hung upon the result of the trial of Bolo Pasha. But Bolo's whole career was a tragical farce, to which even Alphonse Daudet could scarcely have done full justice. Bolo was a Frenchman of the Midi: a Tartarin with the tendencies of a financial Vautrin: a fine specimen of the flamboyant and unscrupulous international adventurer. His first experience in the domain of extraction was as a dentist in the country of his birth. A handsome, blond young man of fine appearance and manners and methods of address attractive to women, he soon found that the drawing of teeth and other less skilled professions led to the receipt of no emoluments worthy of his talents. To take in a well-to-do partner and decamp with his wife and the firm's cash-box was more in the way of business.

So satisfactory was this first adventure that he extended his field of operations, and several ladies had the advantage of paying for his attentions in the shape of all the money of which they chanced to be possessed. Somehow or other he found himself in the Champagne country during the wine-growers' riots, and continued to have a good time in the district while they were going on. But in 1905 the claret region proved more lucrative. For in Bordeaux the charm of his disposition produced so great an effect upon the widow of a rich merchant of that city that she succumbed to his attractions and married him. This provided Bolo with the means for setting on foot all sorts of financial enterprises in Europe and America. He thus became a promoter of the open-hearted and sanguine type, found his way into "society" of the kind which opens its arms to such men, had sufficient influence to become a chevalier of the Legion of Honor, and by 1914 had lost all his wife's money and more into the bargain—was, in fact, in very serious financial straits from which he saw no way of extricating himself. Certain Egyptian friends he had made, who later obtained for him his title of Pasha from the Khedive, were not then in a position to help him.

But Bolo without money meant a German agent in search of a job. It proved easy to get it. He notified the Germans through the Egyptians that he could do good service in France if only he were provided with plenty of funds. He was so furnished with hundreds of thousands of pounds. *L'Homme Libre* said of him that he reveled in the prestige of having money, to such an extent that he believed that money was everything. Rather, perhaps, he had become so accustomed to indulge in pleasures and political and financial intrigues of every sort that he would run any risk rather than give up the game. So it was that he carried on the dangerous policy, if such it could be called, sketched above.

About his guilt there could be no doubt. That he had been closely connected with people in high places as well as in low, and possessed considerable personal magnetism, was clear. All this came out in court, where persons of every grade, from Ministers and Senators to Levantine rogues and Parisian courtesans, passed in and passed out like figures on a cinema film. Bolo, of course, denied every charge, and posed as a financier of high degree, but he was condemned to death, and his appeal against the sentence was fruitless, though he pretended he could make harrowing disclosures. He met his death bravely on April 10th. His fate was a heavy blow to other spies and conspirators.

There was an interpellation on the Bolo trial, a month before his execution, that led to a powerful speech by Clemenceau, in which he declared that he was first for liberty, next for war, and finally for the sacrifice of everything to secure victory. He then made a vigorous appeal to the Socialists to join with the rest of the country in supporting his Government in a supreme effort to free France from the invader. "It is a great misfortune that my administration should be denounced by Renaudel"— then editor of *l'Humanité*—"as a danger to the workers. My hands are to the full as hardened by toil as those of Renaudel and Albert Thomas, good bourgeois citizens as they are, like myself. I have in my pocket a paper in which Renaudel is stigmatized as Clemenceau's orderly; nay, adding insult to injury, he is held up to public obloquy as *Monsieur* Renaudel." Then, addressing the Socialist group, he declared with vehemence: "We have done you no harm, but my methods are not yours. You will not defeat Prussian Junkerdom by baa-ing around about peace." The appeal was quite bootless. On a division confidence in the Clemenceau Government was voted by 400 to 75. The Socialists were the 75. The vote was a direct outcome of the sordid and gruesome Bolo case.

SUMMARY OF EVENTS RELATING TO TREACHERY IN PARIS, JULY, 1917, TO JULY, 1918.

July, 1917.—Clemenceau attacks M. Malvy, then Minister of the Interior, for ruinous weakness towards traitors.

Assails the Ribot Ministry as responsible for the propaganda of the pro-German journal *Le Bonnet Rouge*.

It was shown later that this newspaper had received State support to the extent of £4,000 a year.

August, 1917.—M. Almereyda (*alias* Vigo), connected with Bolo Pasha, M. Caillaux and the *Bonnet Rouge*, arrested and dies in prison.

M. Malvy "explains" the Almereyda affair.

September, 1917.—M. Malvy resigns.

October, 1917.—Debate in Chamber upon M. Léon Daudet's charge of treason against Malvy.

Captain Bouchardon begins investigation.

Proprietors of *Bonnet Rouge* arrested.

November, 1917.—Revelations by Clemenceau in *l'Homme Enchaîné*, which had been going on for a twelvemonth, take effect on public.

Bonnet Rouge trial.

Revelations concerning M. Paix-Séailles's document about French troops at Salonika to have been published in *Bonnet Rouge*. Paix-Séailles in M. Painlevé's *entourage*.

THE ENEMY WITHIN

Clemenceau exposes Caillaux's intrigues with Almereyda, the *Bonnet Rouge,* the defeatists in Italy, and comments on the large subsidies to the *Bonnet Rouge* which enabled it to become a daily instead of a weekly sheet.

Clemenceau forms Ministry.

December, 1917.—Clemenceau examined before Committee of Senate on Caillaux affair.

Clemenceau declares if Parliament would not sanction prosecution of Caillaux his Ministry would resign.

Caillaux's immunity as deputy suspended by vote.

January, 1918.—Captain Bouchardon's report on Bolo Pasha published.

Traces Bolo's career from 1914, his intrigues with Germany through ex-Khedive of Egypt and other Egyptians. Receipt by Bolo of £400,000 from Deutsche Bank.

Bolo buys shares in *Journal,* and tries to buy shares also in the *Figaro* and the *Temps.*

M. Caillaux arrested.

His private safe brought from Florence containing strange papers relating, among other things, to a suggested *coup d'état.*

United States agent at Buenos Aires reveals series of negotiations between M. Caillaux and the German representative, Count Luxburg, having for object the conclusion of a German peace.

M. Malvy arraigned before the High Court of the Senate.

February, 1918.—Trial of Bolo begun. Caillaux, Humbert and others incriminated.

U. S. A. secret service shows that large sums passed from Count Bernstorff, German Ambassador in

Washington, to Bolo for the purposes of German propaganda.

Bolo found guilty and condemned to be shot on February 16th.

M. Malvy's case before the High Court extended.

March, 1918.—Bolo appeals.

Bolo case discussed in Chamber. Socialists attack Clemenceau. Vote of confidence in Clemenceau's Ministry 400 to 75.

Terrible military disasters at Cambrai and St. Quentin due to heavy German attack on positions weakened by withdrawal of British troops.

April, 1918.—Bolo shot.

Caillaux in jail.

Malvy trial continued.

May, 1918.—Caillaux "explains" his connection with *Le Bonnet Rouge.*

June, 1918.—Committee report on M. Malvy's case and fix date of trial.

July, 1918.—M. Malvy found guilty of undue laxity towards traitors and condemned to exile from France.

French Socialists infuriated at M. Malvy's expulsion.

CHAPTER XX

"LA VICTOIRE INTÉGRALE"

IN the endeavor to give a connected statement of the very dangerous German offensive, conducted by their spies and agents in Paris, at the most critical period of the whole war, I have been obliged to some extent to anticipate events in order to show Clemenceau's share in the exposure of this organized treachery. By 1917, as already recorded, anti-patriotic and pro-German intrigues in Paris and France had become more and more harmful to that "sacred unity" which had been constituted to present an unbroken front to the enemy. After the miserable breakdown of Russia, largely due to the Bolshevik outbreak fostered by German intrigue and subsidized by German money, the position was exceedingly dangerous. German troops withdrawn from the Eastern front were poured into France and Flanders by hundreds of thousands, and the Allied armies were hard put to it to hold their own.

At this time, when it was all-important to maintain the spirit of the French army, the enemy offensive in Paris and throughout France became more and more active. What made the situation exceptionally critical was the fact that the rank and file of the French soldiery began to feel that, however desperately they might fight at the front, they were being systematically betrayed in the rear.

While, therefore, Clemenceau, in his capacity as Senator and President of the Inter-Allied Parliamentary Committee, voiced the great and growing discontent of the country with the lack of real statesmanship displayed in the conduct of the war, he also fulminated against the weakness of the wobbling Ministers who, knowing that defeatism and treachery were fermenting all round them, took no effective steps to counteract this pernicious propaganda.

The notorious *Bonnet Rouge* group, however, with M. Joseph Caillaux, Bolo Pasha, Almereyda and others in close touch with M. Jean Longuet and his pacifist friends of the Socialist Party, were allowed to carry on their virulent anti-French campaign in the Press and in other directions practically unchecked. It might even have been thought that these persons had the sympathy and support of members of the Government.

Thus, when M. Painlevé took office on M. Ribot's resignation in August, 1917, the outlook was dark all round. The position of the Allied armies was by no means satisfactory: the state of affairs in Paris itself was not such as to engender confidence: Mr. Lloyd George's headlong speech of depreciation on his return from Italy had undone all the good of the unanimous resolution passed by the Inter-Allied Parliamentary Committee of which Clemenceau was President, declaring that no peace could be accepted which did not secure the realization of national claims and the complete triumph of justice all along the line. In short, a fit of despondency, almost deepening into despair, had come over Allied statesmen. Notwithstanding distrust, however, war-weariness was not spreading among the soldiers and sailors. But among the politicians it was, and German "peace offensives" were being welcomed in quarters which were supposed to be resolute for *"la victoire intégrale."* M. Painlevé's administration was scarcely hoisted into the saddle before it was ignominiously thrown out again. The instability of successive French Ministries was becoming a danger which extended far beyond the limits of France. The unification of the Allied command and the concentration of effort on the Western front had become imperative. The arrest of all those against whom there was serious suspicion of treason, no matter how highly they might be placed, was a necessity of the moment. Vigorous support for the generals and armies engaged in resisting the reënforced enemy was called for from every quarter. So the President, M. Poincaré, found himself in a dilemma. But none of the leading politicians who had been prominent since the war began was prepared to take the responsibility of forming an administration and then acting upon the lines which the situation demanded.

It was at this crisis, perhaps the most dangerous that France has had to face in all her long history, that the President asked Clemenceau to become the Prime Minister. He was then seventy-six years of age and had withdrawn from all those conferences and discussions behind the scenes which, under ordinary circumstances, invariably precede the acceptance of office. The Socialists declared that, no matter what Clemenceau's policy might be, they could not serve under him as President of Council. Clemenceau could not rely upon support from M. Poincaré, and on every ground he was much disinclined to come to the front under existing conditions. But his duty to France and its Republic outweighed all other considerations, and this old statesman shouldered the burden which far younger men declined to take up.

The Socialists went quite wild against him—to the lasting injury, as I hold, of their party and their cause—the Radicals and Republicans themselves were more than doubtful of the possibility of his success. Many politicians and journalists of the Right doubted whether they could make common cause with the man who above all other things stood for the permanence of Republicanism and was the bitter enemy of Clericalism in every shape. Shrewd judges of public opinion stated that his Ministry could not last three months.

But courage, frankness and good faith, backed by relentless determination and the genius that blazes up in the day of difficulty, go far. The whole French people suddenly called to mind that this old Radical of the Bocage of La Vendée, this Parisian of Parisians for nearly sixty years, whatever mistakes he may have made in opposition or in office, had invariably stood up for the greatness, the glory, the dignity of France; that he had voted at Bordeaux for the continuance of the war when France lay at the feet of the ruthless conqueror and Gambetta was striving to organize his countrymen for resistance to the death; that from those dark days of 1871 onwards he had always vehemently adjured his countrymen to make ready to resist coming invasion; that from August, 1914, he had never failed to keep a stout heart himself and to do his utmost to encourage his countrymen even when the outlook was blackest for the Allies; that he had ever been the relentless denouncer of weakness and vacillation, as he had also been the unceasing opponent of pacifism, pro-Germanism and treachery of every kind; that now, therefore, when *la Patrie* was in desperate danger, when Paris might yet be at the mercy of the enemy of whose hideous ruffianism they had had such bitter experience, Georges Clemenceau was the one man to take control of democratic and Republican France in the interest of every section of the population. These stirring memories of the past rose up behind Clemenceau in the present.[1]

Thus it was that the new Prime Minister, coming down from the Senate to read his Declaration to the National Assembly, as the French custom is, was certain beforehand of a cordial reception from the great majority of the Deputies. What might happen afterwards depended upon himself and his Ministry: what should occur on this his first appearance in the tribune after nearly eight years of absence depended on themselves. They took good care that, at the start at least, he should have no doubt as to their goodwill. Only the Socialist minority abstained.

The Declaration itself was worthy of the occasion, and it was a stirring scene when the veteran of the Radical Party, the Tiger of the old days, rose to deliver it to the House, which was crowded on the floor and in the galleries with deputies and strangers eager to hear what he had to say:—

"Gentlemen, we have taken up the duty of government in order to carry on the war with renewed energy and to obtain a better result from our concentrated efforts.

---

[1] CLEMENCEAU'S MINISTRY.

CLEMENCEAU, Prime Minister and Minister for War.
PICHON, Foreign Affairs.
PAMS, Interior.
KLOTZ, Finance.
LEYGUES, Marine.
CLEMENTEL, Commerce ⎫
CLAVALLE, Public Works ⎬ Members of late Ministry.
LOUCHEUR, Munitions ⎪
COLLIARD, Labor ⎭
BORET, Supplies and Agriculture.

We are here with but one idea in our minds, the war and nothing but the war. The confidence we ask you to give us should be the expression of confidence in yourselves. . . . Never has France felt more keenly the need for living and growing in the ideal of power used on behalf of human rectitude, the resolve to see justice done between citizens and peoples able to emancipate themselves. The watchword of all our Governments since the war began has been victory for the sake of justice. That frank policy we shall uphold. We have great soldiers with a great history led by men who have been tested and have been inspired to deeds of the highest devotion worthy of their ancestral renown. The immortal fatherland of our common humanity, overmastering the exultation of victory, will follow, on the lines of its destiny, the noble aspiration for peace, through them and through us all. Frenchmen impelled by us into the conflict have special claims upon us. We owe them everything without reserve. Everything for France: everything for the triumph of right. One simple duty is imposed upon us, to stand by the soldier, to live, suffer and fight with him, and to throw aside everything that is not for our country. The rights on our front, the duties in our rear must be merged in one. Every zone must be the army zone. If men there are who must cherish the hatreds of bygone days, sweep them away.

"All civilized nations are now arrayed in the like battle against modern forms of ancient barbarisms. Our Allies and ourselves together constitute a solid barrier which shall not be surmounted. Throughout the Allied front, at all times and in all places, there is nothing but solid brotherhood, the surest basis for the coming world. . . . The silent soldiers of the factory, the old

"LA VICTOIRE INTÉGRALE"

peasants working, bent over their soil, the vigorous women who toil, the children who help in their weakness—these likewise are our *poilus* who in times to come, recalling the great things done, will be able to say with the men in the trenches, 'I, too, was there.' . . . Mistakes have been made. Think no more about them save only to remedy them.

"But, alas! there have also been crimes, crimes against France which demand prompt punishment. We solemnly pledge ourselves, before you and before the country, that justice shall be done with the full rigor of the law. Personal considerations or political passion shall neither divert us from fulfilling this duty nor induce us to go beyond it. Too many such crimes have cost us the blood of our soldiers. Weakness would mean complicity. There shall be no weakness as there shall be no violence. Accused persons shall all be brought before courts-martial. The soldier of justice shall make common cause with the soldier in the field. No more pacifist plots: no more German intrigues. Neither treason nor semi-treason. War, nothing but war. Our country shall not be placed between two fires. Our country shall learn that she is really defended.

* * * * * *

"The day will come when from Paris to the smallest village of France storms of cheers will welcome our victorious colors tattered by shell-fire and drenched with blood and tears—the glorious memorials of our great dead. It is for us to hasten the coming of that day, that glorious day, which will fitly take its place beside so many others in our history. These are our unshakable resolves, gentlemen: we ask you to give them the sanction of your approval."

Such is a free summary of a Ministerial pronouncement that will ever be memorable in the annals of France and of mankind. It swept the Chamber away as the recital marched on. But organized attacks upon the President of the Council at once followed. Now came the supreme test of the mental and physical efficiency of this wonderful old man whose youth is so amazing. He could read a telling manifesto with vigor and effect. Would he be able to reply with equal power to a series of interrogations in an atmosphere to which he had been a stranger for so many years? Questions, by no means all of them friendly, poured in upon Clemenceau from every part of the Chamber. From his attitude towards Caillaux and Malvy to his view of the League of Nations and his policy in regard to negotiations with the enemy, no point was missed that might embarrass or irritate the statesman who had undertaken to stand in the gap. He showed immediately that he was fully capable of taking his own part. The fervor of the new France was heard in every phrase of his crushing reply:

"You do not expect me to talk of personal matters. I am not here for that. Still, I have heard enough to understand that the criticisms upon me should make me modest. I feel humble for the mistakes I have already made and for those which I am likely to make. I do not think I can be accused of having sought power. But I am in power. I hope it will not be a misfortune for my country. You tell me I have made mistakes. Perhaps you do not know the worst of them. I am here because these are terrible times when those who through all the struggle have loved their country more than they knew see the hopes of the nation centered on them. I am here through the pressure of public opinion, and I am almost afraid of what it will demand of me, of what it expects of me.

"I have been asked to explain myself in regard to war aims, and as to the idea of a League of Nations. I have replied in my declaration, 'We must conquer for the sake of justice.' That is clear. We live in a time when words have great power, but they have not the power to set free. The word 'justice' is as old as mankind. Do you imagine that the formula of a League of Nations is going to solve everything?

"There is a committee at the Ministry of Foreign Affairs even now preparing a scheme for a League of Nations. Among its members are the most authoritative exponents of international law. I undertake that immediately their labors are finished I will table the outcome of it in this Chamber, if I am still Prime Minister—which does not seem likely." (Laughter and cheers.)

"I am not unfavorable to arbitration. It was I who sent M. Léon Bourgeois to The Hague, where a series of conventions were agreed upon which Germany is now engaged in violating. Many believe that a miracle will bring about a League of Nations. I do not myself think that a League of Nations will be one of the results of this war. If to-morrow you proposed to me that Germany should be included in a League of Nations, I should not consent. What guarantees do you offer me? Germany's signature? Go and ask the Belgians what they think of that.

"You never weary of saying that the first thing is for Germany herself to destroy German militarism, but she is far from destroying it; she still holds it fast.

"M. Forgeot wants to make war, but while we are making war he wants us to talk about peace. Personally,

I believe that when you are doing things you should talk as little as possible. Do M. Forgeot's ideas come within the range of practical politics? Do people believe that the men in the trenches and the women in the factories do not think of peace? Our thoughts are theirs. They are fighting to obtain some decent security of life; and when you ask me my war aims, I reply that my war aim is victory in full." (Loud cheers and Socialist interruption.)

"I understand your aspirations, some of which I share, but do not let us make mistakes about war. All these men want peace. But if, while they are fighting, the rumor goes round that delegates of one or other belligerent country are discussing terms of peace—that yesterday we were on the eve of peace, that next day there was a break-off—then we are condemned to flounder about in mud and in blood for years still. That is the way to disarm and discourage us all. For these reasons, I am not in favor of Conferences where citizens of different belligerent countries discuss peace which the Governments alone are able to decide. I want to make war. This means that for the moment we must silence all factious discussion. Is there a man who has been more of a party man than I? I see to-day that I have been far too much of a party man. My program is a military and economic program. We have got Allies, to whom we owe loyalty and fidelity, which must override every other consideration.

"We have not yet achieved victory. We have come to a cruel phase of the war. A time of privation is at hand, a time when our spirit must rise to greater heights yet. Do not, then, speak of peace. We all want peace, we are making great sacrifices to obtain peace, but we must get rid of old animosities and turn solidly against the enemy. Leave all other questions alone.

"There is one on which, however, I must touch. Scandals have been spoken of. Do you think we can have three years of war without Germany trying to keep spies busy in our midst? I complained that our look-out was insufficient, and events have too clearly shown that I was right. I am told to give you the truth. You shall have it. But we must distinguish between crimes and accusations. As the examination proceeds facts will be disclosed which will have their effect. How can you expect me to mention names or reveal fragments of truth? Certain people have been guilty of indiscretion, want of reflection, or weakness. It is not I but the judge who has to decide. You shall have the truth. In what form? If there is any revelation of a political nature to make there is a political tribunal in this country to make it. It shall judge. Just as civil justice must do its work during war time, so must political justice." (A voice: "Caillaux!") "I mention no name. A journalist has freedom as to what he may say, it is his own responsibility; but the head of the Government has a quite different task. I am here to put the law in motion if political acts have been committed which are subject to a jurisdiction beyond the ordinary tribunals.

"Those facts will be brought before the tribunal, but I refuse here to accuse any man.

"Justice is our weapon against treason, and where treason is concerned there can be no possibility of pardon. In any case, you have got a Government which will try to *govern* in the strict, but high, idealistic sense of the word. Where I differ from you, gentlemen of the Extreme Left, is when you want to bring abstract conceptions into the field of hard facts. That is impossible. We shall try to govern honestly and in a Republican spirit. You are not obliged to think we shall succeed. But we shall do our best. If we make mistakes, others have done so before us, others will do so after us. If at last we see before us the long-awaited dawn of victory, I hope—if it is only to complete the beauty of the picture—that you will pass a vote of censure upon me, and I shall go happy away! I know you will not do that; but allow me to point out, as I have a right to tell you, that you have almost passed a vote of censure on me already before listening to my Ministerial program. I challenge you to say that we have made any attempt to deceive you. If we get painful news, our hearts will bleed, but we shall tell that news to you here. We have never given anybody the right to suppose that we constitute a peril to any class of citizens or a danger to the national defense. If you think the contrary, prove it, and I will leave the House. But if you believe that what we want above all is the welfare of France, give us your confidence, and we will endeavor to be worthy of it."

His deeds have been on a level with his words. Bolo and Duval shot: Caillaux in jail: Malvy exiled by decree of the Senate: the *Bonnet Rouge* gang tried and condemned: the wretched intrigue in Switzerland with the poor German tool, Austria, exposed and crushed: a new spirit breathed into all public affairs: the army reassured by his perpetual presence under fire and his unfailing resolve at the War Office that the splendid capacity and intrepidity of all ranks at the front shall not be sacrificed by treachery or cowardice at the rear: the Higher Command brimful of enthusiasm and confidence, due to the appointment of the military genius Foch as generalissimo of the United Allied Armies and the reinstatement of General Mangin at the head of his *corps d'armée*. The Allies, like France herself, are convinced that they have at last discovered a man. Such is the stirring work that Clemenceau has been doing since he took office barely a year ago.

So to-day Clemenceau is still democratic dictator of the French Republic as no man has been for more than a century. When the enemy was arrayed in overwhelming numbers close to Amiens and within a few miles of Calais, when the German War Lords were decreeing the permanent subjugation of the territories they occupied in the West and in the East, when the long-range guns were bombarding the capital and the removal of the seat of government to the provinces was again being considered, the great French nation felt more confident of its future than at any moment since the victories won around Verdun. To every question Clemenceau's answer invariably was, "Je fais la guerre. Je fais la guerre. Je fais la guerre."

Those who doubted were convinced: those who were hopeful saw their aspirations realized: those who had never wavered cheered for victory right ahead.

On June 6th, 1918, the French Socialist group in the Chamber of Deputies made another of those attacks upon the National Administration which, sad to say, have done so much to discredit the whole Socialist Party, and even the Socialist cause, throughout Europe and the world. Pacifism and Bolshevism together—that is to say, an unholy combination between anti-nationalism and anarchism, have indeed shaken the influence of democratic Socialism to its foundations, just at the time when a sound, sober and constructive Socialist policy, in harmony

with the aspirations of the mass of the people in every
Allied country, might have led mankind peacefully along
the road to the new period of national and international
coöperation. The Socialist Deputies in the Chamber held
Clemenceau's Ministry, which they had done their very
utmost to discredit and weaken, directly responsible for
the serious military reverses recently undergone by the
French and Allied armies. They insisted, therefore, upon
Clemenceau's appearance in the tribune. But when they
had got him in front of them their great object evidently
was not to let him speak. There this old statesman
stood, exposed to interruptions which were in the worst
of bad taste. At last he thought the opportunity for
which his enemies clamored had come, and began to
address the Assembly. But no sooner had he opened his
mouth than he was forced to give way to M. Marcel
Cachin. Only then was he enabled to get a hearing, and
this is a summary of what he said:—

"I regret that, our country being in such great danger,
a unanimous vote of confidence cannot be accorded to us.
But, when all is said, the opposition of the Socialists
does not in the least enfeeble the Government. For four
long years our troops have held their own at the front
with a line which was being steadily worn down. Now
a huge body of German soldiers fresh from Russia and
in good heart come forward to assail us. Some retreat
was inevitable. From the moment when Russia thought
that peace could be obtained by the simple expression
of wishes to that end we all knew that, sooner or later,
the enemy would be able to release a million of men to
fall upon us. That meant that such a retirement as we
have witnessed must of necessity follow. Our men have
kept their line unbroken against odds of five to one. They

have often gone sleepless for three days and even four days in succession. But our great soldiers have had great leaders, and our army as a whole has proved itself to be greater than even we could expect.

"The duties we have to perform here are, in contrast to their heroism, tame and even petty. All we have to do is to keep cool and hold on. The Germans are nothing like so clever as they believe themselves to be. They have but a single device. They throw their entire weight into one general assault, and push their advantage to the utmost. True they have forced back our lines of defense. But final success is that alone which matters, and that success for us is certain. The Government you see before you took office with the firm resolve never to surrender. So long as we stand here our country will be defended to the last. Give way we never shall.

"Germany has once more staked her all on one great blow, thinking to cow us into abandoning the conflict. Her armies have tried this desperate game before. They tried it on the Marne, they tried it on the Yser, they tried it at Verdun, they tried it elsewhere. But they never have succeeded, and they never shall. Our Allies to-day are the leading nations of the world. They have one and all pledged themselves to fight on till victory is within our grasp. The men who have already fallen have not fallen in vain. By their death they have once more made French history a great and noble record. It is now for the living to finish the glorious work done by the dead."

This great speech raised the overwheming majority of the Assembly to the highest pitch of enthusiasm. Nearly all present felt that the destinies of France hung in the balance, and that any vote given which might tend to discourage the men at the front at such a time was a direct service rendered to the enemy whose bombs were even then falling in the heart of Paris. The vote of confidence in Clemenceau and his Ministry was carried by 377 votes to 110; and of these 110 more than a third were convinced shortly afterwards that the course they had then taken in order to preserve the unity of their forces as factionists was unworthy of their dignity as men.

Then, too, when the tide turned and the German hordes, after fresh glorious battles of the Marne and of the Somme, were in headlong retreat, Clemenceau, unelated by victory as he was undiscouraged by defeat, repeated again: "Je fais la guerre. Je fais la guerre. Je fais la guerre." Not until the German armies were finally vanquished would the Republican statesman talk of making peace. On both sides of the Atlantic, therefore, as on both sides of the Channel, knowing Great Britain and the United States by personal experience and able to gauge the cold resolution of the one and the inexhaustible resources and determination of the other, speaking and writing English well, he is now, as he has been throughout this tremendous war, a tower of strength to the forces of democracy and a very present help to all who are resolved to break down German militarism for evermore.

CHAPTER XX

CONCLUSION

GEORGES CLEMENCEAU, President of the Council and Minister of War, and Marshal Foch, General in Chief of the Allied Armies, have well deserved the gratitude of the country."

That is the Resolution which, by the unaimous vote of the Senate of the French Republic, will be placed in a conspicuous position in every Town Hall and in the Council Chamber of every Commune throughout France. The Senators of France are not easily roused to enthusiasm. What they thus unanimously voted, in the absence of Clemenceau, amid general acclamation is a fine recognition of his preëminent service as well as of his indefatigable devotion to duty at the most desperate crisis in the long and glorious history of his country. Nothing like it has ever been known. The reward is unprecedented: the work done has surpassed every record.

It is well that the great statesman should be honored in advance of the great military commander. Marshal Foch has accomplished marvels in more than four years of continuous activity from the first battle of the Marne to the signing of the Armistice of unconditional surrender. All Europe and the civilized world is indebted to him for his masterly strategy and successful maneuvers. But France herself owes most to Clemenceau.

Towards the close of this historic sitting Clemenceau himself entered the Senate. He received an astounding welcome. Every one present rose to greet him. Men who but yesterday were his enemies, and are still his opponents, rushed forward with the rest to applaud him, to shake hands with him, to thank him, to embrace him. The excitement was so overwhelming that Clemenceau, for the first time in his life, broke down. Tears coursed down his cheeks and for some moments he was unable to speak. When he did he, as always, refused to take the credit and the glory of the overthrow of the Germans and their confederates to himself. In victory in November, as when he was confronting difficulty and danger in March and July, his first and his last thoughts were of France. The spirit of France, the citizens of France, the soldiers and sailors of France: these were they who in comradeship with the Allies had achieved the great victory over the last convulsions of savagery. He had been more than fully rewarded for all he had done by witnessing the expulsion of the foreigner and the liberation of the territory. His task had only been to give full expression to the courage and determination of his countrymen.

Clemenceau spoke not only as a French statesman, as the veteran upholder of the French Republic, but as one who remembered well the horrors and defeats of 1870-71, now followed, forty-eight years later, by the horrors and the triumphs of 1918. The Senators who heard him and acclaimed him felt that Clemenceau was addressing them as the man who had embodied in himself, for all those long years, the soul of the France of the Great Revolution and now at last was able to show what he really was.

CONCLUSION

This moving reception in the Senate had been preceded by an almost equally glowing display of enthusiasm in the Chamber of Deputies. There, too—with the exception of a mere handful of Socialists whose extraordinary devotion to Caillaux and Malvy blinds them to the genius of their countryman—the whole Assembly rose up to welcome and cheer him. Clemenceau, speaking there, also, under strong emotion, after two stirring ovations from M. Deschanel and M. Pichon, assured the Deputies that the Armistice which would be granted to Germany could only be on the lines of those accorded to Bulgaria, Austria-Hungary and Turkey. Marshal Foch would decide the details which now all the world knows.

But after having dealt with the Armistice implored by Germany, Clemenceau went back to the past and said: "When I remember that I entered the National Assembly of Bordeaux in 1871, and have been—I am the last of them—one of the signers of the protests against the annexation of Alsace-Lorraine. ... It is impossible for me, now peace is certain and our victory assured, to leave the tribune without paying homage to those who were the initiators and first workers in the immense task which is being completed at this moment.

"I wish to speak of Gambetta" (the whole House rises with prolonged cheering)—"of him who, defending the territory under circumstances which rendered victory impossible, never despaired. With him and Chanzy I voted for the continuation of the war, and in truth, when I think of what has happened in these fifty years, I ask myself whether the war has not continued. May our thoughts go back to them and when these terrible iron doors that Germany has closed against us shall be opened, let us say to them: 'Pass in first. You have shown us the way.'"

The French Premier went on to speak of the problems of peace, which could only be solved, like the problems of war, by national unity for the common cause, "for the Republic which we made in peace, which we have upheld in war, the Republic which has saved us during the war." He appealed "First for solidarity with the Allies, and then for solidarity among the French." This was needful for the maintenance of peace and the future of their common humanity. Humanity's great crusade was inspired not by the thought of God but of France. *"Ce n'est pas Dieu, c'est la France qui le veut."*

The Deputies rose again and again. It would have been strange if they had not.

But fine though these speeches were, and impressive as was the Prime Minister's adjuration, that since the problems of peace were harder than those of war, they must prove their worth in both fields—it was Clemenceau's personal influence that gave them their special value. Undoubtedly the splendid fighting of the French and British and American troops and the admirable skill of their commanders had produced that dramatic change from the days of depression from March to July to the period of continuous triumph from July to November. This Clemenceau never allows us for one moment to forget. But he it was who had breathed new life into the whole combination, military and civilian, at the front and in the factories. No man of his time of life, perhaps no man of any age ever carried on continuously such exhausting toil, physical and mental, as that which this marvelous old statesman of seventy-seven undertook and carried through from November, 1917, to November, 1918. His astounding energy and power of work were like those of a most vigorous young man in the height of training. Starting for the front in a motor-car at four or five o'clock in the morning at least three times a week, he kept in touch with generals, officers and soldiers all along the lines to an extent that would have seemed incredible if it had not been actually done. Once at the front he walked about under fire as if he had come out for the pleasure of risking his life with the *poilus* who were fighting for *la Patrie*. The Higher Command was in constant fear for him. But he knew what he was about. Valuable as his own life might be to the country, to court death was a higher duty than to take care of himself, if by this seeming indifference he made Frenchmen all along the trenches feel that he and they were one. He succeeded. Fortune favored him throughout. Then having discoursed with the Marshal and his generals, having saluted and talked with the officers, he chatted with the rank-and-file of the soldiery and rushed back to Paris, arriving at the Ministry of War at ten or eleven o'clock at night, ready to attend to such pressing business as demanded his personal care. And all the time cheerful, alert, confident, showing, when things looked dark, as when the great advance began, that the Prime Minister of the Republic never for one moment doubted the Germans would be hurled back over the frontier and France would again take her rightful place in the world.

And that is not all. Clemenceau's influence in the Council Chamber of the Allies was and is supreme. The old gayety of heart remains but the soundness of judgment and determination to accept no compromise of principle are more marked than ever. Many dangerous intrigues during the past few months, of which the world has heard little, were snuffed clean out by Clemenceau's force of character and overwhelming personality. The French Prime Minister wanted complete victory for France and her Allies. Nothing short of this would satisfy him. There was no personal party he wished to build up, no political object that he desired to attain, no section or party that he felt himself bound to propitiate. Therefore, the other Ministers of the Allies found themselves at the table with a statesman who was something more than an individual representative of his nation. He was the human embodiment of a cause. What that meant and still means will only be known when the dust of conflict has passed from us and the whole truth of Clemenceau's policy can be told.

For my part I have done my best as an old and convinced Socialist, and therefore on some important points his opponent, to give a frank and unbiased study of Clemenceau's fine career. His very mistakes do but serve to throw into higher relief his sterling character and the genius which has enabled him to command success. Read aright, his actions do all hang together, and constitute one complete whole. Comprising within himself the brilliant yet thorough capacity of his French countrymen, he has risen when close upon eighty to the height of the terribly responsible position he was forced to fill.

Therefore his efforts have been crowned with complete victory. Having forgotten himself in his work, the man Clemenceau will never be forgotten. He will stand out in history as the greatest statesman of the Greatest War.

INDEX

INDEX

Adulteration, John Bright on, 215
Albert, 5
Amadé, General, 237
Arago, Etienne, XII, 15, 24, 27
Armistice of 1871, 28
Aumale, Duc d', and Boulanger, 98

Bakunin, 45
Bazaine, Marshal, 24, 28, 33
Barodet, 68, 87, 88
Barrès, M., 299
Basly, M., miners' agent, 197
Bebel and Jaurès on the Fleet, 267
  and the Social-Democrats, 274
Benedek, Marshal, 18
Beesly, Prof., 45
Bellers, John, 262
Berlin, brutality and greed of, 26
Beslay, 38, 43
Billot, General, 171
Bismarck—the forgery at Ems, 24
Blanc, Louis, 5, 32, 78, 86
Blanqui, 49, 53, 55, 56, 59
"Blessed word," the, 9
Blond, Maurice Le, 21
Boer War, the, 242, 243
Boisdeffre, General, 171
Bolo Pasha, 307-316
Bonnet Rouge, arrest of proprietors of, 301
Bordeaux, the Government at, 280
Boulanger, General, xii
  and Army reforms, 99
  as War Minister, 99
  candidate for Paris, 105
  downfall, its effect on the influence of Clemenceau, 109
  elected for the Nord, 104
  enters politics, a candidate for the Nord and the Dordogne, 103
  fails to profit by his success, 108
  flight and suicide, 109

Boulanger, General, his duel with M. Floquet, 102
  his popularity after the Schnäbele affair, 100
  his relations with the Duc d'Aumale, 98
  posted to the command of army corps at Clermont-Ferrand, 103
  his visits to Paris, 103
  deprived of his command, 103
  returned for Paris by a heavy majority, 107
  rides through Paris on his black charger, 106
  the pet of the *Salons,* 101
Brandès, M., Clemenceau's attack on, 283
Briand, M., 229
  as an anarchist, 252
Bright, John, on adulteration, 215
Brisson, M., 78, 171, 177
British statesmanship, blindness of, 265
Broglie, Duc de, xii, 73, 74, 78, 79, 105
Brown, John, and the American Civil War, 47
Brousse, Paul, 104
Buffet, 71, 72
Butchery of peaceful citizens, 6

Caillaux, M., 229
  and a German peace, 300-303
  and Italian defeatists, 306
  and the income tax, 302
  before the Army Committee of the Senate, 305
  the financier, and the income tax, 254
Calmette, M., the murder of, 303
Cambon, Jules, warns M. Pichon in 1913, 281
Camélinat, 38, 43

INDEX

Canrobert, 6
Carnot, M. Sadi-, 96, 126
  President, supports Lesseps, 119
Carrousel, the inscription on the, 150
Casablanca, French settlers at, 237
Caserio, the anarchist, 148
Cassagnac, Paul de, 125
Charles X, 10
Chateaubriand, 6
Church and State, conflict between, 246-251
Cinquet, M., 182
Cipriani, Amilcare, 55
Citoyen Egalité, 4
Clemenceau, as Premier, asks England how many hundred thousand men she could land in North-Eastern France in case of a sudden war, 245
  and Boulanger, 98, 99
  and Boulangism, 104
  and Morocco, 224, 225
  and strikes, 219-223
  and the coal miners, 144-145
  and the doctrine of *laissez-faire*, 146
  and the *Entente*, 128
  and the story of Boaz and Ruth, 148
  and the strikers at Carmaux, 127
  and the wine-growers' agitation, 216-219
Clemenceau's anti-Czarist policy, 128
  appeal to Frenchmen, 275
Clemenceau as a conversationalist, 132
  as a duelist, 133
  as an orator, 131-133
  as doctor at Montmartre, 24
  as Mayor of Montmartre, 27
  as Minister of the Interior, 188
  as municipal dictator, 27
  as one of M. Floquet's seconds at the duel with Boulanger, 102
  as professor of French at Stanford, U.S.A., 20
  as Senator for Var, 187
  at Nantes as a student, 4
Clemenceau's attitude in the matter of M. Wilson's trading in decorations, 95

Clemenceau's attitude towards the Catholics, 59
Clemenceau, author's conversation with, 230
  becomes "suspect" and ceases to be Mayor of Montmartre, 35, 36
Clemenceau's betrothal to Miss Mary Plummer, 21
Clemenceau calls up the State engineers and relights Paris, 202
  the charges against him, 126, 127
Clemenceau's contempt for politicians as politicians, 96
  criticism on the German fête of Sedan, 149
  on the catastrophe of the Charity Bazaar, 148
Clemenceau defends himself in the National Assembly, 126
  denounces M. Ribot, 298
Clemenceau's disregard of monetary considerations, 134
  distrust of colonization by conquest, 262
  duel with Commandant Poussages, 50
Clemenceau, Dreyfus affair, 164-186
  efforts of his enemies to connect him with the Panama scandal, 124
  failure to attain Presidentship of Chamber, 134
  fight for Draguignan, 130
  freedom of speech, 97
  French intervention in Egypt, 93
  French peasantry, knowledge of, 143
  in America, 20
  in prison of Mazas, 15
Clemenceau's individualism antipathetic to Socialist view of collective social progress, 129
  influence in council chamber of the Allies, 337
Clemenceau introduces measure to establish Municipal Council of Paris, 50
Clemenceau's knowledge of Parisian life, 51

INDEX

Clemenceau's letters to the *Temps*, 20
  literary works, 152
  love of animals, 154
  love of Paris, 151
Clemenceau on the "Right to Strike," 193-194
  his reception by the miners at Lens, 194-198
  opponent of Gambetta, 92
  opposed to colonial adventure, 89
  opposed to colonization by conquest, 59
  opposed to execution of Generals Lecomte and Thomas, 35
Clemenceau's opposition to M. Ferry and his support of M. Sadi-Carnot, 96
  powerful personality, 140
  power of work, 133
  reply to Jaurès, 208-211
Clemenceau retires from parliamentary life after defeat at Draguignan, 131
Clemenceau's sense of humor, 52
  speech at Hyères, 229
  speech at Lyons on the miners' strike, 199
  speech in favor of amnesty of Communists, 52
  speech in the National Assembly, 36
  statement of Socialism, 141
Clemenceau the Tiger, 82
  on French intervention in Egypt, 93
  the universal skeptic, 188
  tour of propaganda, 36
  turns journalist, 137
  turns lecturer, 260
Clemenceau's view of Boulangist agitation, 105
  warning after the battle of the Marne, 282
Clemenceau, 1870-71, the war of, 266
Cluseret, 43, 46
Commune, administration of the, 39
  establishment of the, 35
"Communist Manifesto," the, 45
Comte, Auguste, 16
"Coöperative Commonwealth," 45

Constans, M., said to be the cause of the Boulanger fiasco, 108
Cottu, M., indictment of, 123
Courbet, 38
Courrières-Lens colliery disaster, the, 189

Damiens, the assassin, 147
d'Aumale, Duc, 14
Daudet, M. Léon, 299
Delcassé, M., 189
  and Clemenceau, antagonism between, 257-260
  and the Kaiser, 228
  King Edward's courtesy to, 244
Declaration, Clemenceau's, 321-328
Delescluze, 38, 45, 55
Déroulède, M., saves a situation, 243
Dilke, Sir Charles, 91, 227
Dombrowski, 46
Doumergue, M., 229
Dreyfus Affair, xiii, 164-186
Dufaure, 79, 85

Edward VII, King, 237
Eiffel, M., indictment of, 123
Electrical engineers' strike in Paris, 200
Encyclopaedia Britannica: tribute to M. Clemenceau, 238
Engels, 45
England's opposition to construction of Suez Canal, 106-7
Esterhazy, Major, 157-162

Fallières, M., 238
  and M. Clemenceau in London, 244
Favre, Jules, 28
Ferry, Jules, 78, 85, 88, 90, 91, 95, 238
  and colonial expansion, 127
Fez, French delegation at, 226
Flahault, 6
Floquet, 78, 122
  duel with Gen. Boulanger, 102, 103
Flourens, M., his pen-picture of King Edward, 239-241
Foch, Marshal, 333
Fontane, M., indictment of, 123
Fontenay le Comte, 2

INDEX

Foreign affairs in 1908, 237
France and England, a better feeling between, 10
and Great Britain, relations between, 237
the wealth of, 262, 263
Francis Joseph, 18
Franco-German agreement of 1909, 268
convention of 1911, 268-271
Fraser's Magazine, extract from, 39
French Revolution, 5
Freycinet, M., 85, 99

Gallifet, 46
Gambetta, xii, 37, 57, 62-79, 82, 83, 87, 89, 91-93, 234
Gauthier, M., urges the Government to complete Panama Canal, 121
Germany and Morocco, 224
preparations of, 273
Germinat, Admiral, and the Navy, 253
Gonse, General, 171, 178, 182
Grévy, Albert, 78, 82, 85-87, 90, 95, 96
Gribelin, M., 182
Guesde, Jules, 294
Guesdists, the, 129

Haldane, Lord, 227
"sublime confidence" in Germany, 272
"Harum, David," his motto, 60
Haussmann, Baron, 12
Henry, Colonel, 173, 180
the anarchist, 147, 148
Henty, George, 183
Hervé, Gustave, 294
Herz, M. Cornelius, and his part in the Panama scandal, 114, 123-126
House of Orleans, 5
of Bourbon, 5
Hugo, Victor, 14
Humbert, M., 307
Hyndman, Hugh, 39

Income tax, a graduated, 254
Infiltration, German, and France, 290-293

Interpenetration, German, 289
Ismail Pasha, Khedive, 111, 112
Italian campaign, the, 10
Italian Carbonari, 5

Jacques, a liquor dealer, chosen to fight Paris against the General, 107
Jaurès, 132-134, 150, 171, 178, 180, 184-186, 202-213, 237
and peace, 267
in public affairs, 121
Joffrin, 107
Jouaust, Colonel, 181, 182
Jourde, 38, 43
Judet, M., one of Clemenceau's detractors, 125
Junck, M., 182
Junker party and the Crown Prince, 227

Kaiser, the, and preparations for the war, 245
and the King of Spain, 225
and the Sultan of Morocco, 225
King Edward and Clemenceau, 238-242

Labori, M., 175
Labor, Ministry of, and M. Viviani, 257
Lac, Father du, 173
La Justice, 85
Langlois, Colonel, 49
Lauth, Major, 180, 182
La Vendée, 1-3
La Ville Lumière, 14
Lecomte, General, 34, 35, 49
Lesseps, Count Ferdinand, 111-123
indictment of, 123
two estimates of his character, 117-119
M. C. de, indictment of, 123
Lichnowsky's, Prince, revelations, 275
Liebknecht, Wilhelm, 184, 185
Longuet, 38, 295
Lottery Bill, the Panama, 115
Loubet, President, 126
Louis XVI, 5
XVIII, 10
Philippe, 4, 10

INDEX

MacMahon, Marshal, xii, 28, 69, 71-79, 82, 86
Madeira wine and a story about Cette, 215
Malvy, M., and pro-Germans, 297, 298
Mannesmann, Brothers, 236
Marx, 45, 141
Marxists, the, 129
Méline, M., 171
Mercier, General, 171, 182
Michel, E. B., 39
Mill, John Stuart, a dedication to, 16
Montagnards, insurrection of the, 54
Morny, 6
Morocco affair, the, 189
  French policy in, 235
Mouilleron-en-Pareds, 2

Napoleon III, 9-13, 24-26
  chief cause of downfall of, 18, 19
  loss of prestige, 24
  the Court of, 11
  Louis, 5, 6, 8, 10, 18, 19
Naquet, 88
Narbonne and Montpellier, disaffection among the wine-growers, 214
National Workshops, 5
Nicholas, Emperor, 10
1918, June, the Socialists and Clemenceau, 329-331
Noir, Victor, murder of, 24
Norton, M., 126
"Novel with a purpose," the, 158

Orsini bomb, the, 10

Painlevé, M., 318
Panama Canal, a congress of nations called by Lesseps, 113
  and financial corruption, 115, 116
  and opponents of the Republic, 117
  collapse of the company, 120
  horrors on the Isthmus, 115
  indictment of directors, 123
  scandal, the, xii
  scandal, accusation of deputies, senators, and academicians, 122
  Presidents Carnot and Loubet's attitude, 117
Paty du Clam, Colonel, 173
Paris and the Provinces, 8
Peace as desired by Socialist leaders, 267
Perovskaia, Sophie, 55
Persigny, 6
Phylloxera ravages in the Bordeaux vineyards, 214, 215
Pichon, M., 229, 237
Picquart, Colonel, 172, 177, 178, 180, 182, 227
Plébiscite, the, 6, 8, 9
Poincaré and Clemenceau, relations between, 286
Population, concentration of, John Bellers on, 262, 263
  Petty on the same, *ibid*.
Pyat, 43, 44, 45

Radolin, Prince, 236
Railways, the nationalization of, 254
Raspail, 55
Ravachol, the anarchist, 136
Reinach, M. Jacques, and his part in the Panama Scandal, 114
  the tragedy of his death, 122, 124, 125
Rémusat, de, 68
Republic of 1848, 5
Retreat, the great, of August, 1914, 279
Revolution, the French, Clemenceau on, 256
Ribot, M., denounced by Clemenceau, 298
Rochefort, 14
Roget, M., 182
Rollin, Ledru, 5
Rosen, Dr., 236
Rossel, 46
Rouher, 14
Rousseau, M., reports unfavorably on Panama Canal, 114
Rouvier, M., 122, 188
  defends the President in the Wilson affair, 96
  refuses to accept Boulanger as War Minister, 102
Russia, campaign against, 10

INDEX

Sarrien, M., 188, 213, 229
Scheurer-Kestner, 172, 178
Schnäbele affair, the, Boulanger's part in it, 100
Second Empire, the, 4
Shaw, Bernard, 212
Simon, Jules, 73, 74
Social-Democracy, German, and the war, 274
Socialist demonstration against Clemenceau at unveiling of statue to M. Floquet, 255
Party, the, anti-patriotic, 295
Sonnino, Baron, and Caillaux, 306
Spüller, 92
Suez Canal, the, 111

Thiers, 37, 39, 44, 50, 51, 54, 68, 69
Thomas, Albert, 261
Clément, 34, 35, 49
Trochu, General, 28
Tunis, the question of, 89, 90

"*Utrinque paratus,*" 11

Vaillant, 38, 134
and Hervé, and the war, 294
and peace, 267
the anarchist, 136, 137
Edouard, the Blanquist, 121
Venice, the annexation of, 18
Verdun, Clemenceau on the victories at, 251
Vermorel, 36
Victoria, Queen, 26
Viviani, M., 229, 257

Waddington, 84, 85
Ward, Mrs. Humphry, XI
Wilson, trading in decorations, 92
Wine, adulteration of, 215
Working Men's Association, the International, 44, 45
Wyse, Buonaparte, sells concession for Panama canal scheme to Lesseps, 113

Zola, 171-175
the trial of, 177, 180
Zurlinden, General, 157